FAİTHFUL DOUBT

FAITHFUL DOUBT

The Wisdom of Uncertainty

Guy Collins

CASCADE *Books* · Eugene, Oregon

FAITHFUL DOUBT
The Wisdom of Uncertainty

Copyright © 2014 Guy Collins. All rights reserved. Except for brief quotations in critical publications or reviews, no part of this book may be reproduced in any manner without prior written permission from the publisher. Write: Permissions, Wipf and Stock Publishers, 199 W. 8th Ave., Suite 3, Eugene, OR 97401.

Cascade Books
An Imprint of Wipf and Stock Publishers
199 W. 8th Ave., Suite 3
Eugene, OR 97401
www.wipfandstock.com

ISBN 13: 978-1-62564-369-8

Cataloging-in-Publication data:

Collins, Guy

    Faithful doubt : the wisdom of uncertainty / Guy Collins.

    xviii + 208 p. ; 23 cm. —Includes bibliographical references and index.

    ISBN 13: 978-1-62564-369-8

    1. Faith. 2. Belief and Doubt. I. Title.

BL626.3 C75 2014

Manufactured in the U.S.A.

For Kristin, Lyra, and Beatrix

Materialists and madmen never have doubts.

—G. K. CHESTERTON

For the more conscious becomes the belief, so the more conscious becomes
the unbelief: indifference, doubt and skepticism appear ...

—T. S. ELIOT

With knowledge comes more doubt.

—GOETHE

Contents

Acknowledgments

The idea for this book arose out of experiences as a student first at The University of St. Andrews, Scotland, and later at The University of Cambridge, England. I am grateful both to those who taught me, and those I studied alongside. In particular, I owe significant debts to Daphne Hampson and Graham Ward. Their teaching made possible the trajectory of inquiry that this book explores.

More recently, my thanks go to two communities in Hanover, New Hampshire: the people of St. Thomas, and the students of Dartmouth College. Their hospitality to both faith and doubt has been a tremendous gift.

I remain grateful to Jolyon Mitchell, Gavin Hyman, and George Pattison for giving significant help along the way. All mistakes are very much my own.

Thanks also go to those who have granted permission to use previously published material: A stanza of the poem "AD" by R. S. Thomas from *Collected Later Poems 1988–2000* (Bloodaxe, 2004) appears with permission of the publisher on behalf of the estate of R. S. Thomas; Oxford University Press for permission to include in chapter 3 material of my own from "Thinking the Impossible: Derrida and the Divine," *Literature and Theology* 14 (2000).

Finally, thanks go to my wife, Kristin, for seemingly endless reserves of patience and perseverance that helped bring this to fruition.

Hanover, New Hampshire
The Feast of St. Lucy, 2013

Introduction

What is true, then, is an experience of faith, and this is as true for agnostics
and atheists as it is for theists. Those who cannot believe still require religious truth and a framework of ritual in which they can believe.

—SIMON CRITCHLEY[1]

Theology, it seems, is often most influential where it is least obvious.

—MARK C. TAYLOR[2]

And, perhaps, the true communion with Christ, the true *imitatio Christi*, is
to participate in Christ's doubt and disbelief.

— SLAVOJ ŽIŽEK[3]

We live in an age of doubt, and we have been living like this for
quite some time. This work investigates doubt, and the relationship it has to faith. One of the great moments in the history of doubt was
Matthew Arnold's 1867 poem "Dover Beach" and its evocative description of the "melancholy, long withdrawing roar" of a "Sea of Faith" in full
retreat. At the end of the twentieth century the theologian Don Cupitt
drew upon Arnold's poem to frame his own exploration of the history of

1. Critchley, *Faith of the Faithless*, 3.
2. Taylor, *Moment of Complexity*, 180.
3. Žižek, *Puppet and the Dwarf*, 102.

the flight of faith.[4] The genius of Cupitt and Arnold was to crystalize how old certainties have long been ebbing away. However, while the sea of faith has been pulling back for generations, the work of exploring the littoral expanse uncovered in its wake is still in relative infancy. Relatively few theologians have studied the absence of faith, just as few non-theologians have felt the urge to think much about a faith perceived as absent. When reflection on the status of faith in non-theological circles does occur it is frequently assumed that the withdrawal of faith is an epochal event that has its natural conclusion in secularization.

Nonetheless, the triumph of the secular is no longer self-evident or uncontested. Religious faith is in decline, barely on life support in many places, yet it refuses to die. While citizens in the West do not take faith as seriously as they did in the relatively recent past, faith is far from entirely absent. Contemporary theology is always situated within this oscillation between the absence and presence of faith. This manifests on the one hand in theologians plumbing the depths of secular atheist thought. On the other hand, significant thinkers who make no claim to faith are returning to examine the nature of faith. As the atheist philosopher Simon Critchley notes, faith is no longer just for the faithful: it is also a key part of the identity of those he names the "faithless."[5] Others such as Giorgio Agamben have drawn attention to the dependence on the sacred of secularization itself, revealing the hidden theological genealogy of much that is secular within modern Western society.

This work starts from the assumption that both the religious and the non-religious (as well as the undeclared) have much to learn from those like Agamben, Critchley, and Cupitt who venture out to chart the liminal, uncertain, and ever-changing terrain exposed by the withdrawal of the sea of faith. There is also another purpose to this work. It has never been particularly fashionable for theologians not to believe. The theologian is actually in something of a double bind. Unless central tenets of belief are questioned the theologian can never really come to grips with, far less understand, the deep-seated questions of those who do not have religious beliefs. However, questioning belief too intensely can also lead to trouble. At the risk of getting into trouble this work starts from the premise that if faith is to have intellectual, emotional, or spiritual vitality it will need to come to a more serious understanding of doubt. What follows is

4. Cupitt, *The Sea of Faith.*
5. Critchley, *The Faith of the Faithless.*

therefore an attempt at responding to Richard Kearney's suggestion that faith engage wholeheartedly with atheism in order to properly appreciate the divine.[6]

One of the predicaments facing exponents of doubt is the age-old question of whether the path of doubt leads inevitably into plain denial. Remembering the character of philosophical skepticism can be informative at this point. Philosophical skepticism is less the outright rejection of one specific truth than the realization that there may be more than one way of looking at things. It seems hard to argue that such a kind of skepticism might be of considerable help to theology. However, it is also part of the argument of this book that even outright atheism may be a powerful resource for strengthening theology and faith.

In noting that theology is at its most influential "where it is least obvious," Mark C. Taylor invites us to recognize the theological underpinning of disciplines not known for their theology. The original context for this remark was an exploration of the similarity between Charles Darwin's model for evolution and Adam Smith's theory of the invisible hand of the market. Both offer models of complex systems that construct meaning by understanding the interplay between multiple parts and a wider whole. To put it another way, both are secularized versions of the idea of God's guiding providence. Taylor understands that trying to effect a clear demarcation of the theological from the secular can be a losing battle and ultimately incoherent. Evolution and economics may (for some at least) epitomize faithless rationality, but more and more thinkers are discovering quite serious theological genealogies and underpinnings. If theology remains enduringly influential where least obvious, then what could be less obvious, and therefore potentially more influential, than secular questions of doubt, denial, and disbelief?

This is not, of course, by its very nature altogether obvious. Christianity does not have a good track record when it comes to doubt. Skepticism, doubt, and even disarmingly simple questions have all been viewed negatively at one time or another—which is somewhat strange given the history of Christian theology. Christianity has always had an uncanny knack for adapting to different cultures, adopting their various principles and neuroses. It is also hard to think of a single significant theologian who did not explicitly develop theology as the exploration of lines of questioning. During the Middle Ages such lines of inquiry,

6. Kearney, *Anatheism*.

questions (*quaestiones*), were the very lifeblood of theology. However, throughout history theology has been concerned with translating and shuttling between the divine and the secular, adapting to new categories of thought and continually learning from changing contexts. It is a truism, but nonetheless helpful to remember, that there has never been a point of universal harmony within theology. Instead, through succeeding centuries Christianity has continued to morph and adapt against a backdrop of new questions and fresh concerns.

A thought-provoking illustration of this process of change and adaptation is seen in the critique Søren Kierkegaard leveled against the church of his day. Not content with the unchallenging theology coming from the pulpit, Kierkegaard accused the clergy of being cannibals. Kierkegaard could see how nineteenth-century clerics had turned the radical message of Jesus into a set of comfortable social conventions off of which they could make a good living.[7] While Kierkegaard's language may have been intemperate, he realized that Christianity had fused into Christendom, and, along with it, the contemporary concern for ethics and morality over faith. Yet while Kierkegaard and others since have railed against Christianity accommodating itself too much to the world, today the situation is more often reversed. Rarely is Christianity accused of being too comfortable or congruent with the insights of our contemporary situation. More often Christianity is perceived as carrying a torch for views that are distinctly old-fashioned at best, and unhealthily world-denying at worst. To media and the academy alike, Christianity is often identified with criticisms of evolution and denials of scientific methodology. Add to this the perception that sexism, homophobia, and patriarchy are justified in the Bible and you have a recipe for viewing Christianity as a social and intellectual pariah. It is therefore little wonder that many thoughtful people find religion something incomprehensible and alien. Humanists reject beliefs that pit human against human as fundamentally incompatible with highest human aspirations. Atheists correctly note that there is neither overwhelmingly good evidence nor compelling logical arguments for there even being a God. The existence of evil, the hypocrisy of institutional religion, and the moral failings of ordinary believers all add to the case against faith.

In light of all this, it is only natural to wonder whether the divide between critically thinking doubters and religious adherents can ever

7. Kierkegaard's title to chapter 5 is revealing: "The priests are cannibals, and that in the most odious way." *Attack Upon "Christendom,"* 268.

be bridged. Two hundred years ago the German theologian Friedrich Schleiermacher wrestled with similar issues. In the educated opinion of his day, religion was perceived as crude and unsophisticated. In response Schleiermacher penned one of the great apologetic tracts of Christian thought, *Speeches to Cultured Despisers*. Schleiermacher was writing at the height of the Enlightenment, when philosophy and science seemed to be unconquerable. While many religious people feared the new Enlightenment insights, Schleiermacher was convinced that Christianity had nothing to lose from wholehearted engagement with new thinking. He believed that at its heart religion was the "sense and taste for the infinite."[8] To truly understand the infinite Schleiermacher was committed to the notion that educated skeptics might have something to contribute, and something to discover.

There are relatively few of Schleiermacher's mindset in our own age. Pressure to disengage from debate comes from both church and academy. Many churches find appeals to emotions more successful than robust intellectual debate. Meanwhile higher education has increasingly retreated behind a smokescreen of sociology that sees theology and faith as quaint and old-fashioned practices of a dim and distant man-eating tribe. Worse still are the occasional public forays into debate of scientific skeptics and militant believers. In the mud-slinging that accompanies these mercifully rare exchanges, it is hard to discern much on either side to commend healthy debate or mutual understanding. Churches themselves bear a large burden of responsibility for the paucity and shallowness of contemporary debates. Christianity is far from perfect; and there are more than enough good reasons for people not to believe based on the actions and words of professing Christians. This work is not an attempt to argue anyone out of their profound reasons for disbelief. Many of the things educated skeptics do not believe are things that millions of other religious people simply do not believe. A literal seven-day creation, a four-thousand-year-old planet, the subjugation of women to men, the prohibition of shellfish, and rules against clothing of more than one fabric are all to be found in the Bible. However, doggedly believing such things to be timeless truths is profoundly inimical to Christianity and theologically incoherent.

Christianity's worst enemies are not intelligent questioners, but those who produce the most noise in proclaiming their trust in Christ.

8. Schleiermacher, *On Religion*, 23.

This work hopes to present the case for an alternative response to Christianity. This alternative empathizes with those embarrassed at religion while making the case for a form of religious belief that is not entirely intellectually moribund. As such this work is neither a traditional apology for Christianity nor a rebuttal of atheist objections. Instead it is a friendly critique written from the perspective of someone who believes that Christianity's most impressive resources are sometimes better understood by outsiders to the church than insiders.

There is wisdom in the Christian church just as there is wisdom in the critiques and questions of skeptics. If educated twenty-first-century people are to make sense of religion it will be necessary to suspend embarrassment for a moment at the same time as keeping a tight grip on critical faculties. Believers also need to be willing to entertain the question that what they take for Christianity may actually be nothing more than a particularly popular and persistent form of idolatry. Each of these propositions is challenging in different ways for the skeptic and the believer. However, until the thought that something is not quite right with traditional views of Christianity is entertained it will not be possible to discover its uncomfortable truth.

G. K. Chesterton wryly noted how the only good argument against Christianity is Christians. However, just as individual Christians are the first to admit that they are individual works in progress, so theology reminds us that Christianity is still emerging, still being discovered, still "to come." The role of educated skeptics in this is unique: they are not the ones Christianity needs to fear, so much as the ones whose perspective and participation is essential to the future of theology and religious practice.

This book is not an attempt to prove central doctrines of Christianity beyond all reasonable doubt. That does not seem to be a sensible claim to make. Instead, the question that animates this book is whether reasonable doubt can tell us more about Christianity. We will see how theology makes more sense, not less, when doubting is affirmed and critical questions are allowed into the heart of theology. We will also discover how some of the most brilliant and illuminating theology has been inspired by, and originates in, sources and thinkers who have no particular loyalty or commitment to Christian theology. The atheist John Gray has written that Western humanism is itself a child of Christian theology.[9] Atheist

---

9. Gray, *Straw Dogs*.

humanists and religious believers alike therefore share a common theological inheritance. It is therefore imperative to look more closely at the other in order to understand oneself. The remainder of this introduction gives an overview of how the book attempts to do this.

The first chapter explores the nature of the relationship between faith and doubt, and how the two are ineradicably connected. This leads into a discussion of fundamentalism, and an exploration of different forms of fundamentalist discourse. In chapter 2 science fiction is analyzed in an attempt to understand how rationality and religion have been imagined and creatively reimagined in the light of recent philosophical thought. The opposition of faith to reason that was dominant in modernity is not essential and it has been fruitfully reconfigured in both literature and film. This introduces the question of postmodernity, a topic that chapter 3 explores in greater depth through the thought of Jacques Derrida. New possibilities for making sense of religion arise from the decidedly non-theological experience of deconstructive thought. Derrida also reveals the importance of understanding impossibility as a philosophical concept that is not entirely foreign to the theological concept of paradox. Chapter 4 turns to more traditional theological questions with an examination of the dangers of anthropomorphism. Concentrating on the question of hell and the devil, this chapter explores some of the consequences of overly simplistic religious imagery. In chapter 5 more sophisticated responses to questions of evil are explored. The first part explores the question of the nature of evil, while the second part explores Eleanore Stump's case for discerning a reason for suffering and evil. The chapter concludes by noting how the atheist Slavoj Žižek essentially repeats the insight of both the book of Job and Donald MacKinnon in refusing to ascribe meaning to evil. Chapter 6 tackles the question of scriptural understanding, and asks whether there is a way of responding to the thorny problems raised by the Bible. This leads into a discussion of the relative purposes of theology and science, and how different narratives relate to one another. Chapter 7 focuses on atheism and is divided into two sections. The first part examines the links between emancipatory atheists and theologians who have anticipated certain atheist readings of Christianity arising from the death of Christ on the cross. The second part concentrates on the thought of Giorgio Agamben, and asks how his thought might prove beneficial for theology. Finally, chapter 8 returns to the question of how faith and reason might relate. Connections are drawn between the way Kierkegaard, Jacques Lacan, and Žižek theorize subjectivity. Unlike the certainty of the

Cartesian cogito, all three posit a broken, divided notion of subjectivity that requires an understanding of the importance of the other. Using the theme of breach as developed by China Miéville, the chapter argues for a reconfiguration of the relationship between faith and doubt.

In the New Testament Thomas the apostle is portrayed as doubting the resurrection of Jesus. It is significant that for the scriptural writers Thomas's experience is not excised. Instead, his doubts are held up as a legitimate response laden with meaning. Thomas is not deplored, rather he comes across as understandably human, asking for evidence before he commits himself. The question that runs through this work is whether Thomas might not simply be a saint but also a hero for our own times. Thomas's doubts did not derail the Christian narrative so much as draw attention on the marvel of the resurrection. By extension, what if critical skepticism is not a stumbling block but rather the only thing that can save Christianity from itself?

I

Uncertain Truths

I propose to establish progressive stages of certainty ... But the mental operation which follows the act of sense I for the most part reject; and instead
of it I open and lay out a new and certain path for the mind to proceed in,
starting directly from the simple sensuous perception.

—FRANCIS BACON[1]

But eventually I am forced to admit that there is nothing among the things I
once believed to be true which it is not permissible to doubt - and not out of
frivolity or lack of forethought, but for valid and considered reasons.

—RENÉ DESCARTES[2]

AT THE DAWN OF the seventeenth century two thinkers laid down foundations for modern science and modern philosophy. Francis Bacon
affirmed the importance of the empirical, and matters of sense. René
Descartes took the opposite approach, denying that anything could be
proved other than the existence of the mind, and whether it was doubting or cogitating. Both thinkers have come to influence successive centuries of scientific and philosophical thought. While science has taken

1. Bacon, *The New Organon: Or True Directions Concerning the Interpretation of
Nature*.
2. Descartes, *Meditations on First Philosophy*, 16.

1

the Baconian "new and certain path," philosophy has found it difficult to escape the Cartesian emphasis on both doubt and the centrality of the reasoning mind, the cogito. Each in their own way sought a solid foundation for their respective discipline. Yet the treatment of doubt within each thinker was remarkably different.

Today it is philosophically and theologically fashionable to critique the Cartesian reliance on the cogito, especially in light of the negative consequences this has had for our understanding of the status of the body. The dualism that places mind over body has not been healthy for society or theology. In turn, the Cartesian emphasis on the cogito has been connected with the production of other disconcerting dualisms, such as the hierarchical ordering of male over female. However, in the legitimate rush to exorcise theology from an over-dependence on the mind, or cogitation, the important role of doubt within the Cartesian cogito has been neglected. It can be argued that religion and theology have also found themselves divided between Baconian and Cartesian approaches to certainty and doubt. Both are strategies for dealing with doubt, but while both saw doubt as something to be overcome, Descartes also intuits that doubt is uniquely important in developing deeper understanding.

Both Descartes and Bacon assumed that it was ultimately possible to escape doubt by providing solid rational foundations for knowledge. Yet in their different approaches, each created a different route for subsequent scientists and philosophers. As has recently been comprehensively argued, while science has continued to thrive using the empirical foundation developed by Bacon, subsequent philosophy has never been able to agree that Descartes's solid foundations were any bit as firm as he believed.[3] While the history of science is the history of building on the sturdy empirical foundations of Bacon, the subsequent history of philosophy is the story of a continuing questioning and doubting of whether reason alone can ever provide a firm foundation.

The desire to evade doubt was common to both Descartes and Bacon. But Descartes also recognized that doubt played an important role in constituting the subject. It was not simply something to be avoided, it was also a mechanism for helping discover the true foundation of thought. By contrast, doubt for Bacon was merely something to be avoided. At the same time, while Descartes assumed that belief in God was essential to the foundations of his rational system, Bacon's system had no need

3. Gregory, *The Unintended Reformation*, 115–28.

of God. And so while Bacon's system was able to thrive without God, Descartes's system was undermined both by its inability to totally exclude doubt, and also, in time, by the apparent idiosyncrasy of a rational system that incorporated monotheistic belief. Neither Bacon nor Descartes could ever rid themselves of doubt, and as Giorgio Agamben has written scientific method may well have encouraged doubt for Descartes:

> The view through Galileo's telescope produced not certainty and faith in experience but Descartes's doubt, and his famous hypothesis of a demon whose only occupation is to deceive our senses.[4]

Doubts about God and doubts about whether reason could really provide certainty undid Descartes. Yet trust in the verifiable and empirical reality of the external world ensured Bacon's views would remain abidingly influential. While Descartes continues to have a reputation as an arch-rationalist, his thought was never completely able to avoid something theology has always struggled with: the question of uncertainty.

While doubts are important to theology, there are many examples of Christian practice that appear to leave no room for doubt. Christianity has a far from perfect record in accommodating doubters, and for large sections of the faithful doubt appears to be anathema. This chapter examines why doubt presents such difficulties. It will consider the problems raised by uncertainty, and why this creates challenges both for theology and also for some of its ardent critics. The division between certainty and uncertainty, what for simplicity's sake we will telescope as a division between the Baconian and Cartesian, cannot simply be mapped onto the difference between religious and secular thought. Instead, it will become clear how even quite different religious and secular discourses come to resemble one another in the way that they prioritize either certainty or uncertainty. While religious faith can be strengthened when it is recast as a practice of radical uncertainty, too often it has instead been presented as providing ultimate assurance. If, as Descartes thought, doubt is the origin of wisdom, this chapter will explore what happens to theology when doubt is suppressed and only certainty remains.[5]

---

4. Agamben, *Infancy and History*, 20.

5. Although Descartes never used the words "doubt is the origin of wisdom" the persistent misattribution of this phrase to him is powerful testimony to the centrality that doubt plays in his thought.

Bacon, like modern science, allows us to articulate and interpret the world in a more certain kind of way. However, in seeking certainty, this approach has to exclude anything that cannot be verified empirically. God clearly cannot be verified through sense experience, and so God can never be the subject of scientific study for Bacon. By contrast, Descartes was willing to broaden the remit of philosophy to incorporate matters of non-sense experience, like the divine. The tragedy of Descartes is that in seeking to discover a universal framework for reason, he ends up creating a rational system that ultimately has just as negative an effect on divinity and doubt as Bacon. Bacon's exclusion of both divinity and doubt in the construction of his system was successful, and the subsequent history of science bears this out. By contrast, Descartes's attempt to provide certain reasons for God at the same time as affirming the revelatory potential of doubt were not as long-lasting. One legacy of this is seen in the comparative strengths of the scientific and theological communities in academia and public life. Most intellectuals assume that somehow science and philosophy cannot coexist with belief in God. Equally, most Western societies today assume that philosophical or religious beliefs are inherently private matters open to doubt. Neither of these positions would have made sense to either Bacon or Descartes. The rest of this chapter will investigate how it is that the drift toward certainty continues to displace God. Along the way it will also become apparent how doubt is of more utility to religion and theology than has previously been recognized.

The Logic of Certainty

Religious fundamentalism and militant atheism have a number of compelling similarities.[6] Each brooks no opposition, and both are powerfully certain of the rightness of their cause. Despite their very different responses to the question of God, both firmly believe they have a monopoly on truth. Given that many atheists start out as Christian, this is not itself

6. Using the word *fundamentalism* is provocative: it is certainly not a term of endearment. However, it is hard to find a better term to describe those who seek (and profess to find) absolute certainty in their religious tradition. For the purposes of this work, I will take it as self-evident that a (religious or non-religious) fundamentalist is someone who prizes certainty above all. In contrast to fundamentalism we will speak of flexibilism, flexibility, or those who are (religiously or non-religiously) flexible. *Flexibilism* does not appear to be a word, but I think it is eloquently self-explanatory, pertaining to those who seek flexibility over inflexibility. (Of course, fundamentalists could be designated inflexibilists, but this seems a superfluous neologism.)

particularly surprising. The corollary of this is that the religiously flexible and the agnostic also have a great deal in common. While an agnostic is uncertain about the existence of the divine, the flexible tend to be circumspect about their deeply held beliefs. Part of this is because they are, legitimately enough, simply unsure. Such a lack of certainty arises out of the intellectual recognition that faith really does not make an awful lot of sense. While some might see this as evidence that such beliefs are shallow or superficial, by contrast, the question that arises here is the status of imagination in religious belief. Imagination in all its accompanying uncertainty, opacity, and mystery can be a route into religious belief. Yet, for those not inclined to surrender themselves to ambiguity the uncertainties of imagination are something to be shunned. While imagination can be celebrated as a gift, it can also be feared as a distraction.

The religiously flexible and the religiously agnostic are both uncomfortably aware that they do not know all that there is to know. They are open to the possibility of being wrong, and they are aware of the multiplicity of different ways in which others respond to ultimate questions. The key division in faith is therefore not between those who believe and those who do not. Rather, the real religious demarcation is between those who have the hubris to suggest that they "know what is what," and those who have the humility to agree with John Caputo that "we do not know who we are."[7]

As we learn more about the seemingly infinite variety of human life choices it is clear that life is irreducibly complex. While some, like the Amish of Pennsylvania, shun the innovations of technology, most are increasingly dependent on technologies that less than a generation ago were the height of science-fiction. Thanks to the internet, cellular communication technology, and wireless communications we live in a world in which information is now more freely available than ever before. On the other hand, there is a growing digital divide between those who have unlimited access to new technologies and those whose access is controlled or impeded for economic, political, or social reasons. New technology in itself has not resolved the problem of economic inequality. Despite the new-found freedom offered by the internet we are only starting to recognize, let alone respond to, new problems of social exclusion generated by the way new technologies are implemented.

7. Caputo, *On Religion*, 18.

Even when access itself is not a problem, part of the conundrum facing inhabitants of twenty-first-century cyberspace is knowing who to trust. The United States Postal Service or the British Royal Mail rarely concern themselves with seeing mail intercepted or destroyed on an industrial scale. And readers of newspapers and books rarely worry about their purchase infecting other papers and books with an information-destroying plague that renders all literary artifacts useless. However, as digital consumers know, even the most risk-averse constantly place their own data and information at risk. Whether the threat is from spyware, malware, trojans, viruses, or even the virus-protection software itself, we live in an age of information overload and overkill.

Just as we are becoming more fluent in navigating competing information streams, we are also discovering new vulnerabilities in records and data. Where the library of Alexandria stood for centuries, today the life-cycle of a computer is officially accounted as at best five years. And while we can drink from a cornucopia of information on the internet we also have to contend with an entire ecosystem of out-of-date, misleading or purposefully incorrect information. Once one leaves a few select portals whose credentials are trustworthy we find ourselves in the data equivalent of no-man's land. Examining the phenomena of our interconnected age it is hard not to agree with Taylor: "In the midst of these webs, networks, and screens, I can no more be certain where I am than I can know when or where the I begins and ends."[8] Bewilderment is both natural and ubiquitous in the face of such complexity.

This brings us to the paradox of the information age. Marshall McLuhan defined information as a difference that makes a difference. Yet how willing are we to expose ourselves to different thoughts? Just as potential access to information increases so too can reluctance to engage with difference or diversity. This is not a rule for all people and all places, but it does help explain why an exponential increase in the availability of information has coincided not with a great burgeoning of human understanding, but with increasing polarization and failure to understand. There is no common culture transcending economic, political or religious divides. Society today bears less resemblance to the Roman forum or medieval marketplace where everyone had access to the same public space, and more to a series of autonomous silos of affiliation and information

8. Taylor, *The Moment of Complexity*, 231.

that rarely intersect.[9] It is against this cultural pandemonium that we need to locate, and understand, religion.

The explosion of knowledge in the information age is just one small part of a wider set of societal transitions. As the sociologist Zygmunt Bauman has shown, contemporary society is increasingly characterized by insecurity and uncertainty.[10] While life has always provided stresses and challenges, the last hundred years has seen an exponential advance in the rate of societal change. From decreased job security and economic contraction to increased anxieties about everything from terrorism to global warming there are more than enough reasons to be insecure. New diseases and the threat of pandemics have been a recurring theme of recent decades, and whether it is HIV/AIDS, BSE, or the H1N1 virus the general public increasingly lack the ability to discern the difference between legitimate causes for concern and media-inflicted health scares. With more access to information we are becoming ever more insecure as we learn ever more about the possible threats to living the good life. It does not matter whether these threats are significant or relevant. What matters is the overwhelming creation of a culture of fear and insecurity under the guise of the dissemination of information.

Many have noted the powerful connection between pharmaceutical companies and new diagnoses for previously unknown ailments. We now medicate various complaints rather than take the simple steps required to actually remove the need for medication in the first place. Drugs are easy to prescribe, generate revenue, and give patients the illusion of being in control. The United States remains the world leader in the amount of money it spends on healthcare, by a large per capita factor. While overall it does not have a healthier population, it does have a system that produces the illusion of choice and control (for those who are able to afford it). What is less well understood is that a similar mechanism operates in wider society. If insecurity, and the illusion of insecurity, is the illness afflicting contemporary society, the drug of choice has become certainty. Like commercial counterparts in advertising, religious fundamentalism has been enormously successful in both manufacturing and marketing desire. And while the conventional desires of advertising may appear

9. This is not to romanticize the social structures that prevented full and equal participation in both the forum and the medieval market. Access is not the same as participation.

10. Bauman, *Postmodernity and its Discontents*.

ephemeral, there is nothing less ephemeral than the desire for certain knowledge about the meaning of life, the universe, and everything.

It is important to realize that both atheism and fundamentalism have been around for a significant amount of time. Atheism is often viewed as the culmination of modern rationality, while fundamentalism is more frequently imagined as a form of insulation from the demands of modern reason. Against this false dichotomy, it seems honest to recognize how fundamentalism is prevalent in both the religious and irreligious. This is not to say that atheism or religion are inherently reducible to fundamentalism: each has many non-fundamentalist forms. However, in their fundamentalist versions they share a remarkable set of strategies for dealing with the world. At first sight each apparently cuts its cloth from one particular faculty: "reason" in the case of atheism, and "faith" in the case of religion. However, upon closer inspection it becomes clear that atheism depends on a form of faith or fideism just as much as religion depends on a capacity to reason. Each depends for its very existence on the opposite faculty to the one with which it is most identified. Neither Bacon nor Descartes could pass for a fundamentalist, for each in different ways assumed that faith and reason were both important and, in different ways, that both were necessary. Descartes sought to unite faith and reason, effectively under the control of reason, while Bacon sought to delimit the scope of reason to merely empirical things. Neither approach intentionally sets reason against faith, although both cleared the way for the supremacy of reason and along with it later atheist rejections of religion. While the seventeenth century laid the intellectual groundwork for the severing of faith from reason, such an idea would have been unthinkable at the time. Only in much more recent times do we find both religious fundamentalism and atheist fundamentalism suggesting a straightforward opposition between faith and reason.

This is illustrated in Ursula Le Guin's *The Telling* where we are introduced to two different planets, Terra and Akan. On each planet learning is identified as a threat and steps are taken to limit the population's access to the world of ideas, literature, and imagination. On Terra all the books have been destroyed by a theocracy. Nothing except religious orthodoxy is allowed to survive, and the Library of Congress is bombed as a sign of the radical incommensurability of learning and religion. Meanwhile on Akan all the books have been destroyed by the corporation, a completely scientific consumer-producer-led society. On Akan religion is banned, and scientific rationality is the highest form of life. As the narrator notes of both societies: "But they were all true believers, both sides. Secular terrorists or holy terrorists, what difference."[11] When different opinions are systematically silenced, the question of whether this is done in the name of God or of scientific rationality is secondary.

Where religious fundamentalism relies exclusively on faith, it does so in a way that adopts wholesale the language and purposes of reason to articulate how faith is a kind of reason. Equally, where atheist fundamentalism affirms rationality as its central premise, it relies on the language of belief and faith to advocate the singularity, comprehensiveness, and necessity of its trust in reason. There can be no rational basis for the atheist fundamentalist's reliance on reason alone. After all, reason cannot offer decisive arguments for rejecting God, and can no more disprove God than it can agree on what might constitute proper or authentic reason in the first place. Upon closer inspection, reason is as much of a chimera as God: elusive and largely unattainable, but no less important for being so. But for atheist fundamentalists like Christopher Hitchens rejecting God in the name of rationality is a foundational belief.[12] By contrast, other atheists are not able to bow down before almighty reason as having the last word on the subject. They recognize that reason has its limits and that reason may not be able to answer every question. Atheists do not restrict their doubts to deity: they are also able to doubt a whole host of other conceits.

At their respective cores atheist fundamentalism and religious fundamentalism share a singularity of conviction and a certainty of purpose. Emerging in the nineteenth-century religious fundamentalism is a relatively well-understood phenomenon. Before the rise of modern rationality religious faith was inherently complex, diverse, and differentiated. Nowhere is this clearer than in the field of scriptural interpretation. Until the emergence of modern fundamentalism theological scholars across the centuries understood the need for differing interpretations of Scripture. In the Christian West theologians understood that there could never be only one interpretation of Scripture. One of the great religious classics written over fifteen hundred years ago was Augustine's *On Christian*

---

11. Le Guin, *The Telling*, 63.

12. Hitchens, *God is not Great*.

Teaching.[13] In it Augustine went to great lengths to provide a framework for understanding the complexity of different levels of meaning within Scripture. And well before Augustine, Jewish rabbinic teaching took for granted the plurality of interpretations and competing readings that the Torah generates. Yet with the emergence of modern rationality and the claims of universal reason religious fundamentalists sought to transpose the singularity of reason onto the diversity of the scriptural text.

While rabbis and theologians have for centuries argued within their own traditions in favor of often quite competing interpretations, the last two hundred years have witnessed the emergence of popular religious thinkers who suggest that there is but one true interpretation. Such an idea would have shocked the medieval mind, and it would have made no sense whatsoever within rabbinic thought. For them the Scriptures are not univocal, literally speaking in one voice. Instead, the Scriptures are multivocal. The Scriptures speak in many voices with different inflections, and identifying often conflicting and differing levels of meaning is part of the purpose of theology and biblical interpretation.

A good example of this inherent biblical complexity in the Christian world is found in the parables of Jesus, where it is absolutely impossible to find a simple singular interpretation. John Dominic Crossan has shown just how necessary it is to understand the parables not as univocal, but as polyvalent, inherently requiring the creation of multiple different interpretations.[14] For Crossan the point is not that human reason is incapable of making final sense of a parable, true as that may be. Rather, the point is that the parables themselves were designed to preclude the identification of one overarching or final meaning. That parables generate multiple meanings, what Crossan calls polyvalence, is not a failure of translation, but an essential dimension to their theological meaning. Jesus did not speak in the language of modern rationality. The parables were written in a deliberately poetic, contradictory, and ambiguous manner. And we do them violence when we make out that there is only one "ultimate" meaning to them.

Against the polyvalence of the parables, the modern constructions of both reason and biblical fundamentalism share a common commitment to singularity and universality—which is ironic, since neither modern reason nor biblical fundamentalism are particularly universal. They

13. Augustine, *De Doctrina Christiana.*
14. Crossan, *Cliffs of Fall.*

are cultural construals with specific pedigrees and not inconsiderable blind spots. Self-authenticating and self-assured, both depend on a cult of certainty that is the antithesis to the ambiguity, mystery and contradiction found within agnosticism or religion.

Atheist fundamentalism and religious fundamentalism also share a remarkable sense of self-righteousness, literally convinced of the justice of their own cause. They also depend on the opposite form of fundamentalism as evidence of the dangers of straying outside their own system. However, while the two appear to be mutually irreconcilable, on closer inspection it is their shared hostility to other ways of thinking or understanding that makes these twin fundamentalisms distinct from other ways of thinking about important questions. Flexible believers, like agnostics and what we shall call self-reflective atheists, share a common commitment to understanding that no one perspective has all the answers. For want of a better term, we could call their approaches postmodern. The postmodern mind rejoices in the contradictions and inconsistencies of human thought, and it does not try to smooth out rough edges and iron out contradictory folds of thought. By contrast, fundamentalism is inherently uncomfortable with the accommodations and changes needed to adapt to a continually changing postmodern world.

Flexible or conventional believers within all major religious traditions insist on engaging with insights from the contemporary world, finding much of religious value in so-called secular disciplines like the humanities, social sciences and natural sciences. But for both of the twin fundamentalisms it has been convenient to erect a barrier between matters of religious belief and the study of science and the humanities. Much is made of the supposed conflict between science and religion, but the actual conflict is far more complicated. There are forms of science, which can be called "scientism," that are as assured as religious fundamentalism in believing that only their discipline can account for why things are the way there are. Equally, other scientists have a humbler and more sophisticated understanding of their discipline and its limits. What matters is not the discipline so much as the way the discipline is used. Albert Einstein knew that his ability to understand fundamental laws of physics did not constitute an ability to answer the fundamental existential questions. Equally, theologians and biblical scholars know that the Scriptures do not constitute scientific evidence or commentary on the physics, biology or chemistry of the natural world.

While the religious fundamentalist is convinced that the Scriptures contain blueprints for understanding all life, atheist fundamentalists are just as profoundly convinced that human reason offers all the explanation necessary for existence. What remains fascinating is how each mimics the other in making exclusive claims, while at the same time shutting down the possibility of engagement with other approaches. It is for this reason that we should no longer talk of a conflict between science and religion, so much as conflict between fundamentalist belief systems and non-fundamentalist belief systems. Atheists, scientists, and religious believers can be found in both types of system. What matters is not so much *what* we believe as *how* we believe. For depending on how we set about believing we find ourselves more or less open to a much richer and varied content to faith. Marshall McLuhan's thesis that the medium is the message is relevant here.[15] In the field of religion this means that the medium of doubt is an essential part of the message of faith. Faith is not the suppression of doubt, it is the affirmation of doubt. Nonetheless, where faith suppresses doubt, the message is clear: refrain from asking too many questions in case a fragile faith breaks apart.

Since the emergence of science, questions of content, or fact, have become dominant both culturally and religiously. Part of the issue here is that believers have sought to justify belief in terms of the content of their belief. A not inconsiderable irony here is how religious fundamentalists have adopted lock, stock, and barrel the language of scientific fact in their treatment of Scripture. What previous generations would never have viewed as literal or scientific truth, has become invested with a quasi-scientific status by religious fundamentalists. By contrast, the religiously flexible who have been accused of playing fast and loose with Scripture, by being open to non-literal approaches and the complexity of adjudicating meaning "once and for all," are using well-tried, several-thousand year-old modes of biblical interpretation.

Whereas religious fundamentalists imagine that they are being loyal to the text of Scripture, the reverse is true. They are being loyal to a particular Enlightenment view of facts, truth, and certainty. While religions across the world understand the importance of metaphor, symbol, story, and ambiguity, the Enlightenment valued scientific truth over all other forms of truth-telling. In adopting a consistently literal reading of the Scriptures fundamentalists have ignored centuries of Judaeo-Christian

15. McLuhan, *Understanding Media*.

insight into the way to approach the Scriptures. While fundamentalists believe in reading Scripture as the Word of God, they are actually reading it as if it were a set of scientific universal truths. Slavoj Žižek puts it clearly when he observes, "A fundamentalist does not believe, he *knows* directly."[16] Within Christianity this habit of proclaiming one's certain or direct knowledge has always been treated suspiciously, hence the distrust of gnostics, literally those who know. In contrast to Gnosticism that proclaims secret knowledge accessible to a few who "know," Christianity has always been more skeptical.

Contemporary fundamentalist approaches to the Scriptures are simply another version of Gnosticism. The obvious problem with such approaches is that the Scriptures are not science, and never have been. Unlike science most of the claims of the Scriptures are inherently unverifiable through empirical evidence. And unlike science most of the truth claims of the Scriptures concern existential, moral, or spiritual realms. Science is not particularly interested in the question of how to love our neighbor. And even if it were, from a strictly scientific viewpoint it has little to contribute. Whatever love may or may not be, as soon as it is reduced to, or translated into, scientific terminology, we are no longer talking about love.

In defense of scientific methodology we need to be clear that scientists rarely claim the kind of certainty that comes so readily to fundamentalists. Although fundamentalism treats the Scriptures as if they were scientifically and objectively true, fundamentalism does this in a thoroughly unscientific way, entirely lacking any mechanism for revising its hypotheses. Scientists understand that an objective account of what happens in the world, a working hypothesis, can always be replaced by an account that makes more sense and fits the data better. A scientist is aware that there is a discrepancy between the way the world is in itself and the ability of science to understand and observe it. Unfortunately, religious fundamentalism adopts only the claims to objective and universal truth, and not the ability to peer review, revise, and improve upon existing theories.

When a scientist is certain of a particular sequence of cause and effect, what a scientist is really saying is that *to date* all the evidence points toward a particular theoretical understanding. By contrast, when a biblical fundamentalist asserts that God's Word tells them to subjugate women

16. Žižek and Gunjević, *God in Pain*, 191.

to men they are asserting that this is a timeless injunction. Whereas science can imagine the world differently and revise an existing theory, fundamentalists deny the possibility of change. Mainstream religion, like mainstream science, assumes that our understanding can deepen and occasionally even actually improve over time. Part of the irony of the fundamentalist dislike of evolution is that it is a religious reality just as much as a scientific one that human understanding changes with time. The Judaeo-Christian Scriptures make it clear that human beings took a long time to arrive at a place where what we take for granted as moral monotheism could take root. Similarly, any observer of religious history can see theology, like science, has evolved over time. Slavery is no longer theologically acceptable, although only up until relatively recently people continued to turn to the Bible to justify such practices. Theology is not always correct, but like science it can self-correct and update. Biblical fundamentalism is not so flexible.

Memory Loss

One of the most powerful challenges to biblical fundamentalists is the notion of time. It is a commonplace to note that the geological scale by which planetary time is measured in millions of years is decisively repudiated by biblical fundamentalists. What is not so well known is that this is repudiated, not for theological reasons, but for quasi-scientific reasons. There is absolutely no good theological reason why the planet could not be hundreds of millions of years old. It really does not matter to a theologian how old the world is. By the same token, whether Jesus was crucified aged thirty-three or thirty-one can have little interest for theologians. But for the biblical fundamentalist these questions of dating and age matter because they are already committed to taking the Scriptures at face value.

Since biblical fundamentalists read the Bible as if it were a scientific document they overlook the fact that the Bible is an edited set of diverse (and often contradictory) narratives and other forms of literature compressed to tell a story. If biblical fundamentalists understood that two or three thousand years ago scientific methodology was not the context of those writing the Bible they would not make this mistake. But as children of modernity, biblical fundamentalists assume that the facts of the Bible can be treated in the same way as empirically verified scientific facts. Once again we see the great irony of how a fundamentalist reading of the text actually enacts a terrible violence against the text by refusing to admit its own prejudices. And once again we are exposed to the irony of just how contemporary and recent a phenomenon biblical fundamentalism is.

One of the unique features of religious fundamentalism is that it has no sense of shared memory, history, or tradition. In the Enlightenment science and reason mocked tradition as primitive, irrational, and inherently superstitious. Anything that could not be explained rationally was no longer of value. In Immanuel Kant's classic turn of phrase, the point of Enlightenment was that one would dare to know (*audere sapere*).[17] Religious believers reacted to this onslaught in radically different ways. Some, like Kant, sought accommodation, trying to rethink religious categories within the new language of rationality. Some stuck ever faster to the traditional beliefs and practices they had inherited. But fundamentalists seized upon the Enlightenment to extricate themselves from both the layers of tradition and history that had up to this point formed and shaped religious beliefs and practices as well as the specifics of the new rationality.

In yet another profound irony, the fundamental value that both modern rationality and fundamentalist faith share is trust in the Enlightenment promise that highest values are universal, independent of tradition, and clearly knowable. For the modern rationalist reason is the highest value, while for the fundamentalist it is the Scriptures. However, each rely on an Enlightenment attitude that denies the role played by memory, tradition, and history. Each believes we are to be freed from subservience to the ideas of those who have gone before us. And each believes that this new situation requires a radical break with the past.

The Enlightenment is of course old news. Parts of the Enlightenment have been extraordinarily important in developing our future as human beings. The emancipation of women and the end of slavery are key achievements inaugurated, albeit still far from accomplished, by Enlightenment values (not to mention theological ones). At the same time, Enlightenment also rests upon some pretty un-enlightened privileging of the perspectives of, for instance, white Western males at the center of the world. It is impossible now not to be at least somewhat suspicious of the Enlightenment's desire for universal truths as enshrining certain local Western truths over and against the different experiences and wisdoms of

17. Kant, "An Answer to the Question: 'What is Enlightenment?'"

others. Kant may have encouraged us to dare to know, but he never for a moment seriously thought that the "us" he was writing for might include women or those from different cultural or socioeconomic backgrounds.

For those who have been tutored to think that Enlightenment values represent all that is virtuous, and fundamentalist values all that is perverse, it will come as something of a shock to discover how connected they are. But the truth remains that in each case an appeal to universal truth masks deep-seated problems. Tradition, wisdom, and community are all forgotten in the rush to dare to know. For the fundamentalist all that matters is whether you know the text of the Scriptures. While for science knowledge that is unverified is suspect, so for fundamentalists knowledge that is not identified by chapter and verse is no longer important.

As Brad Gregory suggests, the Reformation was a key turning point in the creation of the Enlightenment.[18] With the birth of Protestantism came an explosion of competing religious ideas and the disappearance of any shared religious structure capable of adjudicating between different theological beliefs. After decades of religious wars failed to settle religious disputes Europeans were anxious to find a way beyond the divisions of Protestantism and Catholicism. In Gregory's genealogy, modern reason allied to economic progress emerges as a savior, literally enabling warring parties to finally come to an agreement on questions outside the areas of doctrinal and dogmatic disagreement. The rational pursuit of economic growth becomes a point of convergence across religious divisions, while nonetheless beginning from a shared Christian background. It is not insignificant that Descartes himself was a soldier in one of these religious wars and his philosophical system offers a rational grounding that is inherently non-sectarian, and as capable of being put to use by Catholics and Protestants alike.

Before the Reformation there would have been no suggestion that the Scriptures were somehow universal and free of community, history, or tradition. The belief in the universality and truth of Scripture ultimately depends not on any internal logic, but on a fundamental combination of Protestant Reformation belief and the Enlightenment values that emerge from the Reformation. The fact that such values themselves are increasingly under question and criticism merely serves to illustrate just how hard it is to be a religious fundamentalist in an uncertain world. Founded

18. Gregory, *Unintended Reformation.*

as a religious reaction to the dominance of rationality, fundamentalism has a schizoid relation to truth and reason. It wants to believe in truth and reason, and it believes truth and reason are eternal values free of any grounding in history, culture, or society. With the biases and prejudices of Enlightenment rationality increasingly under question fundamentalism is in a tricky situation. Fundamentalism remains bound to the Scriptures. But it also remains bound to a now very old fashioned trust in unchanging timeless truths that have little to do with the Scriptures. Or to put it another way, in a world where scientific experts and philosophers alike admit they fundamentally do not know everything, fundamentalism is holding on by its fingertips to the idea that its knowledge rests on sure and certain foundations. Such certainty is the bequest of an Enlightenment way of thinking that has long departed the halls of university lecture theaters. Paradoxically, fundamentalism is a powerful reminder of how the quest for knowledge has been deaf and blind to centuries of human experience. The beating heart of fundamentalism is not religious fervour so much as the calculating Enlightenment rationality of one very certain universal truth transposed onto the Scriptures.

On Not Knowing

Admitting that we do not know much about God should be one of the central tenets of orthodox Christian belief (Judaism and Islam seem a lot further advanced on this front). From the great mystics to geniuses like Einstein, Christians have always recognized that our knowledge of God is partial, confused, and far from perfect. And at decisive moments in the emergence of orthodox Christianity the church admitted that it did not and could not understand everything. The Council of Chalcedon in 451 is famous for clarifying the classic understanding of Christ's two natures, human and divine. However, this was not an exercise in explanation. By contrast, Chalcedon affirmed that we do not know how they relate, going on to refute as heresy positions that offered clear explanations of the relationship. While Chalcedon affirmed the complete humanity and total divinity of Christ, the details of how this might actually work were never something it could be clear about.

Chalcedon is less a final word on the relationship between Christ's humanity and divinity, and more of a signpost pointing beyond itself to a mystery that is barely capable of being stated (and even less susceptible to being understood). It is an example of Christianity speaking of faith rather than providing knowledge. Faith in this sense is attitudinal, an orientation to something or other. Just to make things even more confusing, however, faith is also spoken of as a noun rather than a verb. When we hear talk of the Christian faith, people are thinking of faith as a particular set of propositions, a particular "data set" of beliefs. Ironically, throughout history there have been those who have sought to overdetermine and clarify what can be said about such matters. While heresy remains a byword for unconventional or radical thought, the history of Christianity reveals that heresy was as often as not the province of those who sought refuge in the absolute certainty of propositions. Heretics deserve applause for their intellectual honesty and desire to make everything fit neatly together. Unfortunately, such an approach could only succeed by neglecting the parts that did not want to fit neatly together, which for the early church was actually quite a lot. In contrast, what emerges in the run up to Chalcedon as orthodox Christian teaching is the realization that doctrines such as the divinity and humanity of Christ take time to develop and really cannot be easily reduced to a set of definitive propositions.

Unfortunately, the problem with faith as propositional is that this threatens to make Christian ideas sound as if they are propositions of the same ilk as scientific propositions. Unfortunately, few, if any, of the central ideas of Christianity can be reduced to or compared to scientific propositions. To take just one, the resurrection, is to immediately notice that from a scientific perspective there cannot be a resurrection. There can be a resuscitation of a corpse, or a reanimation of something previously dead. But from its earliest telling, the resurrection has never been simply about a dead body turning into a living body. The resurrection also implies some form of transformation that makes the resurrected body not just the old body alive once more. Whatever resurrection might be in the Scriptures (a very open question), one thing no one, disciple or denier, has ever claimed was that the resurrected Christ was a zombie.

Of course, it would be completely understandable to want to simply reject the resurrection as inherently impossible by the standards of science. Resurrection seems to be somewhat beyond the bounds of what science can imagine, especially when we take into account the ambiguity of whether the resurrected one looked much like the crucified one. Reanimation, however, is not scientifically unthinkable. Nor is it logically impossible for someone to pass out and be taken for dead. Yet, neither reanimation nor not-quite-dying is a coherent explanation for what the

New Testament claims happened to the person of Jesus. If Christianity is to speak with a modicum of scientific honesty we need to acknowledge that there are some—indeed, quite a significant number—of beliefs that do not make sense scientifically. The question remains whether making sense scientifically (which I contend resurrection does *not*) also means that such beliefs are entirely devoid of meaning.

On the other hand, what seems uncalled for is the unprincipled adoption of the language of science to argue for beliefs that science cannot justify. Resurrection is one of many other beliefs that cannot be scientifically proven. Approaching resurrection as an object of scientific study presents religious believers with a difficult choice to make. They can side with a traditional scientific response and reject resurrection outright, as impossible, as something that is inherently unverifiable, in a class of its own, and lacking a control group of other resurrections to be compared with. Or they can side with a fundamentalist scientific response and argue that the literal word of the Scriptures clearly reveals a new category of scientific event, that of the resurrection itself. However, both these approaches would be neglecting one important piece of context, the fact that the Scriptures do not even hint at the resurrection as an object of scientific study.

In a similar vein in her wonderful essay on the resurrection, Sarah Coakley notes how modern theological responses to resurrection have tended to divide into two dominant camps.[19] There are those who take seriously Lockean and Humean approaches to verification, who argue that any talk of resurrection is to affirm that there is just as much historical evidence for resurrection as for any other historical event. The other camp is represented by Karl Barth and Søren Kierkegaard, for whom resurrection can never simply be a matter of history. For Barth and Kierkegaard, an attitude of faith is the only way of receiving the resurrection. The historical record can raise the question of resurrection, but resurrection itself is ahistorical, only faith can lay claim to it.

Coakley wants to suggest an alternative between arguing for the certain knowing of resurrection as an historical event and the blind faith of those who believe history cannot contain sure-fire evidence for the resurrection. Using a combination of Ludwig Wittgenstein and a close reading of the gospel accounts of resurrection, Coakley shows how a significant case can be built for seeing resurrection as neither an out-and-out certain historical event, nor a matter of blind trust. Instead, she introduces the

19. Coakley, *Powers and Submissions*, 130–52.

possibility that "we 'perceive' at 'different levels,' according to the development of our devoutness."[20] Taking seriously the idea of different levels of perception accounts for why in the stories almost no one recognizes the risen Christ when they first meet him. It also neatly rescues resurrection from being decisively shown to be either scientifically or historically possible. By contrast, Coakley opens up the possibility that some of the deepest and most critical theological questions can still be grounded in historical reality, while not circumscribed by one particular account of that history. In addition, by drawing attention to how the first women witnesses of resurrection were disbelieved, Coakley reminds us that it is the women who were not legally capable of being witnesses who were the first to witness the resurrection. It may not be too farfetched to suggest that scientific method operates today a little like first-century patriarchy did then: blind to that which it cannot imagine. So to suggest that science cannot see the resurrection is not to suggest that there is no resurrection, simply that resurrection is not a proper object of scientific study.

It is not just outrageous religious beliefs that encourage a response of doubt. We also have to countenance the possibility that for all that science and history are critically important to making sense of the world, they cannot reveal everything. Both Cartesian and Baconian knowledge are good at giving philosophical or empirical accounts of reality. However, there is much of human experience that neither the Cartesian nor the Baconian can capture. A Mozart piano sonata can be described in both a Cartesian and a Baconian fashion, but neither account can properly begin to describe the emotional experience that arises from the music. To be human is not simply to be a thinking machine, and much that is most true in life cannot easily be reduced to either the Baconian or Cartesian. Some forms of knowledge have to be of the order of the women witnesses to the resurrection. Knowledge does not always conform to every scientific or historical desire for objectivity, but may nonetheless be utterly true. Given that the Scriptures have no pretensions to being science, but every indication of being stories, it will be important to explore the genre of narrative in more detail if we are to excavate the truth of stories like the resurrection. This critical subject will be one we return to in subsequent chapters. For now what we have seen is how Scripture itself raises questions that cannot simply be reduced to scientific knowledge. Or, to put it another way, stories like the resurrection (and a great many other strange happenings) show how good the Scriptures are at challenging both the

20. Ibid., 145.

certainties of science and religion. Here the obvious p
tant one: there is much that sounds downright absurd,
in the Scriptures. Yet, perhaps that is the point. Precise
viously *not* scientific, the Scriptures beg to be read nc
literature. And as we shall see, the truth of literature
not) cannot be grasped by confusing it with the truth
and Juliet is not a story that can be explained by offering an interpretation
of what chemicals might have been present in Romeo and Juliet's brains.
In the same way, the resurrection is not going to be explained by recourse
to the pathology lab.

If, as Caputo argues, we do not know who we are, then it also seems
the better part of intellectual valor to argue that we also do not know
much about a great many other matters. Chief amongst these would be
questions of religious meaning. Echoing Augustine, Caputo suggests that
not knowing is actually the highest religious passion. If we do not know
who we are, we are left not with nothing but with a particular form of passion: "The passion *of* not knowing, truth without Knowledge, the restless
heart. *Inquietum est cor nostrum.*"[21] Creeds and councils have produced
many doctrines throughout the centuries, but none of these can ultimately be judged as scientific propositions by scientific standards of evidence.
Scientifically there is no evidence for resurrection. What remains is the
possibility that for the very best rational reasons there are places where
rationality simply cannot take us any further—which is not to encourage
a retreat to a literal reading of Scripture. Rather, it is to suggest that along
with the apostle Thomas a first reaction to the resurrection must be one
of doubt. Nevertheless, in voicing our doubt the question remains, does
doubt in itself offer the final word? Or is doubt a stage in making an attitudinal adjustment toward faith?

Doubting Wisely

The argument of this chapter is that until there is doubt there can be
no faith. The two are co-constituting, inseparable, and intertwined. Faith
without doubt is like a wordless book or a cinema without moving pic-
tures: simultaneously void and nonsensical. Seen in this light, perhaps
part of the point of central doctrines such as the resurrection is to crystal-
lize that even where reason can go no further, doubt can still encourage a
deeper type of thinking beyond simple repudiation or rejection.

21. Caputo, *On Religion*, 127.

But let us be clear that this understanding of the limits of reason
, not the same as the sixteenth-century rallying cry *sola fide*, "by faith
alone." A lot of contaminated water has gone under a lot of denomi-
national and religious bridges in the last four hundred years. And part
of the difficulty is that the return to the religious texts initiated by the
sixteenth-century Reformation created its own monstrosities. What began as a purifying and reformist return to Scripture quickly ossified into
a new form of scriptural authoritarianism. Martin Luther's *sola fide* was
inseparable from a *sola scriptura*, "by Scripture alone." Sweeping away all
traditions and reasons that could not be justified on scriptural grounds
the reformers did enormous damage to religion, even as they sought to
renew and reform it. Indeed, without the Reformation, religious fundamentalism would not have emerged in the way it has.

While Luther deserves respect and admiration for his unerring ability to speak truth to some of the powers of his day, a reappraisal of Protestant pieties is well over due. Luther was rooted in his times, and while his
rhetoric offered liberation it also had dangerous and unhelpful results,
not least in the field of politics and Christianity's relationship to Judaism.
It is also not irrelevant to the current discussion to remember that it was
also Luther who argued (against Erasmus) against doubt: "Anathema to
the Christian who will not be certain of what he is supposed to believe,
and who does not comprehend it. How can he believe that which he
doubts?"[22] By contrast, Erasmus argued, quite sensibly enough, that it
was not possible to know everything for certain.

We no longer live in the sixteenth century, and solutions for contemporary challenges will not be found there. Instead, it is important to
take note of those like James Simpson who have shown how some of the
worst fundamentalist traits began as sixteenth-century "reformist" inventions.[23] If it is possible to discover a more sophisticated way of relating to
God, there also needs to be critical distance from Lutheran Wittenberg
just as much as Catholic Rome or Calvinist Geneva. Solutions to the challenges raised by science and an increasingly complex set of societal shifts
are neither going to be found by retreating into the Scriptures nor by
turning the clock back to the sixteenth century.

Approaching questions of God and questions of faith can only start
to make sense if we peer through the lens of the last two hundred years of
doubt. The theme running through the present work is that unless faith

22. Luther, *On the Bondage of the Will*.

23. Simpson, *Burning to Read*.

arises out of doubt, it is not really faith. Faith needs to have
in the eyes and seen its own reflection. Faith can no lon
as an antidote to doubt. Faith is always in an irreducible
doubt. As Francis Spufford writes of both the experienc
experience of the presence of God, "The whole thing is—has w .
certain right down to the root."[24] Recognizing the uncertainty of life does
not need to lead to projecting certainty onto religious faith. By contrast,
where doubt is banished, certainty intrudes, and faith runs the risk of no
longer being an attitude that affirms what we know to be unknowable.

Uncertainty is not just a social reality. It is also a reality that lies
at the heart of religion. And while religion has been distorted into an
endeavor to find security, true religion has less to do with finding security than embracing the flux of insecurity. God has been portrayed as
the stabilizer of society and religion. But God has also been detected in
earthquake, wind, and fire. Just as religion has historically been at fault
where it tried to control people, religion has also made the mistake of trying to control God. Certainty allows for a more perfect control on both
fronts. By contrast, uncertainty makes it less easy to exercise domination.

The central religious question of our own age is how much uncertainty are we willing to admit in respect of religion? The less uncertainty,
the closer we come to fundamentalism in either its religious or atheist
forms. By contrast, where uncertainty is welcomed as a natural feature of
faith a much larger sea of faith emerges. Part of the purpose of religion
is to offer release from false certainties. Faith requires a movement away
from the firmness of the shore, into the shallows and eventually into the
deeps. To do this requires a willingness to embrace the insecurity at the
heart of faith. Far from being enemies of faith, doubt and uncertainty
enable faith to be something other than a religious rejection of the complexity of life. Descartes and Bacon founded systems of certainty that
sought to exclude doubt from science and philosophy. The fact that their
foundations of certainty have proven unable to coexist with a concept of
God should alert us to the necessary connection between doubting and
believing. The injunction of John Donne, another metaphysical luminary
of the seventeenth century, to "doubt wisely" is worth recollecting once
again.[25] Doubt need not compete with belief. Doubt is instead the horizon upon which faith emerges.

24. Spufford, *Unapologetic*, 72.
25. Donne, "Satyre III," in *Poetical Works*, 139.

2

AFTER REASON

Atheists say they want a secular world, but a world defined by the absence of the Christians' god is still a Christian world. Secularism is like chastity, a condition defined by what it denies. If atheism has a future, it can only be in a Christian revival;

—JOHN GRAY[1]

Religion will not go away; it will not be repressed; it will not succumb to instrumental reasoning. There will be no new Enlightenment.

—GRAHAM WARD[2]

WE HAVE SEEN HOW the question of doubt becomes visible at the same time as developments in the understanding of philosophy and science in the seventeenth century. The rise of rationality also provides the impetus for a flourishing of doubt. Where the Enlightenment witnessed the rise of reason, it also gave birth to a prodigious questioning of religious beliefs. But while Descartes harnessed reason to faith in God, the history of subsequent philosophical endeavor cannot be told without recounting the rise of atheism. The doubt that Bacon represses and Descartes attempts to transform into a basis for certainty increasingly leads to a sustained

1. Gray, *Straw Dogs*, 126–27.
2. Ward, *Politics of Discipleship*.

questioning of metaphysical presuppositions that Descartes and Bacon would never have dreamed of.

The philosophical history of the eighteenth and nineteenth centuries introduces a plethora of thinkers who have challenged religious belief, casting doubt on the existence of God. David Hume (1711–1776) doubted the possibility of miracles. Arthur Schopenhauer (1788–1860) affirmed that God was simply an illusion, a human projection. Karl Marx (1818–1883) challenged the complicity of religion with the forces of economic inequality. Sigmund Freud (1856–1939) saw religion as a primitive way of navigating problems that only psychoanalysis could properly describe or solve. Friedrich Nietzsche (1844–1900) believed religion was responsible for limiting and shackling the human spirit. The precise contours of these histories have been well explored, and have been recounted in detail by others.[3] At this point, it is important to note just how powerful these critiques of religion have remained throughout the twentieth century and into the new millennium. In particular, Marx, Freud, and Nietzsche epitomized the hermeneutics of suspicion, that is, they alert us to the presence of prejudices and presuppositions that can corrupt otherwise apparently transparent appeals to reason. Taken together they provide a thoroughgoing critique of how imbalances in economics, desire, and power corrupt our ability to get to the truth of our world and our own identities. It is impossible to imagine the history of subsequent philosophy without their respective contributions. Nor can the subsequent history of theology or faith be undertaken without a sustained engagement with their thought. As Merold Westphal has argued the insights of these suspicious atheists remain invaluable for theology.[4] Whether a theist, atheist, humanist, or agnostic, we are all heirs to the thought of Marx, Freud, and Nietzsche. Regardless of how seriously one takes their respective critiques, collectively they show how reason can no longer (if it ever could) be thought of as singular. It makes less sense to speak of a single framework of rationality so much as different ways of constructing rationality. The combined effect of the critiques of Marx, Freud, and Nietzsche is to challenge not only the naiveté of certain forms of religious belief, but also the naiveté that there is a single dominant discourse of rationality.

3. There is a vast literature, and other explicitly atheist thinkers who could be added to this list. For an excellent overview see Hyman, *A Short History of Atheism*.

4. Westphal, *Suspicion and Faith*.

The story of secularization is commonly recounted as the rise of rationality allied to the elimination of religion. As people become better educated and more rational, so the story goes, they become more modern and less religious. It is only a matter of time before advancing rationality makes everyone more secular, and religion becomes a thing of the distant past. Allegedly. However, when the idea, to adapt Tolkien's description of the ring of power, that there is "one rationality to rule them all" is exposed as a mirage, then the inexorable decline of religion against the force of rationality must itself be called into question. So long as both reason and religion have been conceived as singular and oppositional the traditional modern fairy-tale of secularization can suffice. In that tale religion and reason are incommensurate. Yet, once the secret of multiple rationalities is revealed, it is only natural to wonder whether any of these multiple rationalities cannot also happily coexist with religious belief. Or to put it another way, if reason is incapable of providing a decisive once-and-for-all argument *for* religious belief (which is surely self-evident) then it is also just as self-evident that reason can no longer (if it ever really could) provide decisive grounds for the elimination of religious faith. While reason may not be able to deliver a *coup de grâce* on either side of the argument, this is not the same as saying that rationality can have nothing to do with elucidating or explicating faith. And although recent history reveals that certain constructions of rationality have been efficiently and effectively marshaled against faith, this does not preclude the possibility of a more harmonious relationship between faith and rationality.

Within the last fifty years the assumptions behind the secularization thesis have been challenged on several fronts. Not only is it no longer obvious that reason is singular, it is also no longer obvious that religious belief is anathema to all forms of reason. Furthermore, as Giorgio Agamben has suggested, secularization has not so much eradicated religion as shifted religion from one sphere to another, that of the secular realm, especially politics, government, and the state:

> Secularization is a form of repression. It leaves intact the forces it deals with simply by moving them from one place to another. Thus the political secularization of theological concepts (the transcendence of God as a paradigm of sovereign power) does nothing but displace the heavenly monarchy onto an earthly monarchy, leaving its power intact.[5]

5. Agamben, *Profanations*, 77.

We will examine the thought of Agamben in more detail later in chapter 6. For now it simply needs to be noted how the doubt (of religious faith) that played an important role in the development of competing rationalities is not unconnected to the doubt that makes it impossible to continue to believe in the undisputed precedence of any one particular form of rationality. Ironically, just as there is no obvious way of deciding *between* the differing claims of different rational systems so there is no longer any obvious way of deciding *against* the different claims of religious systems. In short, the attitude of doubt that initially led to the construction of new rationalities now leads away again from rationality alone and back to other ways of settling questions of meaning. It is in this sense that it is possible to speak of being "after reason." We are both *after* reason, in the sense that we seek reason despite the failure to agree upon one specific version of rationality as well as postrational, or what is sometimes described as postsecular, recognizing that we are no longer living in an age where there is a single framework of secular rationality inherently opposed to faith.

One sign of this dislocation appears in the increasingly visible signs of religion across the globe. What was once envisioned as the triumph of secularism has singularly failed to materialize. While the situation in Western Europe is markedly different from North America and the rest of the world, the philosophical rise of doubt has not always mapped onto a decline in religious belief. Even extremely secular societies like France and Sweden are discovering that religion has not disappeared. The situation is even more marked in traditionally atheist China, which is undergoing unprecedented economic and religious growth. As Graham Ward notes, human beings really do not seem to be voting with their feet for an Enlightenment diet of unadulterated rationality: religion continues to rear up just when you least expect it.[6] As will be seen in subsequent chapters there is also significant evidence of self-identified atheists choosing to engage more deeply with religion. Increasingly it is largely impossible for even the European secular world to ignore the part played by religion both domestically and internationally. In America religion's role is more assured, with even the most secular states (the East Coast and, in particular, New England) reporting much higher rates of religiosity than is common in Europe. And the situation in the rest of the world is almost

6. Ward, *The Politics of Discipleship.*

universally one where religious questions continue to influence, if not dominate, the fields of both private beliefs and public policy.

It may be a coincidence that religion has come to the fore at the same time as new technological innovations. But given the historical interrelation between religion and new technological forms, this is unlikely. The dissemination of sacred Scriptures has always been connected to manufacturing techniques. Religions of the book have required physical texts and for much of recorded history the means of production have been costly and of a concomitant high status. The transition from monastic scriptoria to sixteenth-century printing presses enabled the swift dissemination of old and new ideas alike. By the mid-twentieth century television enabled the construction of a new kind of mass-market relationship to the text in the form of televangelism. The phenomenon of the internet is simply the latest iteration of a form of technological dissemination whose new religious possibilities are barely beginning to be explored. With smartphones the faithful can pray without ever touching the pages of holy books. We live within an age of that is simultaneously dematerializing and reenchanting. What defines the real is no longer as obvious as it once was. No longer do we live in an era of industrialization when all that mattered was the material world. Instead, things that once seemed immaterial, unreal, or impossible are increasingly part of everyday life.

At this point one important word needs to be said about the history of the twentieth century. While it witnessed impressive leaps in scientific and technological prowess, the twentieth century also witnessed some of the worst horrors of human history. The history of rationality has not always been the history of progress. From the Nazi death camps to the purges of Stalin, bureaucratic rationality achieved unprecedented levels of murderous efficiency. The twentieth century reminds us that, while the rise of rationality has been perceived as coming at the expense of religion, it is also possible to interpret this rise at the even greater expense of humanity. While Marx, Freud, and Nietzsche have become well known as pertinent critics of humanity's hubris, history also reveals how unwilling humans have been to face up to their criticisms. It is no longer possible to assume, as our Enlightenment forebears did before the outbreak of the First World War, that the rise of rationality (alongside a decline in religion) will lead inexorably to a happier more egalitarian kind of life. Instead, it seems increasingly plausible to suggest that the rule of rationality does not always equate with an increase in human flourishing. This is not to duck the question of how religion has also played a terribly divisive and frequently deadly role in history. It has. It is simply not possible to pretend that faithful people have been particularly better people than faithless people. Nonetheless, while Descartes sought refuge in rationality from the shadow of the religious wars of the seventeenth century so today the events of two world wars (not to mention subsequent conflicts and ever-growing inequalities) cast just as lengthy shadows over more recent secular thought.

Unless we remember what Edith Wyschogrod has termed the manmade mass death of the twentieth century it is not possible to understand why it is important to challenge those that proclaim they have grasped the truth with certainty and conviction.[7] Ideology, rationality, and religious faith have all promised such certainty at times. One of the questions that animates this work is whether there is a connection between the offer of certainty and a determination to see those who lack the identical certainty as less than human and unworthy of being treated with respect. The history of the twentieth century reminds us that atrocities and genocides have generally been committed by those who profess certainty about their own privileged and certain understanding of the truth. Whether the truth in question is one of race, nationality, faith, ideology, or culture, the privileging of certain truths as being beyond question has always entailed the subordination of particular human beings.

In the previous chapter we saw how atheism and fundamentalism are produced by a similar paradigm that affirms a singular version of rationality and a desire for certainty. Later, in chapter 4, we will explore in more detail what the theological implications of evil are, and whether an interpretation of evil can emerge that does some kind of justice to the horrors of evil. Now, having briefly acknowledged some of the horrific twentieth-century experience of certainty, it is time to address what rationality and religion might look like when certainty is removed from the equation.

In order to do this it is helpful to reflect on the distinction Eleonore Stump makes between two different forms of knowing.[8] The kind of knowing that we most often think about is the kind of knowing *that* something is either philosophically or scientifically (objectively, analytically, or empirically) true. This is the form of knowledge that prevails in the

7. Wyschogrod, *Spirit in Ashes.*

8. Stump, *Wandering and Darkness*, 36–63.

academy and sciences. Whether it is Baconian, Cartesian, or the product of some other scientific or philosophical system Stump gives knowledge *that* something is true the typological label Dominican. Stump notes how St. Dominic always argued for certain objective truths, founding an order that modeled itself on disseminating and arguing for these objective truths. In contrast to this Dominican knowledge there is, however, a form of knowledge that is more personal, experiential, and intuitive, a kind of knowledge that Stump calls Franciscan. For St. Francis and the order that he founds, the subjective, personal dimension of truth is important: and to learn about truth entails entering into a subjective relationship to it. Franciscanly-speaking one can talk of the personal experience of falling in love with another person and that would lead to a certain understanding and formulation of what love is. Domincanly-speaking the same scenario would entail an observer concluding from certain phenomena how two individuals appear to be in love with one another. While we understand that the observer objectively (Dominicanly-speaking) understands the salient features of the situation, we can also appreciate that it is only the actual lovers who (Franciscanly-speaking) have knowledge of the true feeling, depth, and range of their love. Dominican knowledge cannot advance us very far in knowing the true extent of what it means to be in love. Nor can it ultimately provide us with the entirety of the response to the deepest existential and religious questions. It can assert what might be objectively true in any given philosophical or empirical account of reality, but it cannot deal well with the messiness or drama of human experience.

Stump's characterization of Franciscan ways of knowing further underlines that the category of narrative will always be a feature of Franciscan knowledge. It is not impossible for someone who has not fallen in love to learn about falling in love. It is simply easier to learn about love from stories rather than scientific accounts. As Stump explains,

> a story gives a person some of what she would have if she had had unmediated personal interaction with the characters in the story while they were conscious and interacting with each other, without actually making her part of the story itself.[9]

Narrative is particularly conducive to explaining some of the most profound human truths. If we are to begin to release ourselves from the straightjacket of certainty offered by Dominican forms of knowledge, we

9. Ibid., 78.

will then need to entertain the notion that there are important truths waiting to be discovered in narrative.

Stump's Franciscan knowledge recognizes how stories reveal a much more intimate form of knowledge than the propositional knowledge gained by a Dominican or philosophical approach. Her reason for calling this kind of knowledge Franciscan in the first place is the simple fact of how many different experiential stories about the life of Francis have survived. Stories sharing something of the experience of Francis are legion, and together, whatever the objective truth behind them, they present a significant picture of an individual who had a profound experience of God. To be Franciscan was to share in a Franciscan way of being, one that St. Francis typified. By contrast, there are almost no stories about the life of St. Dominic, and his own life is almost completely immaterial to his mission. To be Dominican is to be less concerned with imitating Dominic, and more concerned with learning and sharing the objective knowledge that Dominic taught.

The remainder of this chapter will explore different portrayals of the interface between religious belief, rationality, and questions of doubt. This will be done "Franciscanly-speaking," through the use of narrative. Lacking any pretensions to objectivity, scientific accuracy, or philosophical acuity, narrative allows us to range widely while honing in on the experience of living with questions of faith and doubt. To further free this experiment in thinking from being entirely subsumed by the details of our current historical circumstances we will confine ourselves to science-fiction narratives. This focus allows us to underline the imaginative scope of this chapter, and also to explore esoteric and theoretical arrangements.

Given the fact that for the last three hundred years rationality has been assumed by many to be opposed to both doubt and faith, science fiction offers one way of questioning the veracity of this premise. This is not to suggest that science fiction is entirely ahistorical, lacking context or understanding of the past. However, in studying science fiction it is possible to bring different assumptions about rationality and faith into clearer focus. One of the other great benefits of choosing science fiction is that it is hard to forget the fictitious nature of sci-fi. Being fictions does not mean they are not "true," but it does make it harder to take their accounts too seriously, as if they were somehow the last word on the subject. In focusing on uncertainty as a theme, it is critical to avoid being overly dogmatic about what might constitute alternatives to religious and anti-religious practitioners of certainty. Science fiction makes such dogmatic moves difficult to make since, after all, it is just sci-fi. Through a close analysis of the genre it will be seen how there are a variety of ways of reimagining both religion and science in the wake of doubt without descending into the fundamentalist certainties identified in the previous chapter. In what follows we will identify three different paradigms for understanding the nature of the potential relationship between rationality and religion. While each concerns an ostensibly futuristic story, it will also be seen how these are stories about our current circumstances.

First Paradigm—The Force

The first paradigm is found in John Caputo's reading of *Star Wars*.[10] Caputo contextualizes *Star Wars* within the experience of a post-industrial digital revolution. Unlike the world of Freud, Marx, or Nietzsche our world is no longer either as materialist or as singularly rational. For Caputo the new technologies of cyberspace in particular free us from the dominant physical metaphors of earlier scientific knowledge. No longer constrained by the material world, we now inhabit a world of "cyber-spirits" in which our eyes are opened to the powerful reality of the spiritual.[11] In a world of the everyday, and increasingly unremarkable, marvels of GPS receivers, smartphones, and tablets it no longer seems inconceivable to posit the existence of the non-material. Freed by technology from the supposed limits of the material world we are becoming much more comfortable with ideas that a previous generation would have found fanciful. If it has been traditional to believe in God as the one who connects, it is easy to see how the invisibility of technologies such as Wi-Fi, 4G, and Bluetooth connectivity conspire to make the possibility of the divine more rather than less real.

Caputo identifies the movie *Star Wars* as a potent metaphor for this new techno-religious situation. Although there is no formal institutional church or deity, *Star Wars* has all the accoutrements of religion in the digital age. Describing this situation as "religion without religion," Caputo advocates a way of understanding the divine in a post-Copernican framework that no longer places God at the literal center of the universe. With God displaced from the controlling center, the church too is displaced from its role as guarding and guaranteeing access to God.

10. Caputo, *On Religion*.
11. Ibid., 69.

Within this new post-religious, yet still religious, cosmos the Jedi knights look and act as if they were members of a monastic order with access to both mystical thought and hi-tech weaponry. The ultimate power that binds the universe together is the force, a somewhat nebulous mystical-cum-scientific reality. Religion in *Star Wars* appears not to be the same as contemporary religion. But there is no denying that the underlying philosophy of *Star Wars* is closer to a form of religious belief than to secularism. Religion is not banished in *Star Wars*, it has simply been re-imagined, "teched-up," and harmonized with science. Although the 1960s imagined the death of God and the absence of religion, the world of the late seventies *Star Wars* reveals a new way of imagining religion.

It is illuminating to contrast this with the place of religion in the earlier television show *Star Trek* (first aired in 1966). While *Star Wars* essentially fuses religion and science into a new cosmology there is almost no sign of anything remotely religious in *Star Trek*. *Star Trek* presents a distinctively modern narrative about the pursuit of scientific knowledge, while *Star Wars* assumes that science cannot explain everything. Where Captain Kirk boldly goes where no one has been before, using the latest scientific instruments of exploration, the Skywalker family are privileged by having uniquely religious-cum-scientific prowess that enables them to manipulate the physical universe to great effect. Luke Skywalker does not use technology to save the day, rather his gift is the gift of being able to let go of depending on rationality and technology and instead "use the Force." In Episode IV's final assault on the Battlestar it is not weaponry or technical skill that prove decisive but mysticism—or mumbo-jumbo, depending on your perspective. If for nothing else *Star Wars* deserves acclaim as a movie featuring a scene of passive introspection at its dramatic heart. Where *Star Trek* relies on *The Enterprise* and its crew using their skills to get out of tricky situations, Luke quietly turns off his targeting device in order to meditate or focus, a non-action that results in the eventual combustion of a military space station.

The nearest *Star Trek* approaches to this type of religious-scientific hybridity is a character who has extra reserves of empathy: something still resolutely located within scientific and psychological fields of explanation. To adapt the insight of the German philosopher Immanuel Kant, the worldview of *The Enterprise* is identical to the court of reason that finds God wanting for not having his papers in order. Kant argued that we needed to "dare to know," and he devoted a lifetime to articulating the precise conditions for knowledge and what we could truly know.[12] The subsequent history of modernity is the affirmation of knowledge and rationality as the highest forms of human understanding. By contrast, the story of Skywalker, as Caputo frames it, suggests that not knowing might be an even more profitable line of inquiry.

Within *Star Trek* science has been so successful in effacing and erasing religion that there is almost no sign of it. By contrast within *Star Wars* science works in harmony with religion, and can be used in support of religious knowledge. Even with the remarkably horrible *Star Wars* prequels released at the end of the 1990s, this fusion of science and religion remains. When the Jedi take a blood sample to analyze the density of midichlorians they are scientifically determining the strength of the force. At the same time, the scientific approach to the force by the Jedi is not shared by all. Doubting the existence of the force is also rife in the galaxy, and belief in it seems to be the preserve of the Jedi elite. Dismissed on occasion as Jedi "mind tricks" *Star Wars* presents a range of responses to things that are strictly speaking scientifically inexplicable.

While *Star Wars* remains willing to incorporate elements that exceed the capacity of science to explain them, *Star Trek* remains firmly wedded to the idea of explaining everything scientifically. The voyage of discovery for the *Starship Enterprise* is a voyage into new territory but using the same scientific laws that operated for its writers on twentieth-century earth. By contrast, the science of *Star Wars* is as much religion as it is science. The science of *Star Wars* is not the same as twentieth- (or even twenty-first-) century science, and the difference is not quantitative so much as qualitative. Where *Star Wars* ends the animosity between science and religion by remolding both disciplines into a new *tertium quid*, *Star Trek* merely replicates the old-fashioned Enlightenment supremacy of science over religion. With barely any religion in *Star Trek* (exceptions are made for fraudulent religion) there is also no hint of mystery. Everything in the trekky world can be understood. It may take time, and it may require unexpected technological leaps, but there is nothing inherently mystical or religious that science cannot explain. The *Star Trek* motto of boldly going where no one has gone before is ultimately little more than a reprise of a quite dated Victorian trust in the inevitable power of rational progress. Contrariwise, the world of *Star Wars* is a world of titanic

12. Kant, "An Answer to the Question: 'What is Enlightenment,'" 45–53.

struggle between forces of good and evil, where rationality and progress play second fiddle to being in harmony with the force.

Second Paradigm—The Cylons

There is another important dimension to this new religiosity of these late modern times that neither *Star Wars* nor *Star Trek* fully explores. To understand the possibilities of religion in the postmodern religious and technologically driven world a third science-fiction series deserves critical examination. With almost as venerable a history as *Star Wars* and *Star Trek* the evolution of the television series *Battlestar Galactica* provides a third perspective on possible new configurations of rationality, religion, science, and technology. Originally created in the 1960s but not aired until the late 1970s, the first incarnation of *Battlestar Galactica* consciously adopted a few select religious themes. Using biblical metaphors and borrowing a story of destruction and exile the original narrative arc reprised certain scriptural stories. But with the miniseries and subsequent television series of the new millennium a radically new *Battlestar Galactica* *(BSG)* moved religious and technological themes from the periphery to the center. Not only unafraid to name the divine, *BSG* took delight in putting specific theological disagreements at the heart of its plot. By contrast to the religiously drained world of *Star Trek* or the religiously re-coded world of *Star Wars*, *BSG* is super-saturated with different religious deities, beliefs, and practices. In short, the narrative arc of *BSG* is a profoundly religious narrative.

Before we can appreciate its full significance it is necessary to briefly review the anthropology undergirding *BSG*. One of the novelties of *BSG* was to thoroughly recreate the identity and the values of the artificially intelligent robots, the Cylons. Dedicated to destroying humanity the Cylons of the original series were chrome humanoid figures that clunked slowly. In *BSG* these are reinvented in two distinct aesthetic decisions. There is a new classic Cylon type that has a sleek humanoid form comprising of steel exoskeleton and automatic weaponry. These Cylons do not clunk, instead they are swift and murderously efficient. *BSG* also introduces a new type of Cylon that looks, emotes, and communicates just like an ordinary human being. This second type of Cylons has more in common with human beings than machines, being to all intents and purposes practically indistinguishable.

Right at the start of the series we witness a voluptuous blonde woman (who turns out to be a Cylon) meet an ordinary human officer. She asks him whether he feels alive, whether he is real. Later we meet another identical looking woman, who cannot possibly be the exact same individual, who talks quite straightforwardly about belief in God. Almost without pausing she then quite straightforwardly asks the human she is manipulating whether he loves her. Despite being artificially intelligent, these Cylons display the same range of characteristics as humans. In contrast to the unemotional character Data of *Star Trek: The Next Generation*, these artificially intelligent Cylons appear to have a full range of existential feelings. They inhabit a world that fuses together the religious and scientific, the emotional and the psychological, the material and the immaterial. They can be profoundly emotional, profoundly religious at the same time as being automata who are profoundly mission-driven. And like human beings, there is no polarity here, no opposition between science and religion. For the hyper-sophisticated Cylons there is certainly no sense that religion is any less consequential than science. Gone too is any easy objective way of distinguishing human from machine or artificial intelligence from natural intelligence.

This uncertainty about where to draw lines between humans and machines reaches a head when we discover that Cylons (just like humans) are capable of having theological disagreements amongst themselves. All have similar programing, but various personalities evolve between the twelve different models. As the series progresses the division between Cylons that look human and "real" humans becomes increasingly blurred. Some Cylons do not even know that they are Cylons, programmed as sleeper agents to think and behave as if they are human. Even when these sleeper Cylons are activated and revealed as Cylons it is still not clear where their primary loyalties and desires lie. Neither really Cylon nor really human, they inhabit a form of no-man's land, a hybrid identity. Amidst the breakdown of clear dividing lines between Cylon and human the viewer's sympathies are divided: just as both humans and Cylons are themselves divided over the nature of their relationship.

It is a truism that the dangers of technology are a familiar theme for science fiction. However, in *BSG* a simple struggle between good humans and evil technology is transformed into a much murkier investigation into what it means to exist without such familiar oppositions to fall back on. Who the good guys are is not always apparent. And unlike *Star Trek* that largely avoids questions of religion, or *Star Wars* that drastically reframes religion, in *BSG* it is a set of traditional theological differences that form the heart of divisions between humans and machines. In marked contrast to traditional apocalyptic fare of faithful humans beset by faithless machines *BSG* suggests that faith is just as important, if not more important, to the identity of the artificially intelligent machines as it is to the human colonists.

Whereas *BSG* problematizes any attempt to distinguish humans and Cylons from each other physically, emotionally, or existentially, a critical theological divide separates human polytheists, from Cylons who are monotheistic. Ironically, the language that we often associate with fundamentalism (singularity and certainty) is more likely to come from a Cylon than a human. It is the Cylons who trust that God has "a plan," while the humans struggle to identify the hand of their gods in their lives. In an inversion of the Enlightenment opposition between science and religion it is the superior scientific mindset of the Cylons that professes evangelical belief in God.

By contrast the polytheistic religious life of the human colonials is premised on a respect for various competing religious narratives. Religion for the humans is present in both liturgical practice and everyday language. "So say we all" is a response that can be used as readily at a funeral as at a military briefing. Unlike the religiously empty world of *Star Trek* or the religiously re-coded world of *Star Wars*, religious sympathies and practices are ubiquitous in *BSG*. They are prevalent in the ordinary speech patterns and cult practices of the colonial humans and participation in religious ritual seems important even for those who do not necessarily "believe." The gods are invoked regularly, and for humans always in the plural, even if many of these invocations are profane.

Religious as they are the humans are pluralists who respect the importance of different planetary deities and their cults. Theologically, it is ancient Rome meets contemporary space opera. The world of *BSG* is in many ways a perfect reflection of the thesis of the theologian David Tracy, in his revealingly titled *Plurality and Ambiguity*.[13] In the same way that most of us live daily lives against a backdrop of religious and ideological pluralism and an attendant ambiguity about truth claims, so it is for the humans of *BSG*. Against such human affirmations of religious differences, any whiff of relativism is inimical to the Cylons. There is one truth, and they lay claim to it, as against the humans who recognize com-

13. Tracy, *Plurality and Ambiguity*.

peting interpretations of truth, and in particular religious truth. Cylons are also more likely than humans to show concern for proselytizing. And as witnessed in the opening sequences their singularity of purpose has devastating results for the billions of humans they annihilate. Yet despite the original clarity of will with which they seek to eliminate humanity they are also almost comically nervous about finding and fulfilling God's plan for them. One of their twelve human doppelganger models is modeled on a human priest (and it is worth noting that this particular Cylon character is the least attractive of his peers, simultaneously cynical and murderous). Yet in case this is sounding simply like a straight inversion of a modern secular account of science and religion, it is important to note that even artificially intelligent evangelical monotheists come to have their doubts.

Beyond simple inversion or reversal, BSG reveals a new way of challenging and radicalizing old oppositions between spirituality and materialism, religion, and science. It also sheds new light on what it is to be human faced with the ultimate existential questions. One of the decisive differences between Cylon and human is that Cylons are created with an ability to download. Through a Resurrection ship a Cylon that reaches the end of its physical life can transfer its memories and programming to a new Cylon body. This guarantees Cylons a scientific form of eternal life that is contingent only upon the distance between the dying Cylon and the nearest Resurrection ship. For the humans there is no equivalent guarantee. Like us the colonials have no way of knowing what lies at the end of life, and they are prey to fears and dreams about what death may hold. But when the Cylons lose their Resurrection ship we finally see Cylon and human inhabiting the same galaxy.

For all that Cylon and human start off as radically different, BSG reveals a gradual intertwining of mutual enemies. From a sociological perspective the message of BSG is clear. Religious belief is no particular indicator or virtue or vice. It is part of the background noise of existence, both of artificial intelligence and human existence. Even the great divide between polytheism and monotheism seems largely inconsequential in comparison to the greater political and power divides to do with who controls the military, resources, and decision-making processes. Religion is used, to be sure, to direct and influence the course of events. But we are never properly sure whether the user is *using* or *being* used. Part of the paradox of religion in BSG is that for all that no single individual's religious motives (whether Cylon or human) are ever completely pure, religious practices create meaning and offer redemption. Belief in *BSG* is indispensable to understanding the motivations of both humans and Cylons, but each are also able to critically reflect on their religious framework. If nothing else, *BSG* offers a way of learning how to bathe in the waters of religion without drowning.

Despite having different belief systems, humans and Cylons eventually come to display skepticism and faith in equal measure. For all that the language of religion infuses the series, it is next to impossible to find neat divisions separating the faithful from the sceptic, the cynical from the trusting. In the *BSG* world there is no dividing line between scientific genius and religious belief, and the lines between the rational and the non-rational can be porous. Humans and Cylons are equally capable of finding critical distance from their own religious narratives. Yet while they are capable of skepticism, they also display faith when faced with wider existential questions. However hard they try, God (or the gods) keeps coming back into the picture. *BSG* does not refute the secularization thesis so much as render it meaningless. In *BSG* the question of rationality or religion is answered not so much with an either/or as with a both/and.

For all that the Cylons outclass the humans in their mastery of science and technology, the monotheistic Cylons are still no further along the road to uncovering the fundamental mysteries of the cosmos than the colonials. Equally, for all of the science on display, *BSG* has a thoroughly skeptical and conservative take on technology. The only thing that saves the eponymous battlestar *Galactica* from destruction is the absence of the latest forms of networking technology. As a survivor of the first Cylon war, commander Adama's trust in old-fashioned non-networked technology is the reason they survive when the most modern ships of the line are all remotely shut down by the enemy before being destroyed.

Adama's skepticism toward scientific innovation is one important form of doubt, but is not the only one present in the series. Mistrust permeates many of the most critical relationships for both humans and Cylons. However, more important than this are their existential and religious doubts. Doubt enables creative development as characters on both sides discover new ways of understanding their predicament. Gaius Baltar starts the series adamant that he believes only in the rational world, but through circumstance, specifically the desire he has for a particular Cylon, he is forced to rethink his presuppositions. Faced with a Cylon who is in love with him and who will not simply surrender that love, religious belief slowly but gradually breaks into his life. Similarly, over time the evangelical certainty of many Cylons dissipates as they find themselves closer to the conflicted and conflicting divided loyalties of the pluralist humans. Cylons who have been exposed to humans, particularly humans with whom they begin intimate relationships, eventually begin to share a human universe in which truth is no longer as singular or certain.

Doubt operates here on several levels, but chief among them it is the mechanism by which a more authentic relationship can be found to life, and faith as a natural part of that life. Doubt does not operate as an antidote to faith, so much as a way of transitioning from blind faith to faithful uncertainty. The choice open to human and Cylon alike is not between faith and faithlessness, so much as between an open faith that can weave in new information and a closed faith that resists recognizing things as they are. Evolution has often been used as a metaphor to describe a scientific theory that for many seems to make talk about the divine increasingly incoherent. By contrast, within *BSG* we see humans evolving to take the divine more seriously, just as we see the Cylons evolve to begin to allow doubt freer rein within their self-understandings. Neither path, however, is a path away from scientific understanding. Scientific rationality is one form of truth that operates as a *sine qua non* of both Cylons and humans. What matters instead is the role of doubt in revealing truths that are simply beyond the capacity for science to describe or signify.

To take the example of Adama, again, he does not appear to be overtly religious. Nonetheless, during a funeral service he injects hope to the defeated by revealing a closely guarded military secret, the existence of a previously unknown thirteenth colony. Having lost the other twelve colonies, it is this promise, the revelation of Earth, that infuses a dejected crew with new found optimism. The officiating priest verifies a reference to the thirteenth colony from the Scriptures, assuring the assembly that while it remains a mystery it is part of their sacred story. As we find out later, the military secret is a fiction, invented by Adama to boost morale. For all that Adama believes it to be a fiction, in reading too much into a neglected scriptural reference, doing what could be called a form of military exegesis, he turns things around. As viewers we assume that the existence of Earth is nothing more than a sleight of hand on Adama's part, but as the plot unfolds we realize that there is more truth to the matter than Adama realizes.

Adama's example signifies how scientific rationality cannot always lay claim to the whole truth. From a strictly rational perspective, Adama's suggestion that there is a thirteenth colony is irrational: it is a fiction. Yet, simply being irrational does not mean that there are not good reasons for this thirteenth colony to exist. For Adama it needs to exist for the sake of the cohesion of the crew and for the sake of the future of humanity. Without the hope afforded by the existence of Earth there would be nothing for the fleet to live for. From the perspective of objective reason Adama is guilty of deception. However, from the perspectives of both the colonial Scriptures and the bereaved colonists who have witnessed apocalypse come to their home planets Adama is guilty of little more than bringing hope to those facing hopelessness.

Intermission: Beyond the *Cogito*

In responding to the introduction by Descartes of the *cogito* as the ground of all thinking, women, including the Queen of Sweden are purported to have said (according to Žižek), "My God, for the first time—at least officially—the *cogito* has no sex."[14] While that might seem good news at first glance, one of the gifts provided by the hermeneutics of suspicion of Marx, Freud, and Nietzsche is the realization that rationality is never neutral and objective: this is especially true for a rationality constructed entirely by seventeenth-century men at a time when women were rarely part of philosophical conversations. Even a cursory overview of Marx, Freud, and Nietzsche reveals a rationality that is always invested in something, always born out of a specific context. It would be as impossible to imagine Marx without the history of economic inequality in nineteenth-century Europe as it would be to think about Freud aside from the experiences of an Austrian bourgeoisie seeking therapy or Nietzsche outside of the dominance of Christianity in the late nineteenth century. Equally, aside from their common location in the nineteenth century these famously suspicious thinkers also have the common denominator of being male.

After the nineteenth century it starts to become a little more obvious just how dangerous it has been to adopt as an objective standard any account of rationality that has been almost entirely the preserve of privileged Western male thinkers. Many of those who made the most decisive contributions to the evolution of human reason had some of the most unenlightened perspectives toward those who were different, particularly those who were different in gender. Like other men of their age Kant and

14. Caputo and Alcoff, *St. Paul among the Philosophers*, 166.

Freud, in particular, both had pretty unfavorable and unforgiving views of women. Where this can be seen to negatively impact their professedly rational and objective thought, we have to ask whether their accounts of rationality can be quite as rational or quite as neutral as they would have us believe.

Indications of feminist thought are largely absent from the world of *Star Trek* and *Star Wars*. *Star Trek* is the very model of Cartesian gender-neutral rationality, while *Star Wars* for all that it represents a more postmodern digital age, is largely as untroubled by questions of gender as *Star Trek*. While there is formal equality between the sexes in *Star Trek* at least (this is less clear in *Star Wars*), there is little time spent depicting or exploring the range of gender possibilities that do not encase women in stereotypically traditional or subservient roles. Just as *Star Trek* eliminates religion, so it also eliminates gender: gender differences are literally covered up. By contrast, *BSG* reflects important changes in thought around the development of thought around gender. While the original series in the 1970s had almost no characters played by women, and those that were held minor roles, many of the most active and interesting characters in the remake are women, while explorations of gender differences repeatedly drive both the plot and sub-plots. With Kara Thrace, the lead fighter pilot, we are given a character that combines the numinous messianism of a Luke Skywalker with the cocksure comical self-interestedness of a Hans Solo. Against the fairly one-dimensional nature of characters in *Star Trek* or *Star Wars* complexity is the order of the day for the *dramatis personae* within *BSG*. Moreover, it is the women who are more often key to many of the most intricate plot lines. Against the tokenism of a gender-blind bridge in *Star Trek* where there is really only a male Cartesian gaze, *BSG* allows for true gender diversity. Another remarkable character is the president of the colonies, Laura Roslyn. Both wise and sick (she is fighting cancer) she is simultaneously a strong leader and personally vulnerable, resisting definition as either simply strong or weak. The examples of Thrace and Roslyn reveal constructions of gender that do not confine women to certain roles. So not only is there no inherently hierarchical opposition in *BSG* between science and religion, human and machine, faith and faithlessness, neither is there subordination or polarization of female to male. Questions of gender are not only manifestly important to *BSG*, they are also complex and fluid.

In the last chapter we saw Sarah Coakley's suggestion that the resurrection appearances reveal a certain gift that the women had for recognizing the risen Christ. In the same way, it is the women of *BSG*, especially (but not only) Thrace and Roslyn, who are literally able to see things that others cannot see, or do not wish to see. Both Thrace and Roslyn have revelatory dreams that have an enormous impact in shaping the future for the colonists. And the way these dreams or visions are dramatized one senses there is little room to doubt the experiential veracity of these women. Feminist thought reminds us that exclusively male-produced models of rationality are rarely capable of seeing the whole picture. So-called objective rationality has often excluded other senses, from vision and touch, to sound and feeling. As narratives like *BSG* reveal, humans are not simply rational. We are also physical, psychological, and spiritual. The world of *BSG* literally shows us how sound, vision, touch, and emotion are more capable of conveying truth-claims than the supposedly, objectively rational Dominican truth. It is increasingly obvious that humans are not simply intelligent machines. Indeed, one of the fundamental insights of *BSG* is that if even highly intelligent machines cannot be simply reduced to being intelligent *machines* why should we? If the Cylons can love, fight, dream, sulk, doubt, *and* pray then maybe it is time to allow humans to do the same.

Third Paradigm—Scientific Monasticism

Staying within the genre of science fiction, but turning to literature, two very different novels together form the third paradigm. Each raises important questions concerning the relationship of community to knowledge, and while separated by over sixty years, both suggest a rethinking of the relationship of faith and reason. Despite significant contrasts, each nonetheless offers an illuminating investigation on what might be essential to religion and its relationship to rationality with the passage of time.

Walter Miller's classic *The Canticle of Leibovitz* offers a profound insight into the relationship between religion and technology. Narrated in a post-apocalyptic future we are introduced to monks of various orders who keep the technological torch burning. But unlike the comfortably familiarity of users of science and religion within *BSG*, the *Canticle* reveals a world in which technology survives not because it is necessarily understood and utilized, but because the monks are particularly good at accumulating, preserving, and safeguarding. Like the somewhat overstretched thesis that the Irish monks kept Western civilization afloat during the "Dark Ages," Miller's work highlights the importance of a community as guardians of knowledge.

While most of the monks do not particularly understand the relics and technologies that they host, their awareness that they have technology that is special and worth preserving forms part of their religious vocation. Technology here has both a utilitarian purpose and a symbolic purpose. The preservation of technology enables subsequent study and a retrieval of lost scientific understanding. It also forms part of the religious rationale for the existence of a monastery in the first place, a place of sanctuary for lost technology. Mirroring the centrality of relics in medieval times, so technology operates as a type of post-apocalyptic relic. Thanks to the role of the monks in protecting long forgotten technologies, they have a purpose that is simultaneously worldly and sacred. Their custodianship of technology forms an important part of their religious vocation, giving them a broader non-religious purpose that is recognizable both to those within and without the monastic walls.

Canticle also provides a wonderful insight into the deeply uncomfortable truth that every religious person knows but is often too afraid to admit: we do not understand everything about our religious communities or beliefs. We are formed by ideas, practices, and histories that we have absolutely no control over, and ultimately very little understanding of. The monks in the story are for the most part utterly clueless about what their precious technological relics actually are or might do. The key difference between the monastic communities and the rampant paganism of the world outside the monastery walls is not simply a difference between education and lack of education. Rather, it is the difference between a community formed to pass something on that it has received and communities that seeks only to live in the present. Part of the religious insight is that the decisions of others have shaped us, and in turn our choices will shape the lives of others. Although they do not understand the technologies they protect, the monks know that they are the living connection between the past and the future. With nuclear armageddon having almost entirely destroyed Earth the monks remain the only real link to past learning and the only real hope for a recovery of science and technology. But they are largely unable to participate in understanding the meaning of what they curate beyond the role it gives them of being curators.

In Neal Stephenson's *Anathem*, written fifty years after *Canticle* we see another permutation on the relationship between monasteries, science, and religion. Once again we are introduced to an institutional arrangement for handing on knowledge that calls to mind the monks of *Canticle*. Like *Canticle*, the work hinges on a difference between the secular and the sacred. However, while *Canticle's* monasteries are religious institutions with a mission of accumulating unknown technologies, the *Anathem* monastics have a more complex relationship to technology and science. From a materials science perspective these monasteries are as primitive as those of *Canticle*, lacking in almost any technological development. By contrast, the outside world is replete with hi-tech devices that make secular life easier and more entertaining. Yet, while technology is almost entirely absent from the monasteries, true understanding of science and genuine scientific genius are only found within the students and professors of the monastic communities. *Anathem* therefore presents an interesting divorce between those who understand science and those who utilize technology.

The monasticism of *Anathem* is consequently closer to contemporary scientific communities than religious communities. *Anathem's* monks keep alive the highest levels of science, most notably higher mathematics and physics. The divisions between various religious orders are all divisions between various mathematical ways of forming and understanding community. Stephenson brilliantly overturns modern preconceptions about the way that science, technology, and religion might relate. Whereas Miller's monastics are mere custodians of scientific and technological knowledge who remain recognizably Christian, Stephenson's monks are scientific brains without any particular religious faith or theological commitments whom the outside world turns to when needing specialist scientific advice.

Stephenson's novel tackles head-on the dissonance between our increasingly technological world and the dullards that use the technology. Like the secular users of technology in *Anathem* few understand the science behind most of the devices we use on an everyday basis. Equally, *Anathem* raises the question of the relationship of community and tradition to science. We no longer expect to see high-level scientific research take place in monastic communities. But there is something that resonates about the idea that those free of the clutter of technology might actually be freer to investigate and understand the higher reaches of scientific knowledge.

Like the world of *Star Wars* the world created by Stephenson deconstructs the modern opposition of religion and science. Instead of being separate and antagonistic disciplines, there is a more profound polarity between the learned and the ignorant. The faithful monastics know their science but have little time for superstitious religious belief. By contrast the secular users of technology remain religiously superstitious and scientifically ignorant. The genius of *Anathem* is to expose a supposed dichotomy between science and religion as illusory. A mastery of science does not necessitate the wholesale eradication of traditional religious structures. Just as the Cylons managed to twin scientific sophistication with religious fervor, dependence on sophisticated technology is no logical guarantee that religion will dissipate.

The Future Is Now

Interestingly, one of the themes common to all three paradigms is the presence of a community of religious interpretation who are given the explicit role of guardians of tradition—from the Jedi to the colonial (and Cylon) clergy, to the monastics of Miller and Stevenson. While the precise relationship that these guardians have to science and religion differs, what does not differ is their essential role. The Jedi and Stephenson's monastics may not have the same kind of role in teaching religious beliefs as the priests we find within *BSG* and Miller, but they all contribute to shaping the understanding of truth and rationality within their respective societies. These sci-fi clerics and pseudo-clerics reveal that there is neither scientific nor religious certainty in the future. Instead, what is required are interpretative communities both to conserve knowledge and also to ask the difficult questions, and doubt the simplistic certainties of the wider secular world. Ultimately the one thing that unites these thinking and praying communities within these disparate worlds is their common realization that with the passage of time everything does not get automatically better. Nor do all uncertainties diminish in the face of scientific progress. Rather, the rise of science and rationality creates an accompanying proliferation of new ways of asking old questions, and new ways of doubting conventional truths. In all these works doubt is not something that science and technology can eradicate from human experience. Rather, it is the movement by which humans increase in understanding both the external world of things and the internal world of ultimate beliefs.

Of course, these works are fictions. But they map onto our social reality in which we see rising levels of religiosity at the same time as rising levels of technological sophistication. The thesis that secularization is a necessary accompaniment to rising levels of technological and scientific competency now appears rather quaint. The reach of reason has not swept away religious accounts of the world. Rather, we are seeing new and fascinating ways in which religious life adapts and makes use of new technologies.

In a world no longer dominated by matter that you can touch and feel, the digital revolution is leading inexorably into a spiritual revolution. Technologies that, twenty years ago or even just a couple of years ago, would have seemed impossible novelties or futuristic dreams are now so prevalent that our sense of the limits of the physical world has evolved dramatically. One can play a video game that requires no controller other than one's body and, more to the point, a pre-schooler can also control this just as effortlessly.

The world of the future is no longer ahead of us, we are already living in it. The religious significance of this is barely understood and frequently unacknowledged. As this brief foray into science fiction reveals, science fiction has an uncanny way of holding up a mirror to present reality. Science is no longer in opposition to religion either in fiction or in reality. We therefore need to ask whether the dissolution of the science and religion opposition is an isolated phenomenon or the herald of larger shifts in the way we understand reality.

The Sacrality of the Secular

One theme that stands out from this brief review of science fiction is the difficulty of defining a sacred realm in opposition to things supposedly secular. While modern Enlightenment thought argued for a distinct separation of the secular and the sacred, that is no longer possible. As the Cylons show, it is possible to be a completely rational machine of advanced technological sophistication and still wonder at the mystery of creation. Similarly, contemporary physicists are only now discovering how little they really know about the fundamental composition of the universe. And the more they discover the less the old Newtonian model of science seems to apply. It is not just faith that claims we really "do not know," it is also science. The greatest amount of mass in the universe is no longer the visible world, but dark matter, about which we know very little. In the light of all this, hard and fast distinctions between the secular and the sacred are breaking down all around us, and it is no longer possible (if it ever was) to compartmentalize religion from the rest of life.

Theologically this is nothing new. What is new, however, is the growing sense that the secular and the sacred are *both* increasingly meaningless divisions *and* increasingly necessary categories. Part of the paradox of our contemporary situation is that secular reasons cannot be simply opposed to sacred reasons. Instead, as we have seen with fundamentalism, there is a fracturing of both secular reasoning and sacred reasoning. Fundamentalism in this work is taken to be the dominance of a particularly narrow, certain form of reasoning (that is neither specifically secular nor specifically sacred). By contrast, there are other forms of reasoning that are both secular and sacred that allow room for doubt and uncertainty.

One response to this situation would be to demand greater clarity and a better conceptual distinction between the secular and the sacred. Nevertheless, that would be to misunderstand the seriousness of the dilemma. While understandable, the desire to distinguish the sacred from the secular is always a desire to prioritize either the sacred or the secular. Both the religious and the secular have an interest in creating a division, as both have an interest in prioritizing either the sacred or the secular. By contrast, it seems more honest to admit that the sacred and the secular are mutually implicated, and constitutively dependent upon one another.

Another way of putting this would be to say that without the sacred there is no secular, and without the secular nothing would be sacred. This is neatly illustrated in the medieval world where to be secular meant that you were an ordained religious person who lived in the world (in contrast to an ordained religious person who lived outside the world in a monastery). While we are no longer familiar with medieval social hierarchies, the last three centuries have seen the sacred and secular continue to require each other to make sense of themselves.

While the questioning of the hard and fast division between the secular and the sacred has been recognized for a while, we have yet to see this permeate our theologies and religious life. Part of the problem here has been that rejecting a sharp division is not the same as eliminating the interrelationship. Some churches have done so well at questioning the division that they have simply substituted the secular entirely for the sacred. Removing all references to mysteriousness, transcendence, or the divine, they have entirely secularized rather than retained any kind of dualism between the sacred and the secular. The decline of mainline denominations in much of the West is probably directly related to this banishing of anything that smacks of mystery. Other churches have simply affirmed the centrality of the division between the sacred and the secular, going the other way, entirely retreating into the language of faith while rejecting anything that smacks of secular rationality. We could name the former strategy liberal and the latter strategy conservative, but these labels need to be taken with a pinch of salt. Ironically, neither approach to belief offers a strategy for allowing doubt to be constitutive of religious faith. Each excludes doubt in different ways: the liberal by simply assuming that anything "unscientific" is illusory, the conservative by assuming that anything "unscriptural" is heretical.

What is fundamentally at issue is how the sacred and the secular interrelate. Both strategies of reducing the sacred to the secular or excising the secular from the sacred are doomed. Instead what is required is a third strategy that recognizes both the interrelationship and the necessity of never being able to prioritize one over the other. To truly live in this complex and contested world, and not a world that is the projection of our desire for certainty, it is necessary to name the paradox that the sacred calls for an engagement with the secular while the secular requires reflection on the sacred. Excluding either, or prioritizing one, is theologically incoherent.

From the perspective of Christian theology the realms of the secular and the sacred are never mutually exclusive. A secularity cut off from the sacred, is not true secularity. And a sacrality with no understanding of the secular is meaningless. Throughout the history of theology, theologians have been those who have navigated the complex interrelationship of these two ways of viewing the world. A theology that is purely sacred would have nothing to say to the world. And a world that is exclusively secular does not understand either where it has come from or where it might be going.

The truth of the sacred and the secular distinction is that it is an entirely artificial one. The purpose of theology is to operate not as if this distinction were valid, but to seek points of harmony and contact between the secular and the sacred. This does not mean watering down the sacred and it does not mean colonizing the secular. But it does mean recognizing just how undecidable and uncertain the division between the sacred and secular is. By contrast, where effort is placed in setting up the sacred and secular in opposition to one another one has to ask what it is about the other that is so threatening that the connection has to remain hidden.

It is the argument of this book that secular reasoning flows out of sacred theology. It flows out of a theological tradition that it eventually comes to question. Refusing to engage with those questions is therefore tantamount to neglecting a significant section of the delta of the theological tradition. It is not a coherent theological option. The purpose of theology has always been to translate between the sacred and the secular, revealing the sacrality of the secular and the secularity of the sacred. The doubts of secular reason are therefore not an optional extra, but a fundamental component to the practice of a theology.

Writing from an explicitly non-theological perspective, Agamben underlines just how difficult it is to differentiate the sacred from that which is not. Addressing the concept of sacrifice he notes how the sacred is always implicated in that which is not sacred. Agamben's insight offers a philosophical grounding for realizing that the sacred and secular are always already in relationship. And while he does not offer a way of doing theology, his work is a profound verification of the necessity of a relationship between secular reason and theology. Overtly philosophical, and with no hidden theological agenda, Agamben understands that philosophy will always need to engage with questions of theology and the sacred. As will be addressed later, the profane needs the sacred, just as much as the sacred requires the profane. With thinkers like Agamben we are reminded that it is not just theological wisdom that recognizes the artificiality of attempts to divide the sacred from the secular. Secular reason itself is beginning to discover where it has come from and what implications this has for some of its own deepest beliefs.

If the mystery of the sacred is ever to form part of the vocabulary of contemporary faith it will entail the honest acknowledgment that doubt is central to human life. Doubt has been viewed as a threat to faith when in fact it is the absence of doubt that corrodes and destroys both human reason and faith. Faith without doubt is less a form of faithfulness and more a form of blindness. Faith in dialogue with doubt, however, offers a way of understanding the limits of both reason and faith. Reason cannot explain all, just as faith cannot explain all. The fundamental unwillingness of liberals and conservatives alike to recognize this truth is at the heart of so many sterile religious disagreements. Neither the religious nor the rationalist has all the answers. They do not even have all the questions. What is needed, instead, is a way of thinking through the fundamental place of doubt at the core of all thinking, both religious and non-religious. The inexplicable, that which resists understanding, is at the heart of everything, and it is to the challenge of how to think the inexplicable that we next turn.

3

THE IMPOSSIBLE

And I would say that deconstruction loses nothing from admitting that it is
impossible.

—JACQUES DERRIDA[1]

Human experience, I am contending, comes alive as experience by and
through the impossible.

—JOHN CAPUTO[2]

So this would be for me the great task of thinking today: to *redefine* and
rethink the limits of the possible and the impossible.

—SLAVOJ ŽIŽEK[3]

IF POPULAR ENTERTAINMENT CAN imagine a world in which artificially
intelligent Cylons believe in God, then clearly old oppositions between
faith and reason or the material and the spiritual are no longer culturally unquestionable or unassailable. Far from eradicating religious
belief, increased technological sophistication has simply reinscribed

1. Derrida, "Psyche: Inventions of the Other," 36.
2. Caputo, *On Religion*, 109.
3. Žižek, *Demanding the Impossible*, 144.

the limits of science. However, it is not only science that has found its limits. Contemporary philosophy is also profoundly aware that it cannot make sense of everything. The quest for rational foundations initiated by Descartes and reshaped and refined in recent centuries now seems somewhat quaint.

While the past two hundred years is the story of massive technological advancement it is also the story of increasing doubts about the ability of philosophers or theologians to explain things. Since Kierkegaard and Nietzsche in the nineteenth century, philosophy has been acutely aware of its own inability to provide a firm rational footing. As we saw in the last chapter, in the wake of the failure of the Cartesian project to ground everything in the thinking self, other thinkers sought to explain all in terms that specifically excluded God and sought meaning instead in economics (Marx), power (Nietzsche), or desire (Freud). But while aspects of their thought, including atheism, have remained enduringly influential, the idea that everything can be explained by any one particular system or metanarrative is increasingly philosophically unsustainable. Once the domain of thinkers who sought to explain all, philosophy is now just as often the preserve of those who articulate just how much cannot be explained. Where the early modern philosophies of Descartes, Kant, and Hegel sought to lay foundations, contemporary philosophy, and in particular continental philosophy, is now more interested in exploring just how and why such a task is no longer possible. Where philosophy once sought to make things clear, whole seams of philosophy are now focused on the things that are not clear, including where things appear to be at their most impossible.

After the panorama of the last chapter, this chapter sharpens the focus to a single thinker, Jacques Derrida. Derrida concentrated his work on investigating the difficulties of thought, including what he termed the impossibilities or aporias of key concepts. Derrida once affirmed, "I quite rightly pass as an atheist."[4] Nonetheless, despite his professed lack of religious faith, Derrida's writings have had a significant influence on contemporary theology. Less a foe to faith than benignly uncommitted, Derrida's scholarly criticism unexpectedly revealed a certain durability of the divine. Decades of questioning conventional readings and pressing up against the limits of philosophy might have been expected to lead to a critical rejection of everything theological. Curiously, though, the

4. Derrida, "Circumfession," 155.

more intently Derrida interrogated and doubted the dominant texts, traditions, and tributaries of Western thought, the more space he opened up for fundamental theological questions. At the same time, unlike some other continental philosophers, Derrida does not explicitly argue in favor of religion, nor has he nailed his colors to any theological masts. While he made no secret of his Jewish roots, he was not actively religious. This makes his perspective uniquely important for seeing how an overt and self-professed doubter of religion can still provide immense insight into questions of religious faith.[5]

Through the practice of deconstructing texts, Derrida shows how language inevitably relies on paradox, or *aporia*, to create meaning. Some over-enthusiastic followers (and many of his detractors) assume that this gives a license to wilfully misread. However, the truth is more complex. Derrida's rigorous practice of reading promotes an attentiveness to the text that encourages a broad array of possible interpretations. Far from suppressing meaning, Derrida allows the discovery and celebration of a full range of possible meanings. A champion of the underdog, both in texts and outside of them, Derrida contests dominant theories and readings to produce what are effectively his own minority reports.

As an intellectual with no particular commitment to a determinate form of religious life Derrida nonetheless discovered the necessity of engaging profoundly with questions of faith. A brief litany of Derrida's writing reveals both the variety and breadth of these theological interventions: Derrida has written about the question of prayer in negative theology, mysticism, and deconstruction. He has written about the character of ethics, responsibility to the other, and justice. He has repeatedly explored questions of faith, notably engaging with Kierkegaard. He has explored the challenge of thinking about spirit in Heidegger and Hegel. He has also provided a sophisticated unpicking of the Western Latinate biases implicit in the use of the very word "religion."[6]

Derrida's unpicking of the idea of religion also formed the site for one of his most remarkable religious interventions. Interrogating the idea

5. Derrida is one of three thinkers who, along with Heidegger and Levinas, Christina Gschwandtner identifies as preparing the way for the more explicitly religious thought of subsequent recent continental philosophers in *Postmodern Apologetics?* The theological elements in Levinas and Heidegger are more pronounced (despite their denials and prevarications), which is why Derrida better represents a thinker who practices a more radical doubting of theology, religion, and faith.

6. Derrida and Vattimo, *On Religion*.

of the messianic, he argued for a "messianicity without messianism" at the heart of language. Or to put it in more straightforward terms, Derrida sought to reveal how religious expectations of a divine inbreaking that is "to come" are already present at the deepest structures within ordinary life and everyday language. We will explore this in more detail later. For now, it is important to note that far from excluding religion as a category somehow beneath proper intellectual analysis, Derrida expanded the scope of what might count as the inherently religious nature of language. Characterized as nihilistic and ethically suspect by some of his detractors, a more balanced analysis would stress how he reveals the necessary limitations and blind spots of both metaphysics and ethics.

Derrida's writings on religion are particularly important because almost none of them can be thought of as religious writings. His most explicitly personal religious work is about his own Jewish identity and upbringing in Algeria.[7] However, even there it is clear that Derrida sheds very little light on anything that might be construed as personal religious belief. Instead his purpose is to make connections between his identity and that of another North African, the theologian Augustine of Hippo. Adopting the language of Augustine's *Confessions*, Derrida uses a confessional style that for all it "fesses up," is not overtly confessional in the religious sense. Critics might be tempted to suggest that Derrida is playing his readers or simply relishing the irony of this shared geography with one of Christianity's most famous thinkers. However, something more serious is going on. As Caputo has shown it makes sense to reflect deeply on these "prayers and tears" of Derrida and how his thought invigorates the possibility of theology.[8]

One (not uncontested) reading of Derrida would be to demonstrate that all writing is religious at a fundamental level. Derrida hesitates to state anything as transparently as this himself. However, he repeatedly stresses (and criticizes) the nature of ontotheology, or the theological-cum-philosophical attempt to understand the system by which we attempt to think the truth of being. Derrida recognizes that in using language, everyone, even the most evangelical atheist, is always involved in wider "theological" commitments:

7. Derrida, "Circumfession."
8. Caputo, *The Prayers and Tears of Jacques Derrida.*

> The sign and divinity have the same place and time of birth. The
> age of the sign is essentially theological. Perhaps it will never
> *end*. Its historical *closure* is, however, outlined.[9]

What Derrida means here is that the idea of the sign assumes that there
is a connection between the signifier (the word) and that which is signified (the meaning). Signs point outside of themselves, and the trust that
even the most prosaic of signs can point correctly to what is signified is
directly analogous to the trust involved in some of the bigger signs, like
the word "God" itself. Later, in chapter 6, it will be seen how Agamben
also identifies something essentially theological about the human use of
language.

The idea that there is a proper and pure connection between signifier
and signified is theological, because it entails trust in something outside
the sign providing its meaning. The theory of the signifier and signified
matching up transparently (an idea that is an essential prerequisite to
language) depends upon the idea of something at the center to guarantee
the linguistic stability of the sign. The role of the center (what Derrida
calls a "transcendental signified") is to guarantee meaning by affirming
that signifiers consistently mean what is signified. For Derrida, "There has
to be a transcendental signified for the difference between signifier and
signified to be somewhere absolute and irreducible."[10] In other words,
we need a reliable, stable centerpoint in our language to guarantee the
meaning of our words. However, despite this need for an Archimedean
point in the chain of linguistic substitutions, the transcendental signified
is itself nothing more or less than another point in the chain of signifiers. On Derrida's reading the transcendental signifier, the center point,
is itself already decentered, already part of a slippage between sign and
signifier that cannot be stemmed.

In the history of Western philosophy, this center or transcendental
signified, goes by a number of names. Derrida's work is sensitive to the
multiplicity of ways in which different thinkers have endowed different
concepts with the role of this transcendental center. What is important
to note is that, while God has been one of these "fundamentals" of the
metaphysical visions that Derrida critiques, the metaphysical is neither
restricted to nor defined by an association with the divine:

9. Derrida, *Of Grammatology*, 14.
10. Ibid., 20.

> It could be shown that all the names related to fundamentals, to principles, or to the center have always designated an invariable presence—*eidos arche, telos, energeia, ousia* (essence, existence, substance, subject) *aletheia*, transcendentality, consciousness, God, man, and so forth.[11]

This taxonomy within *Writing and Difference* emphasizes that the plurality of those names for the transcendental signified is part of the issue. The center can never be finally named. Instead, in receiving substitution after substitution it demonstrates that the center only exists as an act of substitution. Thus the center is not fixed, nor is it circumscribed. Rather than being a stable point, it is actually as fluid and mobile as the distance between signifier and signified. This mobility is often characterized by Derrida as play (*jeu*).

Together with his neologism *différance*, play succinctly sums up Derrida's analysis of meaning as constituted in the interstices between words. *Différance* seeks to undermine the privileging of "voice" (presence) by drawing our attention to differences that can only be written, such as the silent "a" in *différance*.[12] Similarly, *différance* inscribes an inherent indeterminacy and movement within the sign by virtue of its own oscillation between temporal deferral and spatial differing. This mobility can also be described as play.[13] The play of *différance* belongs to the middle voice, both passive and active, and resists ready interpretation.

Within the metaphysics of presence the desire for linguistic stability ossifies all the elements of the linguistic chain. In addition to the imagined "solid state connections" between signifier and signified or sign and transcendental signified, the logocentric tradition also supposes an identity within the strict repetition of a sign. By contrast, Derrida concentrates on how the play of *différance* can shift the meaning of even identical words. Each time words are used they take on different meanings and their sense shifts depending on the context. Derrida analyzes this phenomenon of iterability most famously in his debate with John Searle.[14] Iterability understands the fluidity of language to the extent that even an identical repetition of a word or phrase produces a shift in sense. In his response to Searle, Derrida illustrates this by quoting whole sec-

11. Derrida, *Writing and Difference*, 279–80.
12. Derrida explores *différance* in more detail in *Margins of Philosophy*, 1–27.
13. Ibid., 11.
14. Derrida, *Limited Inc.*

tions of Searle's own work. Since each context is always different, even when an identical statement is made, there is always a shift in sense. In the same debate, Derrida also radicalizes the idea of context, by pointing out the essentially illimitable nature of context. By complicating context, Derrida therefore expands and opens it up to linguistic play rather than rejecting it.

Already described in *différance*, and intimately related to the question of differentiation of context, is how the question of time, and the dividing of time, marks the possibility of language. Substitutionary play is not simply a question of spatial differentiation, but also temporal differentiation that is both diachronic and synchronic: both cutting across and alongside. Attempts to describe the transcendental signified of philosophy and language are always inscribed within time's movement just as there is always a spatial rupturing between signs and the center. Timing and spacing both form every act of signification, marking writing as the cleavage of both time and space. As such, writing is less about letteral visibility than the actual process of incision, division, and cleaving. Derrida frames this in explicitly quasi-religious terms as circumcision in his reading of Augustine and Jewish identity. Writing inscribes lines in the pattern of space and time, creating meaning through marks and cuts.

In addition to the axiomatic nature of this dividing aspect of writing, Derrida affirms the necessity of a supplement within writing. All writing is supplementation. This follows from the absence of a center or transcendental signified: without any stable point there can only ever be a continual process of redefinition and reiteration. The reality of supplementation makes finding a point of finality or totality inherently difficult. With a textuality of the supplement, truth emerges only as the contingencies of space and time are accorded a determining value. In other words, Derrida is not arguing for truth to be framed in terms of timeless abstraction so much as timely determinations. Or, to frame it even more concisely, Derrida is arguing that one cannot escape the inherently doubtful and indeterminate nature of what words mean, whatever they seek to describe.

Questioning God

Another set of questions arise as to whether the center might have anything to do with God. If it can we also need to recognize that by extension this "centering" God is probably not very similar to what religious faith has thought by the word God. Equally, if we recognize that the "centering" God does not actually have much to do with God then the question arises as to whether God has meaning beyond that which is presented as guaranteeing stability. Naturally enough some of these thoughts led to deconstruction being identified with a certain hostility toward notions of the divine. However, the only God that Derrida has actual reason to be critical of is the ontotheological view of God as that which gives signs their stable meaning. By contrast, as we will see later, the God of prayer, faith, affirmation, forgiveness, and justice is a completely different subject.

If God is simply a useful way of creating meaning, and if that God is simply a construct of language, then deconstruction is a critique of that God. However, with the passage of time it became clearer that while the ontotheological or metaphysical God has its very existence questioned the erasure of one conception of God does not, indeed cannot, completely remove the divine from the picture.

For all his attempts to displace the metaphysical or ontotheological God, Derrida also showed that the complete erasure of every notion of the divine was fundamentally impossible. Impossibility is not rhetorical hyperbole, however, so much as a key category of Derrida's thought. While it might be possible to deconstruct one kind of language-embedded and language-constituting God, the practice of deconstruction also revealed another opening for deity. Despite having neither a predilection nor disposition for seeking God, Derrida discovered that the ordinary process of making sense of language presents both a "false" God-being that must be rejected, and the potential for a God-beyond-being that is almost impossible to identify—but nonetheless as inescapable as it is inexplicable.

If the divine can not only survive but thrive on the deconstructive thinking of Derrida, this has important consequences for the relationship between critical thought and theology. Against the canard that so-called secular reason inevitably displaces theological thought, Derrida reveals a potentially hospitable relationship to religion at the heart of language. Derrida reveals a certain "sacrality" inherent in language. Yet, unlike earlier twentieth-century process theologians or other liberal theologies, the deconstructive identification of this sacrality is indirect, indistinct, and aporetic. Derrida is not evangelical about finding God under every rock or in every sunset; far from it. Instead, Derrida shows us how attempts to escape (or deconstruct) the legacy of one kind of God can never succeed in completely removing the need to engage with the question of God.

Derrida's central insight is that human language is always fractured and fracturing. While some religious thinkers have wanted to claim religious language as providing an escape from this linguistic brokenness, Derrida reminds us that no form of language can promise us release from this situation.

This has the consequence of making Derrida's thought fascinating to those who are suspicious of reducing God to a set of simple statements. Here is a thinker who reveals the danger of simplistic ideas about God, but does not throw the baby out with the bathwater. No grand Derridean narrative makes the case for God. Instead, Derrida encounters moments of difficulty within texts that are given various names from aporia to the *tout autre* ("wholly other," or possibly "holy other"). These points of resistance within the text are not divine for Derrida. Yet, they are analogous to questions of paradox found in theology. By extension, it is the places that defy easy comprehension, like religious paradoxes, that raise what is perhaps best called the specter of the divine. Here Derrida is remarkably in step with our cultural situation: haunted by a legacy of religion and deity that is not always understood, but that refuses simply to do the decent thing and just die. As Steven Shakespeare puts it:

> Derrida's unheard-of thoughts find themselves touching again
> and again on a strange "theological" dynamic that is neither
> theistic nor atheistic.[15]

While Derrida may not sympathize with or understand religion from within, he is attentive to the nuances of religious language. For through religious language we are given promising ways to doubt the grand narratives or ontotheologies of previous philosophical speculation.

For those wishing to divide up the secular from the non-secular Derrida presents an almost insurmountable challenge. Not immediately identifiable as theological, his work is saturated with theological themes. And yet, while it provides points of intersection with theology, it remains in a clear category of its own: neither irreligious nor religious, neither theological nor anti-theological, entirely lacking in personal faith but profoundly confident of the faithful dimension of language.

One of the strengths of Derrida's thought is his open embrace of paradox. Some of the most vociferous proponents and opponents of theology share a single-mindedness in the way that affirmations or rejections of God are framed. These are practitioners of certainty. By contrast,

15. Shakespeare, *Derrida and Theology,* 45.

Derrida offers a third way of thinking about the divine that doubts the efficacy of a simple yes or a simple no. Like the mystics and orthodox theologians of previous centuries, Derrida can be maddeningly opaque and frustratingly ambiguous. However, if the quest for God is to be a quest for something more than a caricature or cartoon of God, Derrida presents a perspective worth examining.

It is for this reason those of a religious persuasion need to be truly post-Derridean, and deconstruct their models of God. There are plenty of naïve theologies that present a version of God in eminent need of deconstruction. Equally, overly-confident scientific accounts need to get to grips with questions of human language, metaphor, and reference. If God could be proved or disproved by the appeal to either evidentiary or syllogistic reasoning, then debates about metaphysics would have concluded long ago. However, the complex truth is that God resists both proof and refutation not the least because resistance to understanding is built in to the way we use language (or rather, the way language plays host to our ability to think about the world).

One of the ironies of the sterile debates between science and religion is that partisans on both sides fail to understand Derrida. Both seem to be persuaded that there is an objective reality that is framed correctly either by a scientific or a religious metanarrative. And both are equally adamant that their metanarrative is a transparent rendition of reality. By contrast, Derrida reminds us that the only state of reality that is completely transparent and free of the problems of signification is death. All other statements about reality contain something that resists incorporation within the narrative. The point here is very similar to that which Jean-François Lyotard made at the end of the 1970s in his analysis of how it is no longer possible to make total sense of everything through any single metanarrative.[16] Scientific and religious metanarratives both rest on specific narratives, which are simultaneously able to explain much (but not all) within the subject of their story while also resolutely unable to explain much at all within the wider human story. Wittgenstein first showed philosophers how different language games underlie different kinds of activity and different fields of meaning.[17] The language game of sport is not the language game of accounting. Meaning and reference is not the same for each practice, and is not simply determined by the

16. Lyotard, *The Postmodern Condition*.
17. Wittgenstein, *Philosophical Investigations*.

words. Meaning and reference is also determined by the social behaviors and horizons of interpretation that participants bring to their activities. A difference of one point may mean something rather different in a game of soccer or on a trading floor. What constitutes winning in a figure skating competition looks rather different from the winning that is ascribed to a salesperson who leads a particular financial quarter. In the same way, while there is overlap between science and religion there is also radical difference. What Derrida offers is a way of remembering that difference is essential not just to different fields or communities, but also within every attempt to convey meaning.

Divine *différance*

It could be argued that Derrida's gift to theology is threefold. First, we are given the realization that if human language struggles to adequately describe the finite, it can hardly be expected to excel with the infinite. But there is more going on here than simple skepticism. Second, Derrida makes it impossible to ignore the question of the divine. His work shows how both the construction and deconstruction of meaning always raises the specter of the divine. And while deconstruction cannot be the arbiter of what the divine might be, neither can it proffer a decisive refutation of all things theological. If, as he suggests, the age of the sign is essentially theological, then so the age of deconstruction will always already be theological. To call something theological in Parisian intellectual contexts is far from being a term of approbation. Nonetheless, the act of critiquing the "theological" nature of the sign opens up space for a renewed understanding of the sign that also has religious implications. Third, Derrida opens up a new way of navigating the opposition in theology between revelation on the one hand and natural theology or reason on the other. In what follows I want to explore this third gift and what the implications are for other ways of doing theology.

Theologians operate with a variety of clear-cut ideas about revelation and natural theology or reason. For very different reasons they are both heavily invested in the distinction. Flexibilists largely reject the idea of the particularity of a revelation that conflicts with human reason. Fundamentalists largely reject the normative or regulative role of human reason preferring instead the definitive clarity of a revelation. In other words, we have a classic example of bipolar thinking in the theological division between revelation, on the one hand, and reason or natural theology, on the other.

But what if this bipolar division is actually a mirage? What if it is impossible to separate revelation from reason? This would be bad news for both the fundamentalists and flexibilists alike. Bad news for fundamentalists because it requires any appeal to revelation to engage with reason. And unfortunate news for flexibilists because it would require any appeal to the universality of reason to engage with the specificity of revelation.

From a philosophical perspective, Rodolphe Gasché has described *différance* as one of the "infrastructures" that drive Derrida's thought.[18] The terms "infrastructure" or "quasi-transcendental" have the advantage of avoiding some of the metaphysical implications that Derrida is anxious to distance himself from while hinting at questions of the originary. As we saw earlier, the neologism was invented by Derrida to describe a differentiating action that is simultaneously a deferring action. *Différance* incorporates the idea of spatial division, but also the idea of distance in time, deferral. Language is differentially structured and there are no hard and fast linguistic identities. Instead, all is in play and linguistic boundaries and meanings are in constant flux. Among other things this differential way of thinking suggests a reappraisal of some of the clear-cut distinctions that have traditionally structured the way we understand the world. This is why Derrida's thought is sometimes called poststructuralism, in opposition to the structuralism that explained things in reference to opposite poles of meaning.

One of the best examples of structuralist thought is in Lévi-Strauss's use of nature and culture as opposite poles by which to understand society. Derrida realized that the relationship between nature and culture is not as polar opposite as it first sounds, and that in fact the two are related differentially rather than oppositionally. The taboo against incest is what undermines Lévi-Strauss's opposition between nature and culture. The prohibition of incest is a product of culture. But unlike other cultural prohibitions, it is universal, found within every culture, like nature. The incest taboo therefore becomes the point where we see how it is not possible to fundamentally perfectly divide culture from nature. Seizing on this dilemma enables Derrida to point out the inherent limitations in maintaining hard and fast conceptual divisions.

18. Gasché, *The Tain of the Mirror*.

The key Derridean point is that polarities construct meaning by assuming that the meaning of one term excludes its connection with the opposite pole. This not only creates a split, however, but also a sense of hierarchy, with one side of the pole always prioritized. Classic examples of this are seen in the way that the couplets male and female, good and evil, or mind and body have been traditionally opposed. In each case we are given a duality that on reflection really conceals a hierarchy. From Derrida's perspective there is no particularly good reason to suggest, for instance, that females or bodies should be defined as subordinate to males or minds. Instead, what is needed is a differential logic to counter the primacy of static polar opposites that elide and efface much that is more complicated, fluid, and subtle.

Differential thinking can also be brought into fruitful conversation with some of the great polarities that are familiar to theology. Here the traditional distinction between reason and revelation is prime for revision. A structuralist might see the two terms as ineradicably opposed, and a theologian might see revelation as the primary of the two. However, using a differential logic we can contemplate the idea that each might better be understood not as an opposite to the other, but differentially related. So, for example, the most wholehearted attempts to be rational will always be based on something that cannot be rationally argued or proved. In an early essay critiquing Michel Foucault, Derrida points out that this is exactly the situation with the Cartesian cogito and what he terms "the history of madness."[19] Despite the desire of Descartes to set up an entirely rational system, there is nothing particularly rational about the origin of Cartesian reason. Steven Shakespeare explains Derrida's point:

> At the heart of the *cogito* is a hyperbole, an extreme act of self-founding. If the ego founds itself, it can appeal to no rational law other than itself, its own act. There is no reason without this moment of madness at its heart, a moment unsanctioned by any self-evident rule.[20]

The rationality of the self that does the doubting or thinking is not really something that can be decisively proven. Rather, the decision by the *cogito* to see in the self the basis for rationality cannot be justified by appeal to anything outside the thinking subject. While Foucault wants to separate madness from reason, Derrida therefore wants to remind us

---

19. Derrida, *Writing and Difference*, 31–63
20. Shakespeare, *Derrida and Theology*, 84.

that there is a certain non-rationality inherent in reason, something that cannot be rationally proven or argued.

In the same way, it is in the nature of language to never fully or adequately capture what we might wish to describe. On the other hand, applying the idea of *différance* to the question of revelation would challenge suggestions that revelation erupts from nowhere and has no connection to the wider human world of experience, tradition, or reason. Revelation is structurally related to what is not revelation, and *différance* is the understanding that there is no pure and perfect method of communicating free from the constraints and tensions of language. Responding to a text necessitates responding to its context. All Derrida wants to suggest is that we include in that context the otherness that the text itself attempts to repress. Here *différance* operates as that which allows for the analysis of a broader range of nuances of meaning generated by the text than that suggested by one dominant interpreter, even if that interpreter is the author.

This is not to say that context alone explains the entirety of a text. Quite the contrary. Derrida provides an understanding that even the broadest comprehension of context can never capture or contain a text. Rather, the text itself carries layers of context of its own awaiting examination. In this sense, deconstruction is already a form of theology. Like theology it is parasitic on already existent stories, writings, rationalities, philosophies, conceptions, and ideas. Moreover, just like theology deconstruction suggests that however well these are understood something fresh always emerges, something new, something *other*. A properly Derridean view of revelation or Scripture is therefore to view Scriptures as carrying a surfeit of meaning. Scriptures are structurally incapable of being reduced to a single sense. Instead they reveal something other that cannot be completely reduced to the text.

The nature of this relationship between *différance* and theology has been explored in detail by a number of theologians. One of the pioneers is Graham Ward, who first explored similarities between Derrida and the twentieth-century theologian Karl Barth. Ward recognizes how the play of differences reveals an economy of conflicting desires from within which a theological economy can be thought.[21] Within this *différantial* play Derrida avoids the type of absolutism that is characteristic of metaphysics. Drawing attention to the Derridean backdrop of Heidegger and

---

21. Ward, *Barth, Derrida and the Language of Theology*, 231.

Lévinas, Ward affirms the role of *différance* in inhabiting and clearing an area that both is and is not a theological space:

> *Différance* calls the theological into play, lends weight to the ineradicable nature of the theological question in and of language . . . *Différance*, examined theologically, becomes the play between the presence and the impossibility of God.[22]

This interpretation soberly reproduces the indeterminacy of *différance* without eliding Derrida's metaphysical denials with a denial of transcendence. Rather than advocating a closure to the divine, transcendence remains possible and impossible in the same moment. This movement between the impossible and possible marks out the quintessentially Derridean response to both metaphysics and transcendence. Always working within metaphysics, Derrida is nonetheless committed to think the impossible, the extra-metaphysical thought. Concurrent with this tension, the question of transcendence persists in crossing the threshold of Derrida's thought without the possibility of it being reduced to or rejected with metaphysical containment. The questions of metaphysics and transcendence are simultaneously inescapable, yet irreducible one to the other.

Responding to Ward's observation Steven Shakespeare concludes, "Seen in reverse, this means that a certain agnosticism must be preserved within theology, for God cannot be pinned down and defined."[23] *Différance* inscribes uncertainty right at the heart of both theology and philosophy. Unlike Cartesian, Kantian, or Hegelian attempts at metaphysics, *différance* suggests that there is no clear way in which the question of God can be answered. From a Derridean perspective God can neither be proven nor disproven. Instead, questions of God find themselves repeated alongside questions of language and signification.

Derrida's concern with the sign as an essentially theological concept—understood in a derogatory sense—is therefore a critical contribution toward understanding theology's need to extricate itself from metaphysical systems. Even thinking as sophisticated and subtle as Heidegger's thought of Being conceals a potentially hazardous metaphysics. Derrida can sensitize religious and non-religious thinkers alike to such subterranean metaphysics while accentuating the limits of language. In highlighting the liminality of metaphysical frameworks Derrida's

22. Ibid., 232.
23. Shakespeare, *Derrida and Theology*, 191–92.

thought energizes theology with the uncertainty that it needs to be properly faithful.

Tout autre est tout autre

Another important theme is found in Derrida's phrase, *tout autre est tout autre*: every other is wholly other.[24] In English it would also be possible to translate this as "every other is holy other." Mark C. Taylor has made much of the importance of this alterity in Derrida, suggesting that there is a connection between Derridean alterity and the altarity of the crucifixion.[25] Taylor reads Derrida deconstruction as an acknowledgment of the radical otherness of texts and by extension every other kind of other. By contrast, Graham Ward focuses on alterity in Derrida to see the traces of the theological view of God as wholly other.[26] By keeping the question of alterity in play, Derrida offers resources for rethinking the transcendence of God.

The alterity of texts (or of the holy other) reminds us that there is always a surplus of meaning. Something always escapes a complete and final reading. Or to use more theologically oriented language, the question of ultimate meaning can never be answered, and is always deferred. For some theologians this endless deferral smacks of a kind of failure to ever get to grips with the truly transcendental object that is God, undergirding all reality. For them, Derrida is nothing more than a rhetorical dilettante who uses language to avoid talking about the holy, or indeed, any truly meaningful realities. Nonetheless, his thought cannot be quite so easily sidelined. In one essay Derrida goes to great lengths to distance the practice of deconstruction from the practice of negative theology.[27] Negative theology assumes that nothing positive can ever be said about God as God is strictly beyond comprehension. However, despite being a formal practice of "not-saying" anything about God it is also a practice of "saying-quite-a-lot" about God one way or another. As distancing exercises go, Derrida's essay served instead to underline how remarkably close negative theology is to deconstruction. Derrida's lengthy exploration of the mystics reveals how difficult it is for him to decisively separate

24. Derrida, *The Gift of Death*, 82–115.
25. Taylor, *Altarity*.
26. Ward, "Why Is Derrida Important for Theology?," 266.
27. Derrida, "How to Avoid Speaking: Denials."

his way of reading from negative theology. As a result, it does not seem fanciful to suggest that adopting his reading strategies gives theology fresh insights.

This is not to suggest that deconstruction is a form of theology. However, it would seem appropriate to agree with Kevin Hart's analysis that negative theology, theology that denies conceptualizations of the divine, is a form of deconstruction.[28] The central question for Derrida and negative theologians alike is how their discourses prevent language from creating an (idolatrous) God. For both Derrida and the mystics, the God of ontotheology is not the real God. God as an object that can be thought is not truly God for either the mystics or for Derrida. Where the two differ is in wondering whether it can still make sense to speak of another real God beyond the God of ontotheology. This real God would not be a "thing" one could speak of. Which is one of the reasons why Derrida is trying to avoid speaking of God in the first place. We could interpret his resistance to speaking positively of God as the reluctance of a true believing atheist. But we cannot also ignore the fact that both the Jewish and Christian mystical traditions have been reluctant to speak positively the name of God. Their reluctance has not been because they do not believe in God. Instead, they have been wary of the suggestion that their names and formulations for God might actually ever describe God. As Caputo makes clear, "Like negative theology, deconstruction turns on its desire for the *tout autre*."[29] Theologians have always disagreed with those who claim that God is an object, and it is this central issue, that is both substantive and linguistic, that is at the heart of so many contemporary misunderstandings.

The important thing to take away from all of this is that Derrida cannot foreclose the question of God either way. He cannot reject God; nor can he prove God. Rather, what he does is show that at the heart of deconstruction the otherness of the text always raises the possibility of another form of otherness, one who is truly other. The connection with theology is clear when we realize how Derrida's failure to identify God is actually mirroring a central concern of theologians: refusing to make an idol out of our language for God, and remembering that God always escapes and transcends theoretical formulations of deity. As has already been hinted there is, of course, a theological word for the phenomenon

28. Hart, *The Trespass of the Sign*.
29. Caputo, *The Prayers and Tears of Jacques Derrida*, 3.

when meaning appears to be manifest and yet resists simple explanation: paradox.

The Impossibles: Derrida's Paradoxes

Différance is already an attempt to express the paradoxical character of language and deconstruction. As a word *différance* already embodies a degree of paradox. As we saw, only when it is written down does the silent "a" of *différance* distinguish it from *différence* since the graphic dissimilarity is masked in the French pronunciation. On the semantic front, Derrida invests *différance* with the qualities of both differing and deferring but denies it conceptual status. *Différance* is therefore a word unlike other words. Its graphic and semantic boundaries criss-cross existing limits, fashioning a hybrid meaning through the displacement of pure notions of identity.

When transposed into English *différance* retains its singular spelling, as if to underline the paradox of translation. *Différance* denotes, if it denotes anything, a semantic flow between words that frustrates any attempt to regularize or codify meaning. This textual slippage from one word to the next reflects the jagged contact between sign and signifier. With no logocentric system to tie words down to a stable meaning, everything is in flux. Nevertheless, this flux does not preclude questions of ultimate meaning. While it refutes the possibility of ontotheology, it keeps open the question of negative theology, and as an extension of that, the possibility of paradox.

Paradox is actually a crucial theme of Derrida's work well beyond the "paradox" of his non-conceptual concept of *différance*. There are numerous instances in his work where it is paradox rather than any technical deconstructive term that is used to express central motifs in deconstruction. In his discussion of Joyce, Derrida is open about the "paradoxical logic" of the relationship between Joyce's texts.[30] Then, in *The Gift of Death* Derrida adopts the language of paradox in his analysis of sacrifice and time.[31] When he analyzes the potential for nuclear apocalypse[32] or psychoanalysis[33] Derrida again shapes his argument about the nuclear

---

30. Derrida, "Two Words for Joyce," 148.
31. Derrida, *The Gift of Death*, 63–65.
32. Derrida, "No Apocalypse, Not Now," 28.
33. Derrida, *Resistances of Psychoanalysis*, 40.

referent or analysis in terms of paradox. In these and other instances, paradox encapsulates the dissymmetrical nature of language, which in turn connects with the impossibility of truth and the truth of impossibility. Paradox, like *différance* and aporia, is a "normative" feature of making meaning for Derrida. Paradox expresses a rule rather than the exception in Derrida's thought. All analysis, whether literary, philosophical, or political therefore becomes the elucidation of paradoxes.

Unlike traditional theological paradoxes, paradox in Derrida's thought is intrinsic to the ordinary. It is normative rather than exceptional, ubiquitous rather than unique. Paradox exemplifies many of the most mundane concepts under observation by Derrida. Frequently this involves a tension between the two faces of a single idea. With the idea of the gift, this tension is between the significance and identification of a gift. If a gift is to be a gift it must have the significance of escaping the usual economy of exchange. However, the only way that this can happen is for the gift to be a secret event. Once the gift is a secret event, it becomes impossible to identify it as a gift. The impossible possibility of the gift is therefore the paradox of the gift. If it is possible to recognize that a gift has been given it can no longer be a gift outside of the economy of exchange, because it places the recipient in a position of debt toward the giver. Paradox invariably leads into questions of impossibility. Moreover, all the paradoxes and impossibilities encountered in Derrida—from nuclear war to the gift—share a similar contradictory horizon, namely, that of language.

From within Derrida's deconstructive analysis, all concepts are subject to the same contradictory forces that create the paradox of the gift. To name just a few, responsibility, justice, spirit, nature, duty, translation, identity, apocalypse, and friendship also share this sense of paradox. Although Derrida does not always use the language of paradox, these are all paradoxes open to deconstruction. In each case the act of naming itself opens up a rift that echoes the classic tension between the element that is signified and the signifier. This reveals a connection between Derrida's later work on the nature of the gift with that of his earlier analysis of the supplement. Both gift and supplement are concerned with surplus meaning and the necessity of how surplus meaning creates paradox.

Paradox for Derrida carries through the concerns of *différance* rather than contrasting with them. One illustration of this is the similar relationship that they have to time. The deferring activity of *différance* is mimicked by the sense of conceptual postponement within the paradox.

To take the paradox of the gift once again, the nature of time itself is called into question in the interrogation of the gift. It is the time of the gift that helps shape the paradox of whether a gift can be given or received. The gift cannot be thought without some relationship to time also being brought to mind. Paradox emerges precisely as the identity of the gift is seen to be contingent upon a whole economy that follows after it. It is only within a framework of passing time that the gift can be conceived, and yet it is this broader temporal economy that threatens to undermine the very possibility of the gift. The same temporalization affects all the concepts that Derrida analyzes. Sacrifice, duty, and the apocalyptic are other themes that make obvious this connection with temporality. Time really matters in shaping meaning.

One central paradox lies in the simultaneous impossibility and possibility of both the gift and the temporal mode we understand as the present. Their characters overlap and envelop one another, so that to speak of one is to speak of the other. The fact that the word present can refer both to the gift and the temporal mode underlines this mutual interconnection. The question of fulfillment hovers over both, and it is precisely that difficulty that ensures their meaning. Where the question of the gift hinges on the possibility of reception (can a gift be received and remain a gift?), the question of time turns on the decipherability of the present from past and future. Derrida's repeated return to the question of the apocalyptic makes sense within this context. He is not concerned with millenarianism, but with analyzing futurity within the present. A messianic tone also touches his writing here, which we will return to. What remains interesting from the point of view of paradox, however, is that the discourse on the arrival of the apocalypse is paradoxically framed, at one stage, as the apocalypse of the apocalyptic. Traditional apocalyptic thought rests on the imminent influx of the future into the present; and yet this influx is always deferred. Derrida's paradoxical rewriting of this apocalyptic history deconstructs this by suggesting the arrival of an apocalypse that *has* arrived. Here, the "come" of apocalyptic expectancy transforms into the actual event of arrival. Invocation *gives* way to affirmation, as the apocalypse comes to the apocalyptic.[34] The paradox of the apocalyptic, like that of the gift, is once again the impossibility of achievement. As soon as apocalypse is achieved there is no longer the apocalyptic. Apocalyptic thought rests on the same

34. "'Come' does not announce this or that apocalypse: already it resounds with a certain tone; it is in itself the apocalypse of the apocalypse; '*Come*' is apocalyptic." Derrida, "Of an Apocalyptic Tone," 94.

type of deferral that applies to giving. As soon as there is fulfillment, there is an end to the apocalyptic, but while there is no fulfillment there is no apocalypse of which to speak.

If things are sounding a little confusing at this point, that is probably because they are. The possibility of paradox or impossibility remains at the heart of Derrida. While a gift, for example, is strictly speaking impossible, the possibility of such an impossibility is nowhere denounced or derided. This contradiction is most thoroughly detailed in Derrida's eponymous work on aporias. Although aporia is a more oblique, elliptical, and diffuse term than paradox, the two terms are interchangeable. The aporia describes the impossible or rather "a certain possibility of the impossible."[35] Similarly, the paradox expresses the possibility of the impossible.

The undecidability of this "possible impossibility" is nonetheless not confined to the relationship between paradox and aporia. Although there is a specificity to the impossibility of the aporia, it is an impossibility that cuts across the whole of Derrida's thought. The logic of the relation between signifier and signified also incorporates this meeting between the possible and the impossible:

> If it seems to us in principle impossible to separate, through interpretation or commentary, the signified from the signifier, and thus to destroy writing by the writing that is yet reading, we nevertheless believe that this impossibility is historically articulated.[36]

This earliest discussion of *différance* is therefore related to later explorations of aporias. In each case the investigation centers around the interplay between the possible and the impossible. Language thrives on the possibility of the impossible, and the permutations on this theme provide the raw material for deconstruction.

With the aporia impossibility is merely written more clearly. It is impossibility rather than anything else that lies at the heart of the discussion of aporias just as it does of all writing. As Derrida puts it: "The ultimate aporia is the impossibility of the aporia *as such*."[37] Just as negative theology throws into question all and every conceptualization of the divine, so deconstruction thrives on conceptual denial. There have been plenty

35. Derrida, *Aporias*, 11.
36. Derrida, *Of Grammatology*, 159.
37. Derrida, *Aporias*, 78.

of denials trying to distance deconstruction from negative theology, and yet the fact that the denials need to be taken seriously testifies to a certain double-bind.[38] Deconstruction is irrevocably linked to negative theology, even as it unties and subverts the formulations of negative theology. In the impossible thought of the aporia of the aporia there are the same strategies of negation that already serve to distance Derrida from negative theology. The aporia cannot be delineated and is only hinted at in the same way that apophatic theology hints at the divine.

The irony here is that precisely by mirroring the denials of apophatic discourse, Derrida shifts deconstruction away from identification with negative theology. Although the procedure of negation is shared by both disciplines, in deconstruction the "ultimate referent" is subject to more thoroughgoing questioning. For Derrida the analysis of the possibility of impossibility (such as in the aporia of the aporia) is the focus of attention. Derrida can therefore comment that

> deconstruction has often been defined as the very experience of the (impossible) possibility of the impossible, of the most impossible, a condition that deconstruction shares with the gift, the "yes," the "come," decision, testimony, the secret, etc.[39]

It is the concern with this question of impossibility more than any other that distances deconstruction from a reduction to simple nihilism. There is no indication of an interest in nothingness *per se*, rather a fascination with the conditions under which—paradoxically enough—something can impossibly arise out of the linguistic flux. In common with negative theology, Derrida's strategic rejection of onto-theological conceptualization still allows for an ultimate alterity beyond false conceptualizations. In contrast to nihilism the possibility that this ultimate alterity may be another form of death is not decided one way or the other. What is clear, however, is that the possibility of impossibility allows both doubt and faith to coexist as perfectly agreeable relations rather than mutually exclusive polarities. Derrida seems to be saying that one can doubt with every fiber of one's being that a gift can be given, and yet this impossibility may still occur. Having entertained the possibility that such an impossibility

38. "Conversely, I trust no text that is not in some way contaminated with negative theology, and even among those texts that apparently do not have, want, or believe they have any relation with theology in general. Negative theology is everywhere, but it is never by itself" (Derrida, *On the Name*, 69).

39. Ibid., 43.

might be possible, it is hard to see how Derrida can be invoked to refute the possibility that other, even overtly, religious impossibilities might also be possible.

Forgiving Religion?

Derrida is not yet finished with us. In the last decade of his life Derrida addressed several practical ethical and religious questions. In addition to examining opaque textual challenges that refuse to neatly serve up their meanings, Derrida also investigated more concrete social questions. One of the best examples of this is found in a brief and unusually accessible text that deals remarkably straightforwardly with two critical religious questions.[40] In the first essay, Derrida compared the radical hospitality of cities of refuge in the Old Testament with the contemporary Western practice of excluding immigrants or the undesirable *sans papieres* ("without papers"). In the second part, Derrida examines the question of forgiveness.

Derrida suggests that there is something uncontainable and undeconstructible in both scriptural hospitality and forgiveness. It would be natural to suspect that Derrida might want to deconstruct hospitality and forgiveness and reveal that they depend on another term, and that these scriptural practices are somehow neither truly hospitable nor forgiving. However, this is not the tack he chooses. Instead, we are shown that, while hospitality and forgiveness are strictly speaking impossible, this is another type of impossibility that is nonetheless *possible*, nonetheless performed: not the impossibility of that which is never possible.

In the movie *Derrida* we see Derrida visit the prison cell of Nelson Mandela. Later in addressing a university class a student asks Derrida whether his talk of forgiveness is not simply a white man requiring other whites to be easily forgiven for their horrific role in the apartheid regime. But to be fair to Derrida that is not the force or direction of his argument. In his writings, Derrida makes it absolutely clear that forgiveness is truly impossible. However, it is an impossibility that, like the aporias at the heart of language, is nonetheless possible. Forgiveness shares this characteristic with justice, another notion that Derrida excludes from being deconstructed. For Derrida justice and forgiveness are infinite. The desire for justice and the desire for forgiveness, impossible as they

---

40. Derrida, *On Cosmopolitanism and Forgiveness*.

are, are demands that are at the heart of language. Moreover, we cannot ignore them simply because they seem to be impossible to achieve. Once again, in drawing attention to the impossible Derrida's thought suggests profound continuities with a theological tradition that sees God in the impossible.

Strictly speaking the incarnation, the idea that God became a human being, is another impossible. It is this impossible idea, an idea that makes no sense to philosophers or even other monotheists, that forms the kernel of Christianity. Part of what makes Christianity problematic for many is the requirement for certain impossible beliefs to be possible. It requires forgiveness to be possible, even when it is patently so impossible in real life. And it requires God to be found in human existence, something also remarkably nonsensical by the standards of the world. Derrida shows us how other ideas of impossibility are already woven into other more ordinary features of human understanding. If we are to take Derrida seriously, it will entail looking again at whether the impossibility of something is really an adequate reason to deny it.

Closely related to the question of forgiveness is the question of the future. Forgiveness is a way of opening up the future, and it is important to note that Derrida's concern with the question of the future predates later ruminations on forgiveness. In his analysis of political and ethical theories, Derrida consistently puts the question of a politics and an ethics that is *to come*. The thought of arrival (*arrivant*) highlights the inherent incompleteness of these ideas in a way that transforms them rather than rejects them. Messianicity emerges as the continuation of the deconstructive attempt to think through this transformation of concepts. In thinking about the structurally unfinished nature of, for example, justice and responsibility, Derrida brings to the foreground the question of a renewed political and ethical emancipation:

> Not only must one not renounce the emancipatory desire, it is necessary to insist on it more than ever, it seems, and insist on it, moreover, as the very indestructibility of the "it is necessary."[41]

Messianicity grounds all these concepts, in that it is the thinking through of the incompleteness of thought: a naming of that fact that there is always something yet to come. Incompleteness here is seen as the force for meaning within messianicity (rather than the utter lack of meaning required by nihilism that some have attributed to his thought).

41. Derrida, *Specters of Marx*, 75. See also "Force of Law," 28.

The structure of messianicity provides a framework with which to pursue the process of deconstruction. Messianicity generates an awareness of the part played by temporality in the formation of all concepts and ideas. It incorporates an orientation to future completion alongside an affirmation that the seeds of completion are already sown. Here deconstruction emulates the structure of the messianic in religion, while distancing messianicity from an identification with specific messianic content or a specific messianic religion.[42] The elements of promise and call in the religious manifestation of the messianic are mirrored in the way deconstruction treats the notion of emancipation. Promise and call are features of messianicity that anticipate the structure of the messianic itself. Anticipation and vocation are therefore critical to the understanding of deconstruction. It hardly needs to be said that none of these are concepts that are conducive to certainty. Just as there is always room to doubt a specific messiah, so the room to doubt what might constitute messianicity is a central part of messianicity. Thought and language about messianism is inherently unstable, confusing, and open to question. Moroever, this uncertainty is embraced rather than scorned by Derrida, reminding us of the inherent uncertainties, doubts, and aporias that constitute language and thought.

The concept of justice in Derrida also reveals an incompleteness or a surplus of meaning linked to the themes of promise and call. Although Derrida denies the possibility of justice (as of ethics and responsibility) this constitutive impossibility deserves to be read in a similar way to the constitutive impossibility of the messianic. The messianic depends on a non-arrival, waiting, and deferral. But this failure to identify the messianic does not constitute its refutation. Instead, it is essential to it being properly messianic. The whole point of traditional messianism is that the Messiah hasn't arrived yet! In a similar way, the failure to identify justice once and for all is not a refutation of justice so much as the recognition that justice draws nearer only insofar as there is a response to the *call* of justice.

> There is an *avenir* for justice and there is not justice except to the degree that some event is possible which, as event, exceeds calculation, rules, programs, anticipations and so forth.[43]

42. Derrida, *Religion*, 17.
43. "Force of Law," 27.

Justice is greater than simply obeying the calculable, the law. In this way he frames justice within the pattern of messianicity not in order to reduce it to the level of an illusory ideal, but to accentuate the real significance of justice. Justice is quite literally a messianic ideal. As if to underline the religious affinities to this justice, Derrida invokes Kierkegaard to help illustrate the difficult nature of making the just decision. If as Kierkegaard reminds us, the "instant of decision is a madness," so the instant in which a just decision is made "must rend and defy dialectics. It is a madness."[44] The madness of this instant of decision is itself another example of the place of paradox in the work of both justice and messianism. Derrida knows that justice is paradoxical, and it is signficant that he draws on Kierkegaard, the great theologian of paradox.

The discernment of a primordiality to messianicity ensures that deconstruction will always be a question of responsibility, a way of critically responding and reading other texts. For all that deconstruction is parasitic, it is therefore also profoundly "humanist." Refusing any extra-linguistic vantage point, deconstruction remains wedded to a practice that is profoundly ethical. The impossibility of justice, for instance, is a spur to an investigation of undecidability rather than apathy. Where nihilism can call an end to this process, content with its analysis of meaninglessness, deconstruction is relentlessly called to the examination of conditions of possibility. It is the question of possibility, then, that sees the intersection of deconstruction and messianicity. As Caputo explains, "The messianic . . . is deconstruction's passion and deconstruction is impassioned by this impossible."[45] Deconstruction, like the messianic, is an impossible possibility that inscribes the question of paradox rather than simple contradiction or meaninglessness. Deconstruction is, to this extent, affirmatory and anti-nihilist.

From a variety of perspectives it is therefore apparent how deconstruction can be said to be an "experience of the impossible." As an examination of the impossible conditions of thought, deconstruction opens up the field for theological interpretation, not least in its analysis of the possibility of the *tout autre*. Discussing Heidegger, Derrida notes that the possibility of impossibility is actually the condition of truth, a truth that departs from the usual logic.[46] If deconstruction is read in this light,

44. Ibid., 26.

45. Caputo, *Prayers and Tears*, 141.

46. "In the persistence of this apparently logical contradiction (the most proper possibility as the possibility of an impossibility), he even seems to see a condition of

its contribution is toward a *reorientation* to this question of truth that incorporates the insights afforded by *différance*:

> Différance, the disappearance of any originary presence, is *at once* the condition of possibility *and* the condition of impossibility of truth.[47]

Derrida argues for the oscillation between possibility and impossibility, in a way that doubts all claims to certainty, whether they are nihilist or metaphysical. Derrida's thought therefore keeps the question of the divine framed as a (possibly messianic) *question* about the advent of the divine. This "possible impossibility" of deconstruction resists closure. Moreover, it is a "possible impossibility" that opens up space for emancipatory justice rather than apathy, making it possible for Derrida to claim at one point that "[d]econstruction is justice."[48]

What Derrida ultimately, and absolutely unintentionally, gives to religion is the ability to reimagine "impossibles" not as ridiculous, but as essential paradoxes. Believing six impossible things before breakfast like Lewis Carroll's queen has always sounded rather unappealing. Nevertheless, this does not have to be the only way of construing impossibility. As Caputo has recognized, the impossibility that Derrida draws attention to has a lot in common with the ultimate subject of traditional theology:

> For Derrida can say, no less than Augustine, *inquietum est cor nostrum*, our hearts are restless and driven by desire, a desire beyond desire, a desire for *the* impossible.[49]

For too long Christianity in all shapes and forms has laid claim to being completely transparent to either reason or the Scriptures. However, this alleged transparency is only ever created at the expense of doubt. Against such trends, Derrida's impossible thought suggests a recovery of religious approaches that actively militate against being easily reduced to either rational or scriptural explanation. A Derridean reading of religion reminds us to be humble about our supposed insights into theology and faith, and remember that much is "to come." While it may once have been believed that faith and reason could lay everything bare, we now find ourselves in

---

the truth, the *condition of truth*, in its very unveiling, where truth is no longer measured in terms of the logical form of judgment." Derrida, *Aporias*, 70.

47. Derrida, *Dissemination*, 168.

48. Derrida, "Force of Law," 15.

49. Caputo, "The Poetics of the Impossible," 479.

impossible territory where all that is most important is truly undecidable. With Derrida nothing is certain. And it is precisely this attentiveness to the uncertain that makes his thought so enduringly relevant to our contemporary predicament. If faith is a question of uncertainty rather than an affirmation of certitude, then Derrida has much to give theology. We may not be closer to understanding God with Derrida. However, we are closer to understanding how impossibilities and paradoxes might provide occasions for generating belief rather than denial. To reiterate the argument so far, with Derrida we edge closer to understanding how starting from a position of intense doubt leads into some of the most significant questions of religious faith.

4

Diabolical Deities

We shall eventually be no more able to convince men of the existence of a God "out there" whom they must call in to order their lives than persuade them to take seriously the gods of Olympus.

—JOHN ROBINSON[1]

The wise person, as Socrates taught, is one who seeks truth precisely because "he knows he does not know."

—RICHARD KEARNEY[2]

THE FIRST TWO CHAPTERS identified the dangers of certainty, and how fundamentalisms of one sort or another are inimical to doubt. In contrast, the previous chapter reviewed Derrida's thinking through a kind of antithesis to certainty in the ideas of aporia, paradox, and the possibility of impossibility. Derrida's strategy of contesting and questioning leads to an extension of the range of potential meanings, rather than locking interpretation down in one dominant or preferred reading. It is the suggestion of this work that these points of ambiguity and uncertainty can reveal truth more fluently than strategies of certainty that repress doubt. In this chapter, we will explore some of the ambiguities and uncertain-

1. Robinson, *Honest to God*, 43.
2. Kearney, *Anatheism*, 168.

ties raised around the way God has been depicted. The focus will be on identifying problematic conceptions of God—as well as the problematic conceptions of the diabolical that come in their wake.

When God is depicted with any degree of certainty, as is illustrated best by anthropomorphic language for God (language that imagines God to be like a human being), serious problems emerge. However, even something as non-anthropomorphic as philosophical theism (belief in God) rests on defining God with certainty and clarity. In what follows we will concentrate on the implications of these overly clear attempts to define God, and how they lead to the construction of dangerous certainties. By contrast, where the lure of both anthropomorphism and theism is resisted, it becomes possible to remain open to the insights of both continental philosophers who "rightly pass as atheists" like Derrida and the faithful theologians of orthodox Christianity.

At the risk of stating the obvious, it is not self-evident what theologians and philosophers mean by deploying the word "God." We have already seen how the non-religious thinker Derrida and the religious tradition of negative theology both affirm that God must be somehow beyond thought. As the *tout autre*, the wholly other, God cannot be a normal object of study or description. However, while God cannot be spoken of in the same register as a table, this has not prevented from theologians and philosophers from attempting to say something meaningful about the divine. Throughout history theologians have attempted to speak about the, strictly speaking, unspeakable. Moreover, like Derrida, these attempts have also noted what can properly be said of God, pointing out the danger of domesticating or oversimplifying the nature of God.

In order to grasp the significance of anthropomorphic and theistic visions of God it is helpful to recollect the bishop who sent shockwaves through England half a century ago. In *Honest to God* John Robinson introduced cutting edge German theological ideas to an unsuspecting public. A slim volume, it nonetheless ignited a ferocious public debate about the divine. Writing at the start of the secular swinging sixties, Robinson placed God on center stage by suggesting that "the first thing we must be ready to let go is our image of God himself."[3] Robinson's main targets were narrowly anthropomorphic, mythological, and supernatural depictions of God. He specifically attacked the attribution of divine transcen-

3. *Honest to God*, 124.

dence to a deity as either "up there" or "out there." These insights chimed with those of many contemporaries, prompting repeated print runs and national debate. Half a century later the stir caused is almost impossible to comprehend. Written by a member of the ecclesiastical establishment, *Honest to God* was not so much an attempt to defend God as a debunking of a mythological approach to thinking about religion.

Robinson's work became something of a cause célèbre. While many theologians rose to his defense, the work also inspired much criticism and begged many questions. Fifty years later it now seems in certain respects enormously dated, particularly in regard to questions of gender. Nonetheless, it ignited an important public debate and it communicated developments within German academic theology to a wider English-speaking audience. Moreover, with the passage of time, Robinson's own prediction that his work would not have gone far enough seems remarkably prescient:

> What I have tried to say, in a tentative and exploratory way, may seem to be radical, and doubtless to many heretical. The one thing of which I am fairly sure is that, in retrospect, it will be seen to have erred in not being nearly radical enough.[4]

Fifty years later there continues to be a need for honesty about the poverty of language that is used to depict God. Significant questions endure about what it means to talk about God. While much separates Derrida from Robinson, each in very different ways was addressing the same question: How is it possible to talk coherently about anything, and in particular things relating to the divine?

Robinson rejected what he called "supernaturalism" (what Paul Tillich called "supranaturalism") in favor of Tillich's notion of God as the ground of our being. Together with Rudolf Bultmann and Dietrich Boenhoeffer, Tillich provided the theological underpinnings for Robinson to dispense with the supernaturalist and mythological God. Writing as a bishop within the established church, Robinson used these three German theologians to critique the naïve vision of God as the "highest Being." Opting for the metaphor of depth rather than height, Robinson sought to replace the idea of a God envisioned as the exponentially largest version of Superman, a Supreme Being, with a God who was instead the ground of being itself:

4. Ibid., 10.

> When Tillich speaks of God in "depth," he is not speaking of an-
> other Being *at all*. He is speaking of "the infinite and inexhaust-
> ible depth and ground of all being," of our ultimate concern.[5]

Robinson realized that the three-story universe (of heaven, earth, and
hell) of biblical times no longer made any sense to contemporaries. In the
wake of space exploration Robinson saw how the idea that God or heaven
might be located in the sky or space makes no more sense than the idea
that hell might be underground.

While the rejection of anthropomorphism and mythological language of God seemed radical to many of Robinson's readership half a
century ago, another important dimension of this debate needs to be
considered. While overtly anthropomorphic language of God (e.g., father, judge, and lord) has had an enduring appeal (and undoubted biblical
basis), very few thinkers have seriously argued in favor of a solely anthropomorphic God. Writing not long after Robinson the theologian Donald
MacKinnon noted that faced with a straight choice between responding
to God either with agnosticism or anthropomorphism one should always
choose agnosticism.[6] It is better to be unclear about what God is like than
clear that God is a powerful man. However, while anthropomorphism
has been subjected to sustained theological criticism, it still retains a
hold in popular imaginations, both religious and non-religious. Part of
the challenge facing Robinson was that, while he wanted to reject the
theism that views God as a supernatural or supreme Being, at the same
time, "Our concern is in no way to change the Christian doctrine of God
but precisely to see that it does not disappear with this outmoded view."[7]

All this is by way of noting that the more things change, the less
things change. The questions of what is meant by anthropomorphism,
supernaturalism, and theism are still profoundly relevant to public debates about God. It is therefore helpful to turn to recent "new atheist"
rejections of God to see how, despite the passage of time, questions about
the depiction of God endure. Concerns over anthropomorphism, in particular, reverberate as new atheists lend their voices to a fresh rejection
of the cartoon villain that is the anthropomorphic and conventionally
theistic God.

5. Ibid., 46.
6. MacKinnon, *Borderlands of Theology*, 44.
7. Robinson, *Honest to God*, 44.

Christopher Hitchens was able to effect his own rejection of the existence of a Sunday-school vision of God as a grandfather in the sky without being remotely aware that he might be pursuing a quite venerable episcopal line of inquiry.[8] Half a century after Robinson, Hitchens nonetheless made his case with considerable rhetorical flair, aiming not simply for a single metaphor so much as the entire ecosystem of theology and religious belief.[9] The problem is that, while Hitchens is as good as Robinson (if not better) at attacking intellectually unconvincing notions of God, he largely fails to engage with more sophisticated understandings of God found within theological or philosophical traditions. For Robinson exposing the limitations of anthropomorphism and theism was simply a necessary prelude to developing a deeper understanding of God. By contrast, Hitchens assumes the obvious foolishness of a deity constructed in the image of humankind is all that the word "God" is ever capable of signifying.

In recent fiction perhaps the most inventive (and subversive) rendition of classic anthropomorphism is found at the conclusion of Philip Pullman's trilogy *His Dark Materials*. Making their way to heaven Lyra and Will free the Ancient of Days, the Authority. But they are surprised at what they find: "[H]e was so old, and he was terrified, crying like a baby and cowering away into the lowest corner . . . Demented and powerless, the aged being could only weep and mumble in fear and pain and misery."[10] These are powerful and haunting words. Nonetheless, success in showing up the limitations of a childlike construct of God as either a frail or powerful person in the sky should not be equated with success in demonstrating that there is no God at all. It is a little like a journalist finding flaws in a six-year-old's account of the emergence of the galaxy, only to conclude that the discipline of theoretical physics or the existence of the universe is sheer nonsense. Thinking atheists and honest bishops both agree that God is not a man in the sky. Moreover, Robinson was explicit in affirming the atheist rejection of such a God:

> But I have a great deal of sympathy also with those who call themselves atheists. For the God they are tilting against, the God they honestly feel they cannot believe in, is so often an image of

8. Ibid., 126.

9. Hitchens, *God is Not Great*.

10. Pullman, *His Dark Materials*, 926.

God instead of God, a way of conceiving him which has become an idol.[11]

The question nonetheless remains whether there are alternative ways of conceiving and believing in God that are not open to risible rejection. While it is right to deny misleading images, the rejection of misleading depictions should not automatically entail the rejection of all depictions. One can quite sensibly doubt that God is a man in a cloud up on high, but skepticism that there is any other kind of God does not automatically follow. To clarify the particular dangers of an unfettered anthropomorphism the rest of this chapter will investigate two logical consequences of anthropomorphism. First, we shall explore the question of the afterlife, specifically the question of heaven and hell. Second, we shall examine the question of the devil. In each case we will see how anthropomorphic assumptions allow theology to speak with clarity and certainty. However, as will be seen, such transparency and conviction comes at a significant price.

Denying Hell

Unfortunately, much as Robinson and Hitchens might disagree about the implications of their respective critiques of anthropomorphism, it is not possible to sidestep the questions they raise. One aspect of new atheist thought that hits the mark is the recognition of the utter awfulness and ridiculousness of a God who presides over heaven and hell. It seems inconceivable to these atheists that God might reward those who love him with heaven while those who call him by different names, or have the temerity to ignore him, are consigned to hell. For a supposedly loving God, the argument goes, why cannot God love everyone, regardless of whether they return the favor? For many atheists the moral scales are stacked against this jealous God who, not content to demand obedience from us in the present, also exercises a somewhat sadistic hold over our future happiness. We are given freedom, but it is really only the freedom to respond to God. However, if humans exercise their freedom to disagree with God, and fail to give God what God wants, then they find themselves in deep trouble. In this model God judges whether individuals have passed or failed, deciding their eternal destiny as sheep in heaven or goats for the hellfire. Atheists are surely right that there are more than

11. Robinson, *Honest to God*, 126.

a few Christians who believe out of fear for the punishment of not believing. These visceral atheist doubts about the morality and reality of such a God are an important gift to theology.

For centuries there have been apologists for the view that heaven and hell ensure that individuals receive appropriate rewards in the next life for choices made in this life. None, however, have contributed as much to the intellectual respectability of heaven and hell as Blaise Pascal in the formulation of his famous wager.[12] Simply put, Pascal sought to provide a logical argument to encourage making the choice between belief in God versus unbelief. However, it is the characterization of heaven and hell within this argument that is of more pressing concern. Like Descartes and Bacon, Pascal was writing in the seventeenth century during the rise of reason. Pascal's argument is a beautiful exploration of mathematics in dialogue with theology. The argument depends on mathematical values that Pascal assigns to heaven and hell. To heaven he gives the value of infinity, for heaven represents eternal blessedness, everlasting joy, and infinite good. To hell he gives the value of negative infinity, for hell represents absolute awfulness, pain, and alienation for eternity. Pascal then poses the question what makes the most sense to believe in. If one believes in God and there is no God what is the worst that can happen? According to Pascal, the worst that can happen is that one might have foregone certain enjoyments for oneself in the (mistaken) belief that God did not approve of them. But if one believes in God and there is a God, Pascal thinks that there is then the assurance of an infinite reward (provided one behaves correctly). By contrast, if one does not believe in God there are, again, two options. If there is no God, then by not believing in God all one has really done is deprive oneself of the potential good of a belief system, but one has probably not deprived oneself of the full range of human enjoyments. However, the crux of the argument is found in the second of two options to not believing in God. Here, if one believes there is no God and there actually *is* a God, then the full weight of infinite negative rewards (i.e., hell) are one's reward.

It is a very elegant argument. If we accept its premises (the respective values of heaven and hell, and the things that happen to the individual depending on whether there is a God or not) then the only rational choice is always to believe in God. That way the individual can be assured of avoiding hell at all costs, and even if there is no God not much has been

12. Pascal, *Pensées*, 153–58.

given up. However, if the choice is made not to believe in God, there is a chance of ending up in hell for eternity—or not. The Wager makes it clear that the odds of even an infinitesimal chance of going to heaven are better than any chance (however small) that one makes it to hell. Whatever you compute the odds of heaven versus hell, it will always make better sense to wager on heaven, as the rewards are, literally, infinitely better. By the numbers it always makes sense to believe in God, just to avoid hell.

Pascal himself would have hated the idea that he might have provided a distinctively rational reason to choose God. Pascal had little time for the Cartesian cogito, precisely because he believed it placed certainty in reason rather than God.[13] For Pascal, what really mattered was faith, not reasons for faith. It is somewhat ironic, then, that the strength of Pascal's argument is that it purports to rest on a mathematical logic that clearly points to the foolishness of placing trust in anything other than the existence of God. The Wager is the very opposite of a strategy of doubt. Instead, it is a strategy that exploits mathematical probability to attempt to counter other arguments against the existence of God.

However, what if Pascal's premises are simply wrong? What if God is really not dedicated to consigning all those who do not believe in God to everlasting torment? There is no room for a forgiving God in the Wager. Instead, the cold rationality of playing by the numbers to believe in God assures one of at worst somewhat ordinary pleasures, or at best an infinite reward. The Wager is just the kind of argument that, whatever its author's own intentions, might encourage people to believe in God for fear of hell. But what if fear of hell is really not as central to belief as Pascal makes out? What if, *au contraire*, God is not all that fixated upon dividing humans up into heaven and hell? Of course, it does also have to be said that this is only one of the many objections that could be made to Pascal's argument. In the light of religious pluralism, there is also no way that Pascal's argument can discern between different religious traditions and their many different Gods. Strictly speaking the argument has no power to reveal which of these Gods is the one overseeing the gates of heaven and hell.

Pascal's argument rests on an anthropomorphic view of God whose ways resemble less the author of creation and more the high school coach in the television show *Glee* who ruthlessly divides pupils into all those who are outside her cheerleader program and those who are active

13. Popkin, *The History of Scepticism*, 181.

members of it. Seen in the light of attempts by Pascal and others to justify hell it seems that atheists are right to question the intrinsic oddness of believing in a loving God who consigns some to hell and some to heaven. The only problem with this atheist critique emerges if it turns out that the wrong thing is being critiqued. What if Christianity is not dependent upon dividing humanity up into two classes of afterlife? What if we were (remembering Robinson and anthropomorphism) not to doubt the existence of God as a way of avoiding the atheist objections, but instead to doubt the oppositional thinking that divides people up between heaven and hell? Westphal's conclusion to his exploration of the thought of Friedrich Nietzsche and the question of hell is pertinent:

> Nietzsche's critique does not tell us whether there is eternal punishment or not. What it shows is how extraordinarily dangerous it is to believe in hell and in the concept of justice by which it is justified.[14]

There are some very diabolical conceptions of God. Not the least of those, are depictions of God that assume the premises of Pascal's Wager to be true. Atheists are right to raise the alarm at this. However, before conceding the existence of God to atheism, it might first be possible to address some of their concerns about the afterlife.

From the perspective of Christian theology, the type of justice meted out by hell presents more problems than it supposedly overcomes. This is particularly clear from an examination of the New Testament. Even the briefest exposure to stories of Jesus shows how at every possible point in his life he overturned the social expectations of who was an insider and who was an outsider. He consorted with prostitutes, lepers, and tax collectors, the very dregs of society. In the parable of the day laborers, those who work all day and those who arrived at the end of the day all receive the same reward. In the parable of the prodigal son it is the profligate and dissolute son who is rewarded with a banquet fit for a king, while the loyal and hardworking son looks on askance. Time and again, the parables of Jesus proclaim either radical inclusion, or a radical overturning of human approaches to judgment. Where common sense might imply some scale of values in which the holy and faithful are rewarded more than the sinner or the outcast, in the parables it is more often the sinners, the marginalized, and the outcast who are welcomed with open arms. The fact that this same spirit of radical inclusion is also beginning to appear

14. Westphal, *Suspicion and Faith*, 258.

within thinkers within very biblically-based circles is further evidence of just how inimical ideas of hell are to large parts of the Christian faithful.[15]

While it is hard to tie the New Testament picture of Jesus to a bipolar scheme of heaven and hell, he never ceased preaching the proximity of God's kingdom. While the kingdom of heaven may have been translated over time into a heavenly future reward, for Jesus the kingdom of heaven was about the rule of God's love in the present. The word kingdom itself comes from the Greek for the verb "to reign," and strictly speaking the kingdom is more of a verb than a noun—a way of being, rather than a cosmo-cum-geographical location. This perspective is actually rather similar to Philip Pullman's suggestion that heaven is a republic found in the here and now rather than a state of being in a qualitatively different reality. Towards the end of Pullman's trilogy, after a decisive battle that has defeated the enemies of wisdom, Will recounts the teachings of his father: "He said we have to build the republic of heaven where we are. He said that for us there isn't any elsewhere."[16] While many who have sought to affirm the "elsewhere" nature of the republic/kingdom, the stories told by Jesus anticipate exactly this notion that the kingdom should be sought in this world. Perhaps the best example of this is in the portion of the prayer he encourages his followers to pray: "your kingdom come on earth as it is in heaven."

Another illustration of classic theological views of the kingdom can be found in analyzing the radical work of The International Necronautical Society (INS). Founded in 1999 the INS aims to explore death in all of its permutations. In article one of its founding manifesto, the INS affirmed that "death is a type of space, which we intend to map, colonise, and, eventually, inhabit."[17] Article three further states, "We are all necronauts, always, already." For the INS the exploration of death is not something that belongs to a qualitatively different mode of being somehow connected to our individual futures that have not yet arrived. Death is, rather, something with which we live. Something similar could be said about the New Testament view of the kingdom. Against certain popular beliefs that the kingdom concerns some future state that emerges in the afterlife, the kingdom actually seems more connected to a way of living in the present. While necronauts seek to enrich human understanding by

15. Bell, *Love Wins.*

16. *His Dark Materials* (*The Amber Spyglass*), 991.

17. http://necronauts.net/manifestos/1999_times_manifesto.html.

acknowledging the importance of death in the present, Christians seek similar enrichment through an affirmation of the kingdom, also in the present. While there are theological interpretations that posit the kingdom as if it were something that post-dates our death, many of the stories of the kingdom appear to efface hard and fast distinctions between this life and the next. For all that it remains the central subject of their study necronauts recognize that they fundamentally do not know an awful lot about death. A similar reticence concerning the nature of the kingdom as it pertains to the afterlife would be invaluable for theology.

Yet another helpful resonance, if not an out-and-out parallel, can be found in the thought of Giorgio Agamben, whose work will be explored in more detail in chapter 6. Just as there are intriguing connections between Derrida's ideas of impossibility and messianicity, there is also a confluence between the kingdom in the New Testament and Agamben's own theory of the "coming community." Strictly speaking the kingdom or the "coming community" are impossibilities. Yet somehow or other they are "possible" impossibles—despite their seeming unattainability. The kingdom, certainly, does not appear to be a very easy place to get to. The New Testament suggests that it is easier to go through the eye of a needle than for a rich man to enter the kingdom of heaven. The kingdom operates according to a contrarian logic where laborers and wastrel sons are not rewarded according to their just deserts. It is located where those who have been invited to the wedding do not come, while the strangers and aliens in the street outside are brought in. It is a place more accessible to little children than the powerful or religious professionals.

Colby Dickinson underlines the connection here between Agamben's thought and Jesus's declaration that to come into the kingdom we must become like little children: "They are both pointing in fact to an 'impossible' realm of existence that we are yet called to in a sense."[18] The problem with the kingdom, then, may not be that it is, strictly speaking, impossible. Rather, the problem may be that the "impossible" possibility of the kingdom has been replaced with the altogether easier to comprehend and more lightweight concept of life after death. It remains much easier to imagine geographical spaces, even in a post-Copernican universe, than the potentiality of escaping the confining space that is traditional thinking. However, it is surely possible to reimagine the impossible kingdom announced by Jesus using cues from Derrida and Agamben.

18. Dickinson, *Agamben and Theology*, 108.

The Wager assumes that death is followed by a final destination: heaven or hell. By contrast, the thought of the kingdom presents an impossible potentiality that does not have to wait for death before it can be made possible.

Returning to the critique shared by Hitchens and Robinson, if God is anthropomorphically imagined to be a somewhat irascible old man it is not entirely surprising that an anthropomorphic model of the afterlife emerges in which some receive favor and others do not. However, if Robinson, MacKinnon, and the greater part of the entire theological tradition is correct, it makes sense not to ground concepts of the afterlife on a somewhat capricious father figure. The point that requires stressing is that notions about the afterlife, good, and evil all arise out of reflections on the nature of God. If, for example, it is in God's fundamental nature to be love, it will seem increasingly odd to talk about a segregated afterlife with some passing and some failing their celestial entrance exam.

Since Origen in the second century, many theologians have taken issue with the bipolar "pass or fail" scheme of the afterlife. Unfortunately, these universalist voices have often been perceived as being located on the margins of acceptable Christian belief. Universalism is the simple idea that in the end everything is ultimately alright. Universalists believe that no one ends up separated from God, that even the worst offenders are ultimately reconciled with God. In order to understand the limits of anthropomorphism it will be necessary to explore in a little more detail how universalism presents a powerful theological argument against the deity of Pascal's Wager.

While other aspects of Christian belief have been subject to voluminous description and analysis the topic of the afterlife has never been subject to the kind of thoroughgoing treatment that one might expect. And for good reason. *Á la* Caputo, we (whoever we are, whatever our beliefs) really do not know. And, most of us *know* that we do not know. Moreover, while the afterlife itself is relatively underplayed in Christian theology, hell itself is almost entirely absent. The Nicene Creed affirms belief in the resurrection of the body and the life eternal, but it does not specify what that might mean. And while the creed mentions hell, it is only in passing as it describes Christ's descent into the uttermost depths following his crucifixion. Given that the dominant interpretation of Christ's purpose of visiting hell, the harrowing of hell, was to allow those located in hell a chance to escape, it does almost seem as if a perfectly orthodox reading of the creed results in hell itself emptying, if not disappearing, following the resurrection. Even if hell exists at the time of the crucifixion, if Christ's death is somehow about restoring humanity to relationship with God, there is no particularly good reason why hell should not be one of the most serious casualties of resurrection. It could equally be argued that instances of hell in the biblical texts have a cautionary rather than descriptive purpose. The Scriptures do not need to be describing a location or a state of being. They can instead be offering symbolically colorful representations of the results of existential decisions. By contrast, to ascribe reality to hell does not fit with the universalist intuition that Christianity's God is fundamentally all-forgiving and all-loving.

Although hell has had a high profile in the popular imagination thanks to some quite uncompromising scriptural passages and some quite vivid literature (Dante springs to mind), most Christian theology has remained almost entirely silent about hell. The good news here is that any theological revision of hell does not need to worry about conflicting with the Christian tradition because the tradition, given the exceptions already noted, is almost entirely silent on the matter. There are some persistent pointers to a pass/fail scheme: for instance, the references to sheep and goats in the New Testament. However, a few scriptural verses do not make an entire religious system.

Literal interpretations of hell as a place for inflicting punishment (with or without everlasting fire) would be a horrible stain upon a supposedly good God. So maybe hell is simply a metaphor for state of exclusion from communion with God. However, even without a spatial hell of whatever kind, a situation in which hell remains simply a metaphor for a fundamental and everlasting separation from God is also difficult to comprehend. To create and redeem a few while leaving others out (whether in the cold or the heat) seems theologically incoherent.

At this point it might be objected that God creates humans free to choose their final destination for themselves. For freedom to really matter, humans should have both the freedom to choose God *and* the freedom to reject God. Seen in this light, hell would represent the potential for humans to continue to reject God while heaven the potential for humans to choose union with God. Of all the arguments in favor of hell the argument from human freedom is perhaps the most powerful. Unfortunately, it only works if human freedom is determined to be a higher good than any other good, including the good of knowing God. What, however, if the good that is human freedom is not as significant as the good that is enjoying the presence of God for eternity? If God is God, it is hard to imagine that the ability of humans to control their own volition can amount to the highest eternal good. Surely, the goodness of enjoying the presence of God would merit a higher point on a scale of ultimate value than the goodness ascribed to making one's own decisions? To exercise freedom to choose union with God is surely a good. However, eternal separation from God is just as surely *not* a good. Weighing up which of these should take priority is beyond the scope of this work. However, it must be at least possible to imagine a good God who prefers union with everyone rather than just those who make the grade. The possibility of heaven as a fundamental metaphor for union with God, however that is actually conceived, seems necessary for theologians. By contrast, the possibility of hell as a fundamental metaphor for separation from God is not theologically necessary in the same way. Hell adds nothing to Christian theology, and, as has been argued, subtracts a great deal from Christian professions of a loving God. For universalists it is theologically incompatible with the reality of a forgiving and loving God to have a form of religious apartheid in the afterlife.

Agamben draws on an ancient Zoroastrian text about a kind of guardian angel called a *Daena* that has the form of a beautiful young girl.[19] This *Daena* presides at the birth of every person and becomes a silent witness who accompanies and observes them throughout their life. As in the story of Dorian Gray, over time the face of this beautiful *Daena* changes. With every gesture, word, and thought the *Daena* slowly changes so that by the time of death the *Daena* has either become even more beautiful, or absolutely hideous. At death the *Daena* is said to then whisper to the individual she has shadowed through life, "I am your *daena*, the one who has been formed by your thoughts, your words, and your deeds." The *Daena* powerfully reminds us that so long as we are human we will think anthropomorphically. Far better, though, to believe in a *Daena* than the reality of something as antithetical to Christianity as hell. Nonetheless, before hell can be entirely set aside it is necessary to address the question of its chief inhabitant.

The Devil is Not in the Detail

If theology has been relatively quiet about hell, it has been almost completely silent on the topic of the devil and the demonic. In marked

19. *Profanations*, 16–17.

contrast the entertainment industry remains fascinated by the powers of darkness and the commercial opportunities inherent within the notion of an eternal cosmic battle. From television's *Buffy the Vampire Slayer* to cinema's *The Exorcist*, *Dogma*, and *Constantine*, battles between angelic forces and the various powers of darkness are as popular to contemporaries as Dante's vivid imaginings were for the Middle Ages.

While the diabolical depictions of Hollywood and popular television are undoubtedly imaginative, they are not widely known for the depth of their religious or philosophical insights. Drama on the silver and the small screens takes dramatic license with science, history, and philosophy for its own ends. When it comes to constructing worldviews that provide both good storytelling and good visual effects, the cosmologies of popular entertainment are relentlessly dualistic. Good battles evil, and right up until the end evil looks like it is going to win. Until it doesn't.

If the desire for certainty can be likened to a kind of disease, then the dualism of much popular entertainment is one of the most significant carriers of infection. In contrast to most people's first-hand experience in the world of uncertainty and ambiguity, popular entertainment rests upon the dualism in which evil versus good provides the ultimate narrative clarity. However, it is not good philosophy or theology, because neither philosophy nor theology can provide the kind of unambiguous clarity that tales of cosmic conflict require.

A perfectly good example of this type of escapist entertainment can be found in *Devil's Advocate*. A young lawyer played by Keanu Reeves is taken to the top of a shiny impressive skyscraper and offered the world by Al Pacino, his smooth-talking senior. This offer is to all intents and purposes a reprise of the offer made by the devil to Jesus in the wilderness during his forty days of temptation. Just as the biblical devil promises Jesus dominion over the world, so Pacino offers Reeves the chance to command all that his eye can see. It is an absolutely spectacular scene. And the beauty of the city seen from such great height is stunningly ethereal in all of its stone, steel, and glass modernity. But while the setting is modern, the ideas behind the film are somewhat less so.

Within the movie Pacino's character is indeed the devil. He has all of the tell-tale tics of the prince of darkness, from a rambunctious love of sex to his endless capacity to tempt and taint those whose path he crosses. The problem with Pacino's devil, though, is that beyond the single scene in which he offers Reeves the world there is no real connection between

his activities as a fictional devil and religious or philosophical understandings of the reality of evil.

If we take Pacino's diabolical portrayal seriously for a moment, the
best that one could say about his devilishness is that he is quite an under-
achiever. He is able to make Reeves's wife see visions of snakes and other
unpleasant things. He also has an active sex life. However, when all is said
and done the devil is undone by a junior lawyer still wet behind his ears.

There is a series of significant problems here. On the one hand Hollywood dualism presents us with a personification of evil that is instantly
recognizable and comprehensible. Yet, almost without fail the devil in
question ends up being beaten back into hell with relative ease. The overall effect works well in dramatic terms: terrible and awe-inspiring evil
is quashed by the purity of heart of one good person. However, if there
really is such a person as the devil, and if the devil really has been around
for thousands of years perfecting his evilness, why is he always so easy to
beat?

The reason such plots do not stand up is that there is a theological
contradiction at the heart of many popular representations of the diabolical: the idea of a simple battle between good and evil, cosmic dualism, is
all-too terribly clear and certain. Such fictitious representations of the
devil should not be criticized as failures of imagination. Rather, they
should be celebrated as successful representations of dualistic heresy that
equates materiality with evil.

The heresy of dualism is the apparently innocent idea that a good
God is in perennial conflict with a bad God who has dominion over the
world. To some no doubt this sounds like a description of Christian teaching. However, that would be to confuse Christianity with its more lurid
fictitious simulacra. Theologians have always argued against the idea that
the world is the product of an evil creator. Instead, as will be seen later
with Augustine, theologians have contended that God is good and that
the world is created out of nothing other than the goodness that is God's
own being. Yet, throughout history dualism has appealed to those who
have wanted to distinguish between a good God located in heaven and
the evil One who rules over this world and the fires of hell.

At first sight there is a certain logic to dualism. Who has not thought
that some of the most atrocious acts committed by human beings must
have been inspired by some deeply inhuman outside force? Most of us
prefer not to think that human beings are intrinsically capable of geno-
cide, murder, rape, or sexual abuse. We crave some external explanation,

and the existence of an evil force seems to fill that need. However, the evidence points to the fact that humans have committed such crimes (often quite enthusiastically) and will continue to commit them. It is entirely natural to want to explain away the extremes of human behavior, and what better than an evil One.

The problem with this approach, however, is that it shifts responsibility for evil away from those who commit the evil acts to some divine, semi-divine, or quasi-divine figure lurking in the wings. Morally, if we believe the devil is responsible for evil rather than human beings we should be petitioning the courts to exorcise convicted murderers and release them back into the community. And yet even in very religious parts of the world that does not happen. Part of the reason this does not happen is that at some level or other even people who "believe" in the devil do not genuinely think that human beings who commit evil are not responsible for their actions. So if even die-hard believers in diabolical power still think that humans are responsible for their actions the question remains: What is the point of the devil?

It could be suggested that believers in the devil have two logical choices. Either the devil is a force to be reckoned with, a prince of darkness who is competing with God for control of creation. Or the devil is little more than a cheerleader who offers occasional encouraging nods and winks to tempt us into doing things we know we shouldn't. This latter devil is perhaps best exemplified by C. S. Lewis's *The Screwtape Letters*. But contrary to the popularity of that work, if Lewis is correct then the devil is little more than the personification of malevolent desires that have their origins firmly and squarely within human nature. In which case, as Eagleton suggests, we may not need anything more than a brief course in the Freudian death drive to explain the nature of these malevolent desires.[20] Humans are more than capable of wrecking the world on their own. We don't need much help in this arena.

Beyond Anthropomorphism: Augustine

One suspects that few who believe in the devil realize just how much goodness needs to be surrendered in order to create metaphysical space for such an active evil presence. The most important theological argument against the devil is produced by Augustine, famous for stoutly

20. Eagleton, *On Evil*.

defending Christianity from heresy. Augustine is about as far from being a touchy feely kind of happy-go-lucky Christian as it is possible to be. No one ever accused Augustine of being a flaky liberal. Yet, it is Augustine who some fifteen-hundred years after his death continues to set the standard for Christian reflections on the question of evil.

Augustine understood just how prevalent the possibility of evil is. Since he believed he had experienced evil, he spent an inordinate amount of time struggling to work out where evil comes from. For a time he subscribed to a specific form of religious dualism, Manichaeism. However, as he recounts he ended up rejecting Manichaeism largely on account of its inadequate and dualistic understanding of evil.[21] Essentially, Augustine doubted the idea that there were two distinct kinds of being in the world, one good and one evil. Manichees believed that the material world is itself evil, the product of an evil God. He further recognized that as soon as it is treated as a form of materiality the connection is lost between evil and human volition. From personal experience he knew that the temptation to commit wrong acts came from within, even if it could not always be properly explained. Moreover, Augustine did not want to deny the goodness of the material world. For Augustine everything that *is* has to be at some level fundamentally good. While some things are better than others, everything that exists and has ever existed is fundamentally connected with the goodness of God in creating. So when it comes to evil Augustine developed the idea that strictly speaking evil has no being. Evil is no thing. Nothing. For evil is not a thing, rather evil is the word we use when we recognize the utter absence of anything good. Moreover, as Eagleton illustrates in his recent review of fictional representations of evil, this idea that evil is really *nothingness*, really devoid of existence, has continued to exercise a powerful hold over human imaginations.

Augustine imagines evil as the privation of the good (*privatio boni*). So where good is wholly absent, there evil emerges. Note that what Augustine does not say is that this evil has its own being, identity, or personality. None of that would have made sense for Augustine. By contrast, evil is that which emerges when goodness is entirely absent. Perhaps the best recent cinematic rendition of Augustinian evil is the depiction of the Nazgul in the movie *The Lord of the Rings*. The Nazgul are former kings, now ring wraiths, who have so given themselves over to evil that they are depicted as almost entirely lacking in any materiality. Although we see

21. Augustine, *Confessions*.

their clothing, the ring wraiths themselves are almost completely absent, literally all we see of them is dark emptiness under their clothing.

The irony of Augustine is that, while his teaching on evil has been central to Christianity, few have integrated his teaching on evil with reflections on the most famous personification of evil, the devil. But the theological implications of what Augustine is saying are clear. Either there is no ultimate personification of evil. Or, if there is personification of evil that person must also have a fair amount of goodness to exist. Metaphysically a person of pure evil cannot exist within an Augustinian theology. So either the devil is a much *better* person than we first thought, or the devil does not exist, just the lack of goodness that is evil.

At the risk of oversimplifying, it is unlikely that believers in a devil intend him to be a particularly good figure. So the choice remains. It is technically possible to retain the devil within Christianity provided that the devil is acknowledged as quite good, confining himself to occasional nods and winks. The depiction of Satan in the story of Job would fit this interpretation: not only does Satan depend on God to allow him access to Job, God also appears to hope that somehow Satan might even see the error of his ways by learning from Job's faith. Job's Satan is certainly not a particularly powerful force to be reckoned with, and all his power comes from God.

The alternative, to have a metaphysically absolute devil who is total evil, lacking any goodness whatsoever, requires surrendering Christianity in favor of a form of gnostic dualism like Manichaeism. Of course, one could simply agree to doubt the very existence of both the quite good devil and the thoroughly evil devil. Needless to say, simply doubting the existence of the devil does not preclude one from resorting to a personification of evil as a handy linguistic shorthand. Like Santa Claus, the devil can be a helpful cultural device that enriches our language and our imaginations. However, the linguistic benefit disappears as soon as such fabulous constructs are invested with too much certainty or treated as dogma.

A good illustration of the theological implications of the classically Augustinian position on evil is found in G. K. Chesterton's story about a secret policeman called Thursday.[22] Thursday is under the command of a chief policeman called Sunday. When Thursday, at Sunday's request, infiltrates an anarchist group he discovers that Sunday is also the chief of

22. Chesterton, *The Man Who Was Thursday*.

the anarchists. Later as Thursday tries to flee this arch-anarchist version of Sunday he realizes that he simply cannot get away from him. Whether appearing as ultimate good or ultimate evil, Chesterton's message is clear, there is not one power for evil and one for good. The one who is all-powerfully good is the same as the all-powerful evil, just Sunday. Sunday does not have an opponent with a similarly high status. Instead, he is the head of both the anarchists and the police. In contrast to the neat separation of good and evil offered by Manichean dualism the model offered by Augustine and Chesterton is complex, begging as many questions as it answers. It also has much in common with Derridean understandings of impossibility. Where anthropomorphism offers simplistic certainties, Augustinian and Chestertonian orthodoxy is altogether more complex and undecidable.

Beyond Being

Part of the problem that faced Robinson was that, at the same time that he rejected the anthropomorphic God of a Supreme Being "out there," he also affirmed a Tillichian God that was pure being. While being, or the ground of being, sounds more promising than a man in the sky, a demythologized God can be just as dangerous as the fully mythologized anthropomorphic God. While it is easy to reject anthropomorphic visions of God after even cursory reflection, the God of the 1960s liberal theology posed just as many profound questions. If God is a metaphysical object, even when known as the ground of being for Tillich and Robinson, then does God not continue to be just another (albeit very powerful) object? The problem with this approach is that it assumed that God could be understood with reference to other beings. By contrast, the God of theological tradition, like the God of Derrida's "atheological" tradition has always been beyond conception, and beyond being.

To put it another way, if God is not a big man in the sky, surely God is also not simply the biggest being in the cosmos or even the being that somehow grounds the cosmos. While the first option seems quite ridiculous, the contention of much modern theology has been that the latter two options are absolutely spot on. The problem with these latter kinds of God-as-being, Super Being, or ground of being is that they continue to define God immanently in terms of the creation, rather than acknowledging divine transcendence. However, if God is to be God, then surely

God cannot be understood as just another component or fundament of existing beings.

Theologians know that they do not believe in the existence of God. To exist implies that there will also be a time of non-existence. Everything experienced in the world has some form of existence, and everything will at some stage cease to be. From the relatively short life of a butterfly to the somewhat larger lifespan of the polar ice caps, all that is known of this world is temporal, and all passes out of existence. To exist is then to have the possibility of non-existence. However, language about God does not speak about a form of being that came into existence and will in time go out of existence.

This fundamental difference in the relationship to existence between the divine and the beings of this world means that it is not possible to speak about God in the same way that we speak about other beings. For Thomas Aquinas this is why we can only speak analogically of God. God's being or goodness is not the same as our being or goodness. For God to be God, it is required that God transcends the usual human categories of thinking about existence and non-existence. To be fair to Robinson, he recognized how the transcendence of God might be lost in simply turning from metaphors of height to metaphors of depth. While it resolved the problem of the simplistic positing a God as a supernatural being "out there," the depiction of God as the ground of our being simply introduces other dangers. Whether God's being is a man in the sky, a superlative being, or the ground of being the issue is not with size or scale, but with the fundamental idea that there is an ontological equivalency between the being of God and the being of creation. Such an equivalency would lead to a univocity, the idea that we can speak of God or creation in the same voice, or with the same categories of understanding. However, the contention of Aquinas and the theological tradition is that univocity, or the collapsing of finite being into Divine Being, is as dangerous an over-simplification as anthropomorphism.

The real problem within theology, once again, is where it suggests a univocity, or the ability to be too clear about questions of the divine. Whether that clarity is found in anthropomorphic visions or the modern demythologizing theologies of the 1960s, the issues are the same. When God is believed to have been made comprehensible, whether through simple or complex metaphors, God is lost. God cannot be thought, and to think that God has been conceived is to commit either a horrible philosophical category error or an act of great hubris.

The dark side of theology is found in theologies that lay claim to too much univocity or transparency. It is not only fundamentalism that seeks to reduce the complexity of God to something much more comprehensible. A similar strategy occurs within more flexible theologies that determine God to be a process or aspect of nature. The problem with such theologies is that they tend to maximize the comprehensibility of God while minimizing the alterity, or the holy. By contrast, if God is the author of creation, rather than some kind of metaphysical giant within creation, then that God cannot be fully comprehended by that creation. To take our cue from Aquinas, we would be better off speaking analogically. Or to take our cue from Derrida, we might want to consider approaching matters differentially. If God is divine, and not simply a super-thing, God is both fundamentally beyond being and fundamentally beyond our comprehension. Theologies (whether fundamentalist or flexibilist) that claim to be able to explain all are therefore committing the unfortunate theological error of forgetting their origins and taking for themselves the place of deity.

5

HOLY AGNOSIS

It is sheer nonsense to speak of the Christian religion as offering a solution
to the problem of evil.

—DONALD MACKINNON[1]

God doesn't give his reasons or share anything with us: neither his motivations, if he has any, nor his deliberations, nor his decisions. Otherwise he
wouldn't be God, we wouldn't be dealing with the Other as God or God as
wholly other [tout autre].

—JACQUES DERRIDA[2]

HAVING NOTED THE DANGERS of overly anthropomorphic views it is time
to delve deeper into the problem of evil. Terry Eagleton is surely right to
suggest that, "Ideas of evil do not have to posit a cloven-hoofed Satan."[3] At
the same time, the rejection of the devil as anything other than figurative
does nothing to explain or mitigate the problem of evil. It still remains
to be seen how evil might be construed without descending into anthropomorphism and the dualistic oversimplifications of Manichaeism and

1. MacKinnon, *Borderlands of Theology*, 92.
2. Derrida, *Gift of Death*, 57.
3. Eagleton, *On Evil*, 16.

Hollywood. The problem of evil, and the question of whether it can ever be explained, is therefore the central concern of this chapter.

From the outset it is important to acknowledge J. L. Mackie's classic philosophical rendering of the problem of evil. An atheist, Mackie argued that it is fundamentally incompatible to believe in the following three propositions: (1) that there is a good God, (2) that God is all-powerful (omnipotent), and (3) that there is evil.[4] It is possible to wholeheartedly agree with Mackie that it does appear to be nonsense to suggest that all three premises can coexist if one takes them at face value. While a case can be made for disagreeing whether the Christian God is in fact the same as Mackie's God of philosophical theism (omnipotent and good) this is not the issue at hand. Consequently, in what follows no attempt will be made to argue with Mackie about his central premises. Instead, from the outset, it is important to admit that (as Mackie believes) by the standards of rationality, and in the terms that Mackie sets out, the problem of evil really does appear to be indissoluble from a strictly philosophically theistic perspective. So, rather than attempting to solve the problem as presented, we will assume for now that this problem is inherently unsolvable from the perspective of theism. The problem can be instantly solved by turning to atheism (a perfectly reasonable response), and rejecting the existence of a God who is good and powerful. It can also be solved by rejecting that there really is evil (an inherently unreasonable response, what Mackie labels one of several "fallacious solutions"). It can also be solved by simply rejecting either the goodness or the omnipotence of God (a response that seems perfectly possible, with the abandonment of the latter being the focus of many recent theological responses). Instead of opting for any of these perfectly valid ways to dismiss or evade Mackie, we shall entertain the proposition that Mackie might, indeed, be absolutely correct, and that belief in God is by its very nature *not* able to offer a solution to the problem of evil.

This might strike some as providing a very good reason not to place one's trust in God. However, it seems just as reasonable to suggest in the light of the broader argument of this work that it might precisely be the capacity for the problem of evil to generate doubts about its solution that ensures its truth. Mackie's lucid presentation of the three premises to understanding the problem of evil may make it sound like a mathematical problem whose only solution is in abandoning one of the three premises.

4. Mackie, "Evil and Omnipotence."

However, it is also possible to agree with Mackie on the insolubility of the problem of evil for theology without abandoning belief in God simply because of its insolubility. Maybe what we have in the question of evil is a paradox, aporia, or impossibility that simply resists our understanding. Maybe the attempt to make sense of evil is actually the *real* problem raised by evil, not the idea that evil and God are somehow contradictory. Theology is not calculus. It cannot construct beautiful equations where everything always makes sense. It is, instead, closer to art. It can describe, imagine, inspire, tell stories, and point to great mysteries. It is less good at offering certitude or problem solving. Moreover, as shall be seen, the insolubility of the problem of evil seems to be something of a theme within theology.

It is important to underline that one question that will not be entertained is whether or not there is evil. Mackie is correct in affirming as "fallacious" solutions that argue that there is, in fact, no evil in one sense or another. Although evil is difficult to define, it will be assumed that this is not simply a linguistic problem. The prejudice underlying what follows is that it is not possible to deny the problems raised by evil by simply claiming that evil is illusory, fabricated, or mythological. It is possible to dispense with the devil and hell as the product of anthropomorphic mythology, but such a move does nothing to explain the question of evil in the world. It also seems counterintuitive to allow for skeptical denial of the existence of evil or nihilist affirmation that evil is somehow indistinguishable from good. Neither denying evil nor claiming that there are no standards from which to judge anything evil offers a way of dealing with the severity of human experiences of evil. At the same time, attempts to explain what evil is or somehow minimize evil also present considerable difficulties. One suspects that for many the greater question, in the face of evil, is should there not be absolute clarity about what is evil and what is good? In what follows it will be suggested that it is precisely the need to be honest about the reality of evil that stands in the way of acquiring any such certainty or clarity. That evil exists cannot be denied. Where things get a lot trickier is in working out precisely what it means to describe something or some action as evil.

For many thinkers the question of evil has also been allied to an uncertainty about what evil really is. It is natural to have significant doubts about not just the possibility of evil coexisting with God, but the very nature of evil itself. Counter to those who might see this as deeply problematic, or an example of less than rigorous thinking, the working assumption in what follows is that the ambiguity that arises out of these types of questions might itself be an essential part of thinking rigorously. Or, as Derrida might put it, maybe there is an impossibility at the heart of the problem of evil—without that making it any the less true.

The Banality of Evil

One of the problems of not believing in the devil and not believing in an independent evil agency is that it becomes very hard to explain why evil might exist or where it might come from. Augustine's teaching on evil as the *privatio boni*, the absence of good, may be intellectually coherent, but it does not offer a terribly robust response to some of the more hideous excesses of human evil. Positing a devil intuitively appears to explain evil a lot better than positing an Augustinian cosmology in which everything is good and things that are thoroughly not good simply don't exist.

The difficulty with this line of argument is that the apparent explanatory power of the idea of the devil is illusory. It provides the illusion of certainty and clarity about where evil might come from, but such certainty is ultimately unhelpful, if not dangerous. Simply positing a devil does not explain why that is the case, or why a good God would allow it to be the case. By contrast, the strength of the Augustinian approach is that it does not offer false certainty—because it is unable to offer any kind of certainty. Augustine's approach still begs questions, yet it does so in a way that does not diminish the reality of evil by attributing it to some unknown force. It is therefore appropriate to salute Augustine precisely for *not* solving the problem of evil. Having rejected the false solution of dualism, Augustine instead remains content with the creative ambiguities of believing in the goodness of God and evil as the lack of goodness.

If theology adopts Augustine's account of evil one can see why Donald MacKinnon would think that Christianity does not offer a solution to the problem of evil. Remaining within an Augustinian tradition offers a description of the problem and a rejection of a particular dualistic attempt at explanation. However, it does not offer (nor does it seek to offer) a fundamental explanation for evil. In this way Augustine's teaching on evil should be commended for keeping certain important questions open, as it does not provide anything like a final explanation to the problem of evil.

Hannah Arendt was working with an implicitly Augustinian view of evil when she famously concluded her discussion of the trial of Adolf Eichmann with the words, the "banality of evil."[5] For Arendt, evil is not the product of some exotic, supernatural, mysterious force. Evil is, rather, the product of banal, dull, and, unexceptional human beings who commit terrible acts or make their commission possible. Arendt's focus on Eichmann's part in the Holocaust does not attempt to produce a grand explanation for evil. Instead, her careful examination of Eichmann's character revealed someone utterly unexceptional, a bureaucrat more concerned with his career and party politics than the lives of the millions he was sending to their deaths. Recent scholarship suggests that Eichmann was probably not the unwitting perpetrator of the Holocaust portrayed by Arendt. However, an Eichmann more actively responsible for the evil of the death camps does nothing to change the insight that the nature of evil. The evil committed by Eichmann, and that which was committed under his direction, was effected not through supernatural power, but through the banalities of train timetables, logistics, and the bureaucratic jockeying of petty officialdom.

Why some commit evil and others do not is something neither Arendt nor Augustine are able to explain. However, what they do point to is the inherently ordinariness and tediousness of evil. Augustine understood that the impulse toward evil is within every human being, and that there is nothing particularly supernatural about the way that human beings often allow themselves to become agents of evil. As against the Hollywood depiction of evil that was investigated in the last chapter, Arendt and Augustine both imply that evil is something that has no particular direction or purpose. Affirming the banality of evil dethrones evil from its dualistic role as a spiritual power independent unto itself. Evil in this theory is not self-caused by some independent metaphysical power so much as the effect that occurs whenever the good is rejected—for whatever reason (or lack thereof).

This point was recently made by John Milbank. Defending the Augustinian theory of the privation of the good, and affirming Arendt's analysis of the banality of evil, Milbank questions those who follow the alternative route of Immanuel Kant in attempting to provide metaphysical grounds for theories of "radical evil." The temptation when faced with the enormity of the horror of the Nazi death camps is to allow evil the

5. Arendt, *Eichmann in Jerusalem*, 252.

kind of metaphysical independence and status that can allow us to account for such horrors by creating a reason for them. However, against that temptation, Milbank reminds us that to claim any positive status to the nature of evil is to grant "a ghostly theoretical victory" to Hitler.[6] Against those who see in the death camps a pure form of radical evil, Milbank wants to deny the possibility that such evil is a point of revelation against which all our thinking of evil should be judged. Here Milbank's purpose is not to underplay the history of the Holocaust so much as to underline Arendt's thesis that evil is the product of banality rather than metaphysics. It is worth noting that Žižek also agrees on the importance of Arendt's reading of evil:

> As Hannah Arendt was right to emphasize, the unbearable horror of Auschwitz resides in the fact that its perpetrators were NOT Byronesque figures who asserted, like Milton's Satan, "Let Evil be my Good!"—the true cause for alarm resides in the unbridgeable GAP between the horror of what went on and the "human, all too human" character of its perpetrators.[7]

Žižek, Milbank, Arendt, and Augustine agree that evil is not a transcendent being of its own. For them the true danger when facing the question of evil is to imagine evil as an independent force to be reckoned with when in fact evil has no independence or autonomy. Evil is, rather, parasitic: emerging only when good is reduced, deprived, or rejected.

It is worth noting another pertinent connection to Kant. While Arendt is largely critical of the internal contradictions of Eichmann's attempts to defend and explain his actions (on her reading he often ignores the most helpful evidence, while implicating himself and outright contradicting himself at other times), when it comes to Kant Eichmann successfully explained his actions in terms of a Kantian construal of duty. Part of Eichmann's defense was the admission that he was following orders. For Eichmann this constituted his duty, as a servant of the state. Nowhere in Arendt's account does Eichmann emerge as particularly relishing the elimination of the Jews, nor even personally benefitting (at a time when others were) from the disposal of their property. Instead, his particular relation to evil seems to have been that of the archetypal bureaucrat: doing his duty without regard for what he was really doing. Whether or not this is actually true of Eichmann, it is most certainly true of many other

6. Milbank, "Darkness and Silence," 290.

7. Žižek. *On Belief,* 38.

twentieth-century experiences of evil. Evil may well be the product of malevolence and psychosis, but it is also what happens when good people do nothing, or else, when good people allow themselves to be used for evil.

Milbank and Arendt remind us that attempts to imagine evil as something greater than the Augustinian reading end up actually enlarging and valorizing evil. Like traditions of God that speak only in terms of what cannot be known of God, so evil appears to be one of those topics where it is best admitted just how little we understand. Some might object that denying the devil or the metaphysical independence of evil is to grant evil a freer reign. By contrast, Augustine, Arendt, and Milbank suggest that evil arises out of disordered human desires that originate within quite unremarkable human beings. Within this way of thinking, to imagine evil as greater or more metaphysically independent than it really is risks exculpating from responsibility the actual doers of evil.

If questions of faith always involve uncertainty, that uncertainty becomes pronounced when it comes to evil. Contrary to popular interpretations of the story of Adam and Eve, theology cannot tell us why there is evil or where it comes from. All theology can honestly do is highlight the fact that evil is a part of human life. Moreover, within the Scriptures, God appears to accept that evil is part of the way things are at the same time as being righteously indignant about it. The story of Job and the story of Jesus are both unflinching in reminding us that the world is far from perfect and that suffering and evil form part of the horizon of existence. However, nothing within the stories of Job or Jesus completely comprehends, still less answers, the problem of evil. Quite the contrary. Each can be read as a response to evil: but neither is an explanation.

The story of Job is entirely concerned with reminding humans just how much they do *not* know about where evil comes from, why it happens or how we might avoid it. Žižek hits the mark in noting what many religious believers are never quite able to see:

> Job's properly ethical dignity lies in the way he persistently rejects the notion that his suffering can have any meaning, either punishment for his past sins or the trial of his faith, against the three theologians who bombard him with possible meanings—and, surprisingly, God takes his side at the end, claiming that every word Job spoke was true, while every word the three theologians spoke was false.[8]

8. Žižek, *The Puppet and the Dwarf*, 125.

Equally, when the story of Jesus climaxes in Jesus embracing an awful and evil death on the cross, this neither sugar coats, nor does it explain. Both Job and Jesus reveal the reality of evil, and that evil has profound consequences. However, their central lesson, if it makes sense to speak of such a thing, is surely that evil is not something that can be avoided, and that belief in God does not come packaged with a comprehensive answer to the problem of evil.

Beyond Augustine? The Challenge of Eleonore Stump

In her magisterial exploration of the question of human suffering and evil, Eleonore Stump proposes an explanation for why evil might coexist with God based on the thought of Thomas Aquinas. Through an impressively close reading of the narrative of Job and three other biblical stories of suffering, Stump explores whether there is a way of reconciling God's goodness with the reality of humans who suffer evil. Stump suggests that a reason for suffering can be found in the fundamental desire that God has for relationship with humans. On her account, it is through suffering evil that humans grow closer to God. Interestingly, trust in heaven is a *sine qua non* of this argument, but hell is optional. Without trust in heaven and eventual union with God the argument fails. For in the face of awful suffering, the only way of finding meaning is to have faith in God and attain union with God. While such union with God begins through faith in this world, in the face of the most terrible suffering the potential union with God in heaven is sometimes the only vindication for those suffering evil.

As was noted in chapter 2, Stump introduces an important typological distinction between Franciscan and Dominican knowledge. While she believes it may not be possible to immediately detect a Dominican (objective or third person) response to the problem of suffering, there is nonetheless a Franciscan (subjective or second person) response to be found in stories. Stump decisively rejects "objective" suggestions made by theologians that there is a general purpose to evil and suffering that either makes the individual a better person or provides some benefit of utility to others.[9] She recognizes how ultimately inhumane and preposterous it is to suggest that moral growth to the individual or utilitarian benefits to

9. Stump specifically distances herself from the perspective of John Hick in *Evil and the God of Love*.

others might somehow justify one person's suffering. At the same time, she does not want to abandon the idea that God allows suffering as a means for humans growing closer to union with God.

Stump therefore takes issue with readings of the story of Job that purport to show that there is no reason to the story of his suffering. Instead, she argues that the awful suffering of Job has the very clear result of bringing Job and God much closer together. By the end of the story Job is a veritable hero, and an intimate of God. Pointing out how Job is portrayed as having a more profoundly personal experience of God than any other figure in the Scriptures, Stump argues that suffering is that which enables Job to attain a closer union with God. Job is recognized as remarkable for his faith before the privations of Satan, but both attempts by Satan to dislodge Job's trust in God fail miserably. Note here how Satan is able to do nothing without having God first lift his protection from Job. Stump further notes that God's relationship with Satan appears to be more loving than combative, and that the Satan who tempts and attacks Job is able to do nothing without God's permission. This is a complex and nuanced view that tries to make evil distinct from God while recognizing that it is sanctioned by God. What it is not, is the cosmic dualism of Hollywood or the Manichees. Rather, like Chesterton's depiction of Sunday, it introduces the idea that evil only happens because God allows it. Of course, Satan fails miserably in attempting to destroy Job's faith. Noting this failure, Stump suggests that for all the evil that befalls Job he attains a status equivalent to Socrates: one universally recognized as the human being who continues to trust in the goodness of God despite the privations that he suffers.

Stump's thesis here is that throughout this suffering, Job continues to be close to God, trusting in divine goodness. Furthermore, Stump realizes that only a story told Franciscanly-speaking can demonstrate this kind of truth. It cannot be demonstrated objectively, it can only be experienced dramatically in the second-person account of a story. The problem in this, of course, is whether the story that has Job remaining steadfast in faith despite evil, and essentially conquering his suffering, can provide a response to the question of other evils. Alternatively, it could simply be viewed as a remarkable testament to a remarkable character. It is important to recognize that Stump does not need Job to be an historical character to make this argument. Whether or not Job is historical, the story of Job reveals a God who is in a profound relationship with the person who suffers. God on this account takes responsibility for the well-being of the person who suffers by being close to him. In Stump's view, it is Satan who is the originator of suffering (the evil of the story), while God acquiesces. Here the diabolical is only capable of introducing evil into the world once God has agreed to suspend the protection of his hedge that surrounds Job. So, while Satan is theoretically an independent contractor of evil, in real terms Satan receives the contracts only after first soliciting them from God.

Stump recognizes how the story of Job has more frequently been read as *not* providing any kind of answer to the problem of evil. As we saw with Žižek and MacKinnon earlier, this is also the point that David Burrell underlines in his examination of Job.[10] Indeed, both Stump and Burrell recognize that the interlocutors of Job who offer to explain why he suffers have their explanations roundly rejected both by God and by Job. Both also identify the remarkable feature of the Job story resting in the fact that God actually responds to Job. Where Stump differs from MacKinnon, Žižek, and Burrell is ultimately in whether or not God's response provides enough of an explanation for why evil might be allowed. For Stump the attention itself merits being treated as an explanation for evil, while for the others the Job story underlines the rejection of the possibility of producing any kind of theodicy (an explanation of evil).

In Stump's interpretation, the question is whether the fact of God simply being responsive and close to faithful to Job can be counted as a solution to the problem of evil. To reframe things a little, it has often been said that God is found in suffering and evil. However, to suggest that finding God in suffering and evil provides a full account for the necessity of suffering and evil seems a stretch given how many people appear precisely *not* to find God in such circumstances. Empirically it simply does not seem true that suffering and evil bring people closer to God. Surely, one of the reasons why Job's story is so powerful is that it is so absolutely remarkable (and by extension, for many, unfathomable). Job's faith is not diminished, and he grows closer to God. Nevertheless, while that growth toward God may account for Job's experience of evil, it is hard to transpose that experience to others who suffer evil. When one stops to consider what evil and suffering have done to alienate people from God in the course of human history, it is hard to turn that argument on its head and suggest the exact opposite, that evil and suffering are themselves the mechanisms by which God draws closer to individuals.

10. Burrell, *Deconstructing Theodicy.*

In essence Stump's argument with the Job story is that God is present to Job through his suffering, while not offering any explanation, and that Job nonetheless remains faithful (despite being told by God not to expect to understand why the evil happens). However, it is not obvious that this can really be described as providing a solution to the problem of evil. Remaining faithful and trusting in the midst of suffering certainly mitigates evil, but in what sense can God simply acknowledging the suffering predicament of a creature be equated with solving the problem of evil?

It does seem true that suffering and evil can bring individuals closer to God, at least for Job and for many particularly faithful individuals (one thinks of the mystic Simone Weil). Yet, it is hard to be convinced that faithfully enduring evil and trusting through faith that God has not abandoned one can be given the status of an *answer* to the problem of evil. While Stump's readings of Job and other stories are deft and insightful, it is not immediately apparent how she can incorporate other first-person accounts of evil and suffering that see faith destroyed and diminished. The narrative of the Scriptures and certain extraordinary figures may point one way, but surely the multiple narratives of the past two millennia point in an alternative direction to the harmonious reconciliation of evil and suffering with belief in God?

Stump addresses precisely this issue by quoting an impressive range of psychological studies revealing that many types of trauma do result in increased senses of psychological integration for the sufferer. She identifies these as "support[ing] the connection between suffering and psychic integration at issue for the Thomistic defense."[11] However, this needs to be put in context. Stump's central argument is premised on the idea that Franciscanly-speaking the stories of Job, Abraham, Saul, and Mary offer an account of truth that reveals an individual drawing closer to God while also attaining their heart's desire *even while suffering greatly*. It is only through their sufferings that each figure attains an increased integration of the self in relation to God. However, in none of these cases do they receive an answer from God for their sufferings *during* their sufferings. Rather, it is only with the benefit of hindsight (and in these scriptural cases, remarkable and miraculous goods) that the sufferings are either alleviated or explained.

---

11. *Wandering in Darkness*, 459.

While biblical stories of faith in the midst of suffering are indisputable, it is not obvious how once one turns from biblical stories into the world one can argue that the integration that psychologists detect can necessarily be equated with increased proximity to God, the contention upon which the argument of Stump and Aquinas rests. Stump might object that this places an artificial division between personal integration and God, and that God desires personal integration. So any kind of psychological integration must ultimately lead one closer to God. However, as soon as she shifts her focus from the emphasis on faith that is found in the Bible to the experience of integration found in psychology it is not entirely clear how the two can be completely equated. Worse, since Stump quite sensibly rejects any utilitarian benefit either to society or to the individual accruing as a result of suffering, is not the appeal to increased psychic integration just one such apparently quantifiable benefit?

In short, Stump presents a powerful way of imagining how God seems to have drawn close to four very different biblical characters. But can we really presume that the experience of suffering and growing in faith of these four (who receive remarkable gifts in terms of their knowledge of God) be readily transposed to those who do not have God speaking to them quite so clearly? Moreover, even if we assume that most people undergoing traumatic experiences were to see some quantifiable psychological benefit, to propose that such a benefit answers the problem of evil is no less problematic than those who argue that evil brings much good in its wake. What if the price of the benefit of growth does not outweigh the original suffering and loss? Stump would, one imagines, reply that for Aquinas the benefits of growing close to God and joining God (and those one has lost) in heaven outweigh all suffering and evil. However, the hope of heaven as the justification for evil and suffering does not appear to be an argument that can be marshalled in real life to those who are actually enduring suffering and evil. Saying that everything will be better in the next life as the only consolation we can provide in this life can hardly be treated as a resolution to the problem of evil.

Part of the problem here has to do with the inherent ambiguities associated with the question of faith. Another part has to do with the ambiguities inherent in stories. In essence, Stump's analysis conveys to others what in the stories only appears by faith to the person experiencing suffering. And while there is ambiguity for the person in the story who relies on faith, so there is also ambiguity for us who listen to the stories. For most of the stories those who endure suffering and evil cannot make sense of their suffering while it is going on. Equally, the reader of the story must also wonder exactly what the truth quotient of the story is (although, as Stump rightly notes, some truths only story can convey, and the intimate experience of another's life is surely one of those truths). Nonetheless, Stump knows that neither faith nor story can be totally explained or proven. The entire account is, in essence, haunted by undecidability and doubt. Just as Derrida affirms our inability to know God's reasons,[12] so Stump makes a remarkably similar point in an important passage on how God cannot explain the reasons of their suffering to the individuals who suffer:

> God cannot explain his reasons without losing them. And the reasons that justify God's allowing human suffering are also the reasons that justify God's failing to explain those reasons to the sufferer. The benefits that, on Aquinas's theodicy, come to the sufferer are benefits defeating even the suffering of the hiddenness of God's reasons for allowing particular individuals to suffer as they do.[13]

This passage gets to the heart of the matter. Assuming Aquinas and Stump are correct, and that God allows suffering because suffering draws the sufferer closer to God, then it is only a lived life that can show this to be true. Only from within, or in hearing a story of a second-person account, can we see how one person might find this to be true. However, to extrapolate from several admittedly fairly unique stories that this is how suffering and evil work in the Scriptures is not to prove that this is how suffering and evil can always be understood. As Stump notes in the story of Job, when the comforters try and tell Job that there is meaning to his suffering both he and God rebuffs them. In other words, it is essential to Stump's account that the meaning of suffering and evil can only be approached from within, or from stories that take us as close as possible to first-person experience. However, as soon as we start to talk in the third person objectively about the nature of suffering and evil we run the risk of turning into one of Job's comforters who God and Job both reject.

While Stump's presentation of Aquinas constructs a possible explanation for why God *might* allow evil and suffering, it is in the nature of the limits of theology that it cannot be proved. Structurally, it is open to doubt. Such a theodicy can, of course, assist an individual who suffers in

---

12. See the quotation at the start of this chapter.

13. Stump, *Wandering in Darkness*, 410.

offering hope. However, it cannot exclude or deny the fact that the existence of suffering and evil still remains hugely problematic and difficult for so many.

It is worth at this point comparing and contrasting Stump with Eagleton. Both believe that evil can, indeed, be comprehended, but what they mean by this is very different. Both also owe a considerable debt to Thomas Aquinas. As a result both believe that the work of becoming a person is the work of becoming more integrated with oneself and with God. Stylistically they also have much in common. Eagleton's analysis of evil, like Stump's, relies on the examination of narratives for its explanatory power. However, unlike Stump, the narratives Eagleton chooses are predominantly drawn from secular fiction, from William Golding to Flann O'Brien. While Stump's work focuses on showing how evil and suffering do not have to prevent the flourishing of a relationship with God, Eagleton's focus is on trying to understand how evil presents itself in the world. The point for Eagleton is simple. To understand evil better we need to understand the split that occurs not within the relationship between God and Satan or the devil, but the splits that occur within individual human beings. He does not say it, but here the story of the *Daena* is again directly relevant: every choice we make has the effect of changing us for good or for ill.

As alluded to earlier, Eagleton suggests a Freudian reading of the death drive is ultimately the explanation for how individuals are evil. Fragmented and directed toward death, humans are not misled by some diabolical agent, merely capable of allowing themselves to be handed over to destructive dimensions that lie within their own volition. The problem is that, while Eagleton helps explain *how* humans might be evil, this still does not explain *why* it should be so. Indeed, at one point he makes it clear that evil in terms of its own identity is inherently pointless (something one imagines Stump would agree with).[14]

So there is much within Stump's and Eagleton's attempts to understand evil that overlaps. However, while Eagleton stresses how the choreography of evil is to destroy and disintegrate, Stump reminds us how suffering nonetheless can hold out the possibility of individual integration. The reason that Stump can propose a potential reason for evil is not that she believes any more than Eagleton and Augustine do that evil has its own reasons. None of the thinkers we have examined believe evil

14. Eagleton, *On Evil*, 84. Eagleton repeatedly stresses that evil itself is a desire for nothingness allied to sheer purposelessness. This is also very Augustinian.

has agency or direction at a metaphysical level (or, indeed, any level). Nonetheless, while Eagleton and Augustine concentrate on exposing the essential meaninglessness of evil itself, Stump is asking a different question: how an individual might find meaning within suffering and evil for themselves.

One does not need to be a theologian to understand that humans are remarkably adept at finding meaning out of even the most remarkable meaninglessness. Or, to put it another way, why should an individual *not* claim that through their suffering they grow closer to God? Just as one cannot prove that it does, neither can one prove that is does not. The genius of faith lies in the fact that questions of faith are inherently beset by a certain indeterminacy and doubt. It is also important to remember, as already noted, that Stump's professed purpose is not to produce a theodicy (an explanation of why there is evil) so much as a defense (a *possible* explanation for why there might be evil that does not conflict with any evidence in the world as it really is). This reluctance to claim for her work the status of *the* actual explanation so much as *a* possible explanation actually brings her closer to MacKinnon, Eagleton, and Augustine than might otherwise appear at first sight.

To conclude, none of the writers we have examined offer a response to evil that decisively answers the problem of evil. While Stump comes closer than any of the others, even her impressive argument ultimately places responsibility for finding meaning in suffering and evil in the faith of the individual. In essence, MacKinnon's advice that we not speak too clearly about that which we do not know (at least until we experience it) still has value. Even those like Job who grow closer to God as a result of their suffering never discover *why* there is evil. All faith can offer is a methodology for living with uncertainty and questions while making it possible to draw closer to God. Saying that we do not know why there is evil does not have to be a retreat from intellectual honesty. Nor does it have to entail a denial of the potentially transformative nature of suffering and evil in the lives of those who experience it. Clearly, suffering and evil have transformed individuals in growing closer to God, as surely as others have been profoundly alienated from God by their suffering.

One of the great strengths of Stump's approach is that she does not seek to provide an objective rejoinder to why there is evil. Her argument is not a proof for why there is evil, so much as a story that can be told about how evil was, for certain individuals, something through which they grew closer to God. Although her thesis rests on being able to argue that suffering draws us closer to God, Stump reminds us just how little can be known when it comes to trying to make sense of another's suffering from outside:

> [A]s I have been at pains to show, neither suffering nor the benefits defeating suffering are transparent. It is not true that a person has them if and only if he knows that he does. A fortiori, they are opaque to outside observers.[15]

If another's suffering (and any putative benefits) cannot be transparent from the outside (and rarely from the inside) then there are no grounds for being able to claim objectively that it is true that there is a meaning to evil or suffering. Stump's account answers the question of why it would be possible for God to allow evil and suffering if it were possible for an individual to grow closer to God with a faith as remarkable as that of the biblical stories. In this scenario only a subjective relationship to God through faith can constitute what must always be a personal answer to the why of suffering. And yet, on Stump's account even within faith the reason for suffering and evil has to remain occluded and hidden from the person who has faith.

The previous chapter suggested that one of the most important reasons for doubting the devil must surely be that picturing personal agency behind evil gives evil too much meaning, too much clarity, too much certainty. Stump also shares a similar reluctance to allow too much meaning, too much clarity, or too much certainty, into the scheme by which faith might emerge as the ultimate meaning of suffering and evil. As we saw in the story of Job, God himself knows that the reason for evil remains so incomprehensible to the suffering Job that all attempts to explain what is going on by the comforters are rejected by both God and Job. If there is anything to be learned from this story it is surely the reluctance to overdetermine the objective meaning of evil even if it may be possible to formulate a subjective way of coping with it through faith.

The experience of faith for Job, Abraham, Saul, or Mary was not an experience of knowing why they suffered. They did not have answers, but they did have varying degrees of trust, as well as different degrees of doubt. The strength of Stump's position must surely be in drawing attention to how responses to the question of evil emerge through individual lives, appearing as she notes "fractally" through the concrete lives and experiences of different people in different ways. Ultimately, there is no

15. Stump, *Wandering in Darkness*, 413.

overarching comprehensive answer to why there is evil. Instead, what Stump beautifully articulates is how faith cannot explain evil so much as provide a strategy for responding to evil that does not allow evil to win. The faithful believe that through faith in God certain individuals have managed to draw closer to God through their suffering, but that same faith cannot provide them with an answer to why they suffered evil. Instead, faith gave them a way through which their doubts and uncertainties could be transfigured. There is nothing about this experience of faith through suffering that allows evil and suffering to be easily explained away, lessened, or overcome. Instead, faith provides a survival strategy premised on attaining proximity to God in this life and the next. At the same time, just as suffering and evil can draw some closer to God, they also push others away. So while faith may offer subjective hope for living in the middle of uncertainty, suffering, and evil, what it cannot offer is an answer to the problem of evil.

The healthy agnosticism toward understanding evil encouraged by Donald MacKinnon allows for doubt to be seen as an essential part of theology. By contrast, the explanatory tactics of Job's comforters aim at erasing doubt by producing a rationale for evil and suffering. However, as both God (in the story of Job) and Žižek observe, it is not possible to identify reasons for suffering and evil. More than anything else, the story of Job serves as a powerful reminder that nurturing doubt is not inimical to faith. Job trusts in God at the same time as being unsure about the reasons behind his suffering. In this way, the experience of faith in the face of suffering and evil does not diminish doubt so much as depend on doubt to ensure that it remains faith.

6

True Fiction

[T]he attempt to read literally and timelessly from the surface of the text, whether by zealots or sceptics, is a modernist aberration that lacks any historical sense or proven communal context.

—DAVID FERGUSSON[1]

Christianity is postmodern because it is not founded on anything other than the performance of its story. It cannot be established against nihilism, but only presented as a radical alternative, as something else altogether.

—GERARD LOUGHLIN[2]

THE LAST CHAPTER ADDRESSED the importance of stories in shedding light on some of the most difficult questions surrounding evil and human suffering. Narrative is an important category of thought that allows for a sophisticated exploration of truth claims. This chapter investigates in more detail the connections between fiction and truth. Up to this point it has been shown how stories can be used to convey truth in ways that are difficult, or at least counter-intuitive, for philosophy and science. We have also seen how stories found in the Scriptures might be able to point to truths that other disciplines cannot. It is now time to tackle the broader

1. Fergusson *Faith and Its Critics*, 175.
2. Loughlin, *Telling God's Story*, 21.

question of the Scriptures. Neither science nor philosophy, the Scriptures are a veritable mélange of different genres.

While the Baconian and Cartesian both aim for certainty and clarity, the Scriptures have tended in the opposite direction. A challenge to common sense, confusing, and at times infuriatingly opaque, the Scriptures represent almost everything that science and philosophy have attempted to eradicate. For many the Scriptures are a stumbling block, a leading cause for skepticism or doubt, if not simply apathy, confusion, or incomprehension. In what follows it shall be assumed that the capacity of the Scriptures to elicit all these responses (and many others) is neither inconsequential nor immaterial. To approach the Scriptures requires the admission first and foremost that these are a collection of writings that are simultaneously breathtakingly odd and mind-numbingly strange. In what follows, we shall also explore how the fabricated, fictional, and often unworldly elements with the Scriptures might also be part of a deliberate truth-generating strategy.

Ruffian or Saint?

It is helpful first to begin with an illustration. In Adam Thorpe's novel *Hodd* a famous icon of good triumphing over evil is radically reinvented. Thorpe's Robin Hood lives in the forest in the thirteenth century, but aside from that he could hardly be more different from the Robin Hood of popular legend. However, it is not simply the inverted nature of Hood that captures the reader's imagination. Thorpe's work is also an impressive portrayal of textual transmission and the issues that accompany both the telling and interpretation of narratives. Thanks to Much's monastic quill we are treated to a wonderful first-person perspective on Hood and his band of distinctly un-merry men, wanton women, and captives. Much symbolizes the power of institutional religion through the permanency of his mastery of writing. However, in Thorpe's retelling it is not solely Much's written story that creates the Hood of legend. Much is also responsible, quite inadvertently, for the beginning of the folk ballads celebrating Hood through his own oral musical storytelling. He recounts his own surprise at hearing his own songs sung back at him, much embellished. And it is the power of these songs, together with stained glass designed to ward off the presence of Hood, that create and sustain the legend of Hood.

Thorpe's novel is a fascinating exploration of the competing narratives that surround one person. As the novel progresses it becomes increasingly difficult to unequivocally separate original historical event from subsequent literary representation. Hood nowhere speaks for himself, and is instead only heard through the perspective of Much, a not entirely trustworthy source. The further we dig into his writing the more any moral certainties start to unravel. There is also a powerful sense of never being able to decisively identify the original truth of Hood. The more one finds out about the circumstances under which his one surviving literary witness writes the less one really knows. This is heightened even further as we only encounter Much through the lens of a soldier who discovers his text during the First World War. Stacked like Russian dolls, there are several narrative layers between the modern reader and the original Hood.

In addition to pointing out the difficulty of knowing the truth or distinguishing fact from fiction, Thorpe's *Hodd* also reveals how popular caricature can not only replace, but also potentially invert, a truth that is more complex. While we never understand the entire textual transmission from the thirteenth century through to the First World War, the reader is left in little doubt that sheer happenstance, or ill fortune depending on your perspective, conspire to turn a ruffian into a saint.

When it comes to reading the Scriptures the experience of *Hodd* has much to teach us. While unlike Much's manuscript the Scriptures have not been physically hidden for the last seven centuries they have undergone the same kind of fate as Hood. On the one hand their supporters have turned a blind eye to some of the more outrageous and indecent parts. For them questions of authorship and textual transmission are irrelevant, as all has been penned by a divine maker. In this scenario all Scriptures should be treated equally, and all should be understood as the final word. On the other hand, opponents of Scripture have largely condemned the Scriptures for not meeting standards of rationality or morality that are themselves the product of several thousand years of religious history. For them the Scriptures are parochial and beneath contempt precisely because they dare to be what they actually are, a collection of writings spanning centuries written by different people facing remarkably different circumstances.

Both the cheerleaders and the detractors of the Scriptures fail to understand the importance of diversity, complexity, and competing narratives in the Scriptures. The Bible, a singular noun, is a remarkably unhelpful designation in the English language for this enormously complicated library. Understanding these writings as plural, as Scriptures, is an important first step toward understanding what they really are. Just as Thorpe demonstrates the importance of at least three distinct storytellers in shaping our understanding of Hood, so the Scriptures can only be understood as the product of multiple writers. Unfortunately both the sternest critics and most earnest enthusiasts conspire to treat the Scriptures as if they were a singular product of a single author. Yet while God has been described as the author of our salvation in the Scriptures, nowhere is it written that God is the author of the Scriptures themselves. Of course, biblical fundamentalists affirm that the author is God, but this does not really help comprehend the tremendous diversity of perspective and context to the various books of the Bible. If one is to claim God as the writer of Scripture one must also affirm that God allowed a veritable plethora of differing and contradictory perspectives into the authorial process.

Theologians and philosophers have spent much time addressing these questions of understanding, or what is more precisely called hermeneutics. Named after the Greek messenger god Hermes, hermeneutics is the science of interpretation. Hermeneutics teaches that not all letters get delivered in a timely way, and not all missives reach their correct destination. Hermeneutics attempts to understand the forces at play in interpretation, and in particular why certain kinds of understanding are either privileged or ignored. When it comes to the Scriptures, there is also the question of why some texts made it into the canon and others did not. The Scriptures evolved through time, and different churches have often played the roles of hermeneutical communities deciding which texts to include and which to exclude. There are no Scriptures before a community of faith. In *Hodd's* terms, communities of faith play the same role Much inhabits in relation to Hood: it is through their necessarily imperfect interpretative actions that the Scriptures come to be.

In the world of academic biblical studies few doubt that the Scriptures are plural and diverse. A single-source author might make sense for a fundamentalist, but the idea of a singular writer responsible for the great range of literary genres is fanciful in the extreme. Even when parts of the Scriptures appear to have a family resemblance scholarship has long taught us to be open to alternative possibilities. What may appear to be written by Paul at first sight may well not have been written by Paul, but may be using the name Paul in a similar manner to the way in which modern brands are used. *Nike* or *Adidas* may not have actually made the running shoes that are the subject of our desires, but this does not stop them from calling them their own if they "fit" the brand identity that they wish to be offering their customers. While today we do not particularly concern ourselves which factory makes the sneakers, just which brand name they bear, so the ancient world was a lot less obsessed about authorial identity. It is entirely natural for different books in the New Testament to be associated with certain names of certain disciples or schools of thought. Just as no one today seriously thinks that an individual historical personage called Mr. Nike signs all *Nikes*, so no ancient reader would have been overly concerned about whether a man named Luke, John, or Paul really wrote every word ascribed to him.

Since the mid-nineteenth century it has been common knowledge that the name carried by certain books of the Bible is not necessarily the name of the historical individual who wrote it. It has also been taken for granted that most books were not set down concurrently with the events that they appear to record. Very few of the books of the Bible are anything like contemporaneous, and the vast majority were, like Much's manuscript, written up significantly later. In certain cases it is not even a matter of decades but hundreds of years. And in still other cases, there is significant debate about whether the events of the narrative had any historical grounding. Like the story of Hood, some of the narratives found in the Scriptures are out-and-out fiction. They are fiction in the sense that they refer to characters and events that were the invention of the writer. While fundamentalists will revolt at such claims it is natural for others to cheer, especially those who identify with Friedrich Schleiermacher's "cultured despisers" of Christianity.[3] However, as Hood surely shows us, not all fiction is untruth. Or not all that is made up is entirely without meaning, merit, or deeper significance.

Returning to Much it is clear that his manuscript is as much a fiction as the songs of the minstrels in praise of Robin Hood. There is actually no way of verifying that Much's manuscript is any closer to the truth of Robin Hood than the legendary tales of benign derring-do that is the traditional account of Robin Hood. From a strictly historical perspective, Much's manuscript offers a convincing account for the popularity and the positive feelings associated with Robin Hood. Yet, this is about all that can be said. One cannot independently verify that the negative portrayal

3. Schleiermacher, *On Religion.*

of Much himself is in any way non-fictional, and there is no way of knowing that he is not simply spinning us a yarn that simply happens to be exponentially more inventive than that of other ballad singers. There is no way of knowing for sure. But on the strength of the evidence of Much's text alone it would make sense to revise positive approbation of Robin Hood in favor of something more circumspect and less favorable.

Returning to the Scriptures, there are no independent points of reference inside the Scriptures and few outside. While there are other histories and mythologies, legal codes, and biographies that intersect with the Scriptures, it is never entirely clear whether these are more reliable or less reliable. Parts of the Scriptures may be just stories, but that does not mean that sources outside of the Scriptures are anything more than stories either. While there may be a vast difference between a Roman legal code and the writing of an early Christian, neither text is value free or objectively neutral. The hermeneutics of suspicion encourages a wariness about swallowing whole from any particular text. Just as the Scriptures have multiple axes to grind, so do the other independent sources that are either contemporaneous or covering similar material. Historiography can teach us how to weigh sources and where to ascribe greater weight, but fundamentally historiography can never produce an entirely objective neutral account of historical events.

For a long time scholars have appreciated that the interpretation of texts requires acknowledging some bias, perspective, hidden agenda, or simple prejudice. Some of these are well hidden, others not so. Some are conscious, others merely an unconscious part of the wider context in which the text is written. What literary theory also teaches is that these biases are not simply within the texts. They are also within us. Indeed, it would be impossible to approach a text value-free unless one were to first rid oneself of every value. A reader without any values would discover about as much from a text as a pebble might learn from a beach. Being partial and understanding partially are essential features of human consciousness. While we strive not to allow prejudices, blind spots, or peccadilloes to overly determine our perceptions, each of us would be much less than human if we did not have them.

In approaching the Scriptures, if one intends to treat them seriously and not simply as comic books, it is necessary to understand and celebrate this. It is important to have a hermeneutics of suspicion in which the question is asked: Why this particular story and this particular outcome? Whose interests would it be in? Who benefits? Who has most to lose?

Equally we also need a hermeneutics of retrieval and re-enchantment in which we are allowed to wonder what this all means. What was the purpose of this story? Where is it leading us? What happens if we suspend our disbelief just for a second? What is this story asking of me?

There are two significant problems that face those who read the Scriptures. One comes from taking them too seriously, and not being able to countenance a hermeneutics of suspicion. The other problem stems from treating the Scriptures as singular rather than plural. Singularity implies a consistency and uniformity that simply does not reflect the polyvalence of Scripture—the ability to generate multiple and competing meanings. Unlike scientific discourses that value consensus and unanimity, Scripture is an inherently complicating and confusing discourse. When someone tells you that they have understood Einstein's theory of relativity the correct response would be to cheer. However, if someone claims to have understood the Scriptures it would be preferable to extract oneself quickly and quietly. The fact remains, that the more interesting parts of the Scriptures resist most attempts at understanding. That this has been obfuscated by those who claim to have understood them is one of the great tragedies of biblical interpretation.

Babel

A powerful scriptural example of this twin need for a hermeneutics of suspicion and recognition of scriptural pluralism is the story of the tower of Babel. Built by humans in order to reach the heavens Babel is the scriptural version of Prometheus. In Greek mythology Prometheus steals the fire of the gods and as a result is cursed, forever associated with overreaching and attempting the unnatural and hubristic. Ironically, Prometheus has become something of an icon in his own right for scientific achievement. He symbolizes reaching for the skies and pressing the natural limits of human understanding. The tower of Babel is built for the same original purpose, to advance human understanding by placing humans at the apex of creation. However, while today the metaphor of reaching for the sky conjures up images of positive, entrepreneurial and indomitable spirit the same was not true in the Scriptures. In the book of Genesis God is recorded as deconstructing the tower of Babel and scattering the humans who have built it. Against the human impulse to conquer and comprehend, the God of Genesis sows deliberate confusion.

Moreover, this confusion is a deliberate strategy aimed not at crushing but at liberating. Where humans seek uniformity, God quite literally encourages diversity and pluralism. The scattering of tongues and cultures in the aftermath of Babel portrays God as more interested in the ability of humans to be different than to find unity. The babble of Babel is what is important. By contrast the homogenizing and domineering reasons for constructing the tower spur divine dissatisfaction. What is not in doubt is whether humans are able to build to the heavens. What is at issue is whether this is an enterprise that is worthy of human endeavor. Those who attempt to portray the Bible as a singular edifice built on a solid foundation also run the risk of turning the Scriptures into a latter-day Babel. Scriptures that should be understood in plural and competing terms, have increasingly been given Babel-like uniformity. While Genesis records God's deconstruction of Babel, the task of deconstructing the Scriptures remains one of the most pressing challenges for people of faith.

Part of the purpose of God deconstructing Babel was to challenge the idea of one particular perspective coming to dominate the world. Ironically, this is exactly the kind of notion that fundamentalists have come to invest in the Scriptures themselves. Yet, far from being the last word on any given subject the Scriptures more often than not are writings that initiate further conversations. Babel introduces uncertainty to the human quest for understanding, and it is key to understanding the Scriptures that this uncertainty and confusion is divinely inspired. As Derrida puts it:

> The "tower of Babel" does not merely figure the irreducible multiplicity of tongues; it exhibits an incompletion, the impossibility of finishing, of totalizing, of saturating, of completing something on the order of edification, architectural construction, system and architectonics.[4]

By speaking out the word "confusion," YHWH passes on a proper name that valorizes linguistic indeterminateness. The impossibility of translating this name becomes linked to the necessity of accepting the confusion that the "mistranslated" name names. Ironically, YHWH determines translation as a theological activity in the very moment that perfect translation is proscribed. With Babel theology can interpret the field of linguistic differences as theologically significant. God affirms that the

4. Derrida, "Des Tours de Babel," 165.

substitution of one word for another lies at the heart of divine communication. Theologically YHWH inaugurates translation in the "confusion" that marks the proper name. YHWH instructs the sons of Shem (those whose own name means "name") to participate in the proliferation of language rather than to seek finality.

In Derrida's reading of Babel we see the necessary connection between translation and the God of revealed Scriptures. As against the complicity between structuralism and metaphysics, the scriptural God rejoices in the flux of language. The confusion at Babel is God's own deconstruction of metaphysical accounts of language. Against the logic of dualistic and structuralist thought, God's self-naming affirms the need for unceasing translation in which the economy of *différance* emulates the divine distrust of univocity and literal communication. Caputo endorses this identification of deconstructive and divine hostility to totalizing understandings. Whether or not deconstruction is on the side of God, he suggests that "it is clear that God is on the side of deconstruction . . . calling construction to a halt, disseminating the Shemite tongues, and making translation necessary and impossible."[5]

God's name can never be captured and Babel reinforces this nameless naming. In confusing God's own name, God queries all other naming acts and subjects them to the same economy of translation. Again, we have Derrida to thank for realizing how the need for endless translation is an essential part of connection between God and humanity:

> The sacred surrenders itself to translation, which devotes itself
> to the sacred. The sacred would be nothing without translation,
> and translation would not take place without the sacred: the one
> and the other are inseparable.[6]

The metaphysical anchorage afforded by knowledge of God's proper name is erased just as the banner of translation is unfurled. By condemning the human desire for linguistic totality God is also rejecting "techno-economic" and political totalizations that the tower represents.

In contrast to fundamentalist readings that seek certainty, the story of Babel is a reminder that the idea of one powerful universal human interpretation is diametrically opposed to the depiction of the divine in the Scriptures. God does not hope that humans will all sing from the same hymn sheet, so much that humans might discover different

5. Caputo, *The Prayers and Tears of Jacques Derrida*, 54.
6. Derrida, "Des Tours de Babel," 204.

interpretations and perspectives. Or to put it in terms of the current argument, Babel reveals a God who is happier living with uncertainty and confusion. Babel is in many ways analogous to the certainties of the scientific and fundamentalist projects, a literal projection of the desire to conquer the heavens. However, against this natural human desire to have everything completely understood and utterly certain, the destruction of Babel reveals a God more interested in mystery and ambiguity. In short, the God of Genesis is a God who doubts that it is healthy for humans to think they have conquered the heavens.

The Book of Nature and the Theological Origins of Science

Returning to the question of how to interpret the Scriptures, Wesley Kort offers an important set of insights.[7] Kort suggests that we know something to be scriptural by understanding how it pulls us in and pushes us out. The Scriptures act centrifugally and also centripetally. First, they are the texts that demand us to engage with them, in this sense they are centripetal, pulling us in. And unlike other literary texts, something about the way Scripture pulls us in speaks to our sense that this text might point to something decisively important. A good novel can capture our imagination and attention. A really good novel can do that without us even realizing. By contrast, Scripture pulls us in because of transformations that it suggests to the reader. But things cannot stop there. If Scripture only acts on us centripetally, if we are simply sucked in, then we run the risk of fundamentalism. There is nothing wrong with acknowledging that we find ourselves centered by our sacred texts, or that we find that the Scriptures reveal big existential and human questions. However, for a reader to find herself centered in Scripture, rather than obliterated by Scripture, she will also experience the centrifugal force of Scripture moving her out to engage beyond its pages.

Scriptural study that is not centrifugal, that does not require us to ask deep questions of non-scriptural material, is fundamentally mistaken. Yet where Scripture engages with us wholeheartedly we will also find the need to expand our horizons and engage beyond the limits of the canon. Kort's scriptural analysis also includes an analysis of cultural and historical transitions, first to the modern and then to the postmodern. Kort

7. Wesley Kort, "Take, Read."

demonstrates how it is the centrifugal action of Scripture that contributes to the creation of nature as a book to read alongside the Bible. Since the Scriptures suggest an understanding of the action of God in the world, interpreting the Scriptures requires an identification of God's world as another kind of sacred Scripture, another book. The idea that there is a book of nature is a very traditional Christian idea. It was common in the medieval era, and in the seventeenth century it provided an important spur to the development of science. If the scriptural account of creation is to be believed, then the created world is also a work of God just as much as the Scriptures themselves.

Ironically, while the created status of creation is something that religious people of every stripe and creed agree upon, the implications are not always worked out consistently. For some, the natural sciences become a way into understanding God. For them the book of nature is something worthy of a lifetime of study, and the ultimate rationale for understanding the connection between disciplines as varied as theology, physics, biology, and the natural sciences. One important example of this initial work came in the eighteenth-century argument of William Paley. In what became the teleological argument, he suggested that a person coming across a watch would assume that there was a watchmaker simply based on the evident design, regularity, and order that the watch signified. By extension Paley went on to suggest that our world is like the watch, and that its own order suggests that the cosmos was designed, and therefore has a designer.

What is interesting is not whether or not we agree with the argument. What is interesting is that Paley and many other religious individuals saw absolutely no incommensurability between reconciling the observations of the natural world with those of theology or religious belief. In short, the book of nature was not a rival book that set out to deceive. By carefully observing it, nature could cast more light on the splendor of God's world.

So what happened to divert theology from the promising path of reconciling the natural sciences and theology? It simply makes no sense, as certain fundamentalists suggest, to think that science is misleading and that creation can hold no clues for understanding God. To reflect more on this strange turn within certain scriptural readerships, it is necessary to recollect just how interrelated science and theology really are.

If Kort is to be believed it is not simply that theology creates the book of nature. More audaciously, theology, or rather, the faithful reading of the Scriptures, also creates science. We are so used to hearing of the conflict between religion and science that this naturally comes as a bit of a shock. We have been accustomed to assuming that theology and science are antagonistic and exclusive, and it is possible to enlist as evidence the church's condemnation of scientists from Galileo to contemporary stem cell researchers. However, there is an unfortunate problem with such a thesis.

While the church was horribly slow to adopt the heliocentric view of the universe of Copernicus and Galileo, it is often forgotten that this very same church had been the driving force within Western Europe behind scientific study. It is not just that universities themselves were religious institutions, which throughout the medieval and early modern eras they were. More importantly, it has been forgotten just how dependent theology itself was on the philosophical and protoscientific insights of non-theologians like Plato and Aristotle.

The supreme irony of Christian theology in particular is that as a discipline it depends to a significant extent upon those who are not Christians. Scripturally it depended on affirming the witness and truth of the Old Testament, the Hebrew Bible of the Jewish people. Theologically, as it attempted to understand the stories of Jesus in the New Testament, it needed to acquire significant philosophical acumen from wherever it could find it. Where it found it was in Greek thought, and in particular in the use made by medieval thinkers such as Thomas Aquinas of Aristotle for everything from understanding grammar, rhetoric, and logic to the more highly developed nuances of neo-Platonists on the nature of the divine.

The mystery is not that Christian theology was so heavily dependent on outside thought. The mystery is that so many faithful Christians have been so remiss in acknowledging the intellectual and scriptural heritage upon which the ornate cathedral of theology is built. Remove all traces of the advanced thought of the Jewish and Greek worlds in the development of Christian theology and there is little left.

Returning to the origins of science, what happens in the early modern period is that Christianity gives birth to a scientific understanding that is fundamentally compatible with Christianity. This is illustrated in one of the leading scientific lights of this time, Isaac Newton. Newton is both a driver of scientific revolution and mindful of how new scientific discoveries will gel with what he believes to be his own pre-eminently rational understanding of God. The remainder of this story of the rise of science is not entirely unlike the story of Oedipus. Science continues merrily enough to begin with. But eventually, blissfully unaware of its parentage, science attempts to eliminate that which has brought it to birth. The remarkable thing about this account is just how impressively secure science believes itself to be in its reasoning powers. Only because theology believes in the ordered regularity of the created world is science endowed with the idea that universal laws underwrite the universe. Science is itself an utterly theological enterprise, insofar as it believes that there is regularity and meaning to the way the universe is constructed. However, it is this fundamental theological belief in the meaning of what it studies, something that cannot be scientifically proven, that science internalizes, allowing it to cut the umbilical cord. In the same way that Descartes doubted all to create the sure foundation of his *cogito*, so science doubts the ability of other disciplines to create meaning in order to create the sure foundation that scientific method can itself generate meaning.

The tragedy of the last couple of hundred years is not that science and theology are fundamentally opposed. The tragedy is that religious believers who ought to know better have forgotten the often quite religious origins of science. Yet, even more tragically, having forgotten where science received its trust in an ordered creation, religious people have rejected belief in an ordered creation that can be better understood through theories like that of evolution in favor of a creationism that conflicts with science. Theology created the idea of an ordered universe, without which science would have been unimaginable. So while science has managed to sustain the religious belief in a creation that is essentially comprehensible, regular, and predictable, many readers of Scripture have not.

One of the great achievements of science in recent years has been to expose just how little we really know about the physical universe. At the highest levels of theoretical physics it is becoming clear just how incorrect the Newtonian scientific model was. The world is not as ordered or as regular as seventeenth-century faithful scientists believed. Instead, the world of contemporary science is a confusing and impenetrable world of quarks, chaos theory, Higgs Boson particles, dark matter, and other opaque discoveries.

Ironically, we are now seeing new possibilities for a new convergence between science and religion. Scientific discoveries increasingly point to what little can really be said about the fundamental structures of the universe. We still share the optimism of the seventeenth century that we can know increasing amounts about the material world. However, unlike the relatively fixed theories of Newtonian physics, we are all now post-Einsteinian, living in the shadow of the theory of relativity with, as yet, no grand unified theory of everything.

Far from this being a problem, as knowledge of what we do not know increases, science and religion find themselves, once again, sharing the same world. In each case, it is increasingly important to recognize the fluid nature of what we hold to be true. Just as the Large Hadron Collider continues to provide data that will stimulate new scientific thought about atomic particles, so religious communities must recognize the provisionality of their own fundamental beliefs. This is not to suggest that there is no such as thing as truth, or that one can never intrinsically know the truth. However, it is to suggest that both science and religion appear to be pointing in the direction that truth is more complex and elusive than was thought in the seventeenth century. Or to put it another way, it seems increasingly sensible to doubt that things are either simple or certain.

To clarify, any theory of scriptural interpretation that suggests that there is only one truth to the Scriptures seems to rest on a fundamental misunderstanding of truth in Scripture. The Scriptures are not a truth-generating machine that outputs the same truth regardless of who is operating the machine. Kort's theory reminds us that much like the constant movement of the planets in this solar system, the Scriptures are always exerting gravitational pull and push on their readers. Nothing is stable for science or for biblical hermeneutics. As Derrida suggests, the center is death. By contrast, the truth of the Scriptures, like the truth of the solar system, is profoundly dependent upon the perspective of the observer. As it was with Einstein's breakthrough in theories of relativity, so it is with scriptural study. Where observers start from different points (as they always do) the truth will, naturally enough, also be different. Affirming that the Scriptures can generate multiple truths in relation to multiple readers should encourage us that they are functioning properly. By contrast, to imagine that the Scriptures can be restricted to one meaning or one narrowly defined range of meanings would be to misunderstand how they managed to generate truth in the first place.

As literature, the Scriptures demand readers who can respond to and engage with the ambiguities and uncertainties within them. Repressing these ambiguities and uncertainties restricts the ability of Scripture to connect to different readers with different interpretations. What makes Scripture sacred, then, is not that it has a singular or predetermined meaning. What makes it sacred, is the sacred nature of the interpretative experience. Reading or hearing Scripture is not simply listening to the text. Reading or hearing Scripture involves surrendering one's own sense of self to the text (being pulled in), while allowing the text to send one out again. It is this dynamic, the centripetal and the centrifugal, which allows Scripture to be transformed from literature to sacred Scripture. In this account it is not anything intrinsic to the text that is sacred. Rather, it is the move from merely being an observer of the text to being engaged by and with the text that constitutes what is revelatory and sacred about Scripture.

Paying Tribute with a Little Help from Augustine

So what makes the difference between good readings and bad readings of a text? For Augustine it was a given that the Scriptures could produce multiple readings.[8] While Augustine did not think there was only one good reading, he did nonetheless recognize that there needed to be a mechanism to distinguish good readings from disreputable readings. When faced with contradictory readings Augustine suggested that interpretations that did not maximize our understanding of God's love should be rejected. By contrast, interpretations that increased our understanding of God's love should be given precedence over others. This simple rule, what he termed the rule of faith (*regula fidei*), was Augustine's central hermeneutical key. Augustine would not have understood the modern perspective that assumed there is only one singular correct interpretation. Instead, he assumed that the Scriptures generate multiple interpretations and that the rule of faith was needed to decide between the beneficial and the detrimental. For Augustine the Scriptures are the story of God's love for us, and so any interpretation that builds up love must be part of the Scriptures, while readings that seems to take away from love cannot properly be part of the Scriptures.

Identifying love as the hermeneutical key enables Augustine to decide between different, ambiguous, or competing readings. What Augustine does not explore in detail is whether this affirmation of love is itself a factor in making Scripture inherently difficult to interpret or ambiguous. However, if the consideration of love is the deciding factor for Augustine it is also worth examining whether the rule of love might generate more or less complexity and ambiguity. To put it at its simplest, many

8. Augustine, *De Doctrina Christiana*.

stories are love stories, and many of those love stories are the stories of misunderstandings, confusion, and failure to recognize the nature or depth of love. From Beatrice and Benedick in *Much Ado About Nothing* to the romantic comedies of Jennifer Aniston and Hugh Grant, the idea that love is not always immediately transparent to the lovers is a cultural staple. Let us assume for a moment that such love stories are genuine attempts to reproduce something of the mystery of love, and not simply misleading narratives. If that is the case, then there are some helpful clues to be found in the interpretation of Scripture once we accept the genre identification as a love story.

Love stories relate the affirmation of one person's love for another. However, in the average love story it is not the affirmation that takes center stage so much as the difficulties that create a situation in which love is unrequited. One pretty major difficulty has been the fact that the subject of one person's love, the beloved, is not aware of the lover, or, if aware, not responsive in a positive way. Even should the beloved and the lover reach the stage of mutually requited love there is always the possibility that external circumstances prevent them from fully sharing the fullness of their love. Whether these external circumstances are geographical, matrimonial, cultural, or familial, the love story is always a story that is fraught with the possibility of unrequited love and the possibility that love is either unrecognized, rejected, or simply misinterpreted. The roles of lover and beloved in a love story are not stable. They are vulnerable both to each other, but also to their wider context. At the same time, the ambiguity and uncertainty that attend to loving or being loved are not somehow peripheral or secondary. To expose oneself to another in love is to expose oneself to uncertainty and ambiguity. It can also be argued, building upon Augustine, that to expose oneself to the Scriptures as the story of God's love will have a similar effect. One would think very poorly of a modern-day Romeo who held back from taking the risk of loving Juliet until he could confirm in all certainty that she really loved him. In the same way, it seems nothing less than honest to admit that there is no good reason to allow oneself to hold back from the interpreting Scriptures simply because all interpretations are inherently uncertain and ambiguous. It may well be that the Scriptures are not a love story, and simply the stories of those who have deluded themselves into thinking that they are. However, as we shall now see, even this delusion may not be as insuperable a problem as it first appears.

A good example of a story that may or may not actually be a love story is Suzanne Collins's *The Hunger Games*. Set in a future dystopian version of North America, poverty is endemic, and there is huge economic inequality. Following a failed rebellion, every year people of the twelve poor districts send two children to the wealthy capitol as tributes to participate in gladiatorial combat to the death. This serves both to provide amusement (the ultimate in reality television) and remind the citizenry of the wages of rebellion. Into this premise Catniss Everdeen and Peeta find themselves selected as tributes. As part of their preparations they are interviewed, and on live television Peeta confesses that if he wins he will never be able to see the person he loves. When pressed why he reveals that it is because he loves the other tribute from district 12, and only one of them can return home alive. This detail becomes even more important during the games when we see Catniss and Peeta start to work together to protect one another. Written from the first-person perspective of Catniss *The Hunger Games* makes it absolutely clear that at the start of their time together Catniss herself does not have feelings for Peeta. Nonetheless, as events unfold Catniss and Peeta start to inhabit the story that Peeta has revealed to the interviewer. Even though she does not feel anything for Peeta, during the game and constantly on camera, even Catniss learns to play the game *as if* she loves him in the hope of better appealing to the audience, advisers, and sponsors.

The denouement for Catniss and Peeta comes when a rule change is announced that allows for two winners from the same district to return home. Continuing to cooperate they manage to eliminate their final rival. Unfortunately, once they have done so they are not rewarded with victory, but with another rule change revoking the previous change. Now each must kill the other to have a chance of victory. It is at this point that Catniss, who has not appeared to have any genuine love for Peeta, decides that if they cannot live together they must both end their lives. Motioning to Peeta they prepare to swallow poisonous berries in a double suicide pact. The choreography is identical to the sacrifice of Isaac by Abraham, as it is only as their hands are raised ready to feed themselves the berries that they are interrupted for a third time—and told that they can after all return victorious together.

This brief summary highlights something crucial about the nature of love and the nature of fiction. The reader never knows whether Catniss and Peeta really love one another. It is entirely probable that Peeta loves Catniss but that Catniss does not love Peeta. Equally, it is entirely possible that neither loves the other, and that both are simulating love to gain advantage within the game. Love cannot eliminate ambiguity or complexity. Rather, it generates it. However, what the story also shows is that even the simulation of love can have the effect of love. When faced with the prospect of seeing the games end with no victor, the game makers choose to allow both to live. One reading of this story is that whatever Peeta's motives, Catniss simulates love for strategic reasons. She understands that the simulation of love has already helped the two of them up to this point, and she takes the risk that continuing to simulate love will also bring a reward (that both might after all be allowed to live). Whether Catniss and Peeta really love one another is strictly speaking undecidable. As readers we just don't know. It appears to the gamemakers and audience that they love one another. Equally, it appears to the reader that Catniss is simply playing along. But the effect of her (fictitious or real) love is the same: it is the only thing that can subvert the games and allow both to live. Either way, one of the things that can be said quite clearly about this love is that it is a desire brought about by the other, something we will return to in the final chapter.

Theologically it seems that there is much of value in the depiction of love in *The Hunger Games*. Catniss already has moral authority in the story for substituting herself for her little sister Primrose who was originally selected as a tribute to enter the games. And so even if she does not love Peeta for real, it is already clear to the reader that Catniss loves her sister for real. She is not heartless or merely scheming. *The Hunger Games* is therefore less a story about teenage romance of the order or Romeo and Juliet, but more a story of a latter-day David (Catniss) standing up to a Goliath (the capitol). However, as befits our postmodern times, it is not clear to us or the inhabitants of the capitol the full extent of what is going on.

The Hunger Games affirms how love is never totally transparent. We cannot completely understand Catniss and what motivates her. Nevertheless, by choosing to act *as if* she loves Peeta she stands a chance of redeeming the situation for both of them at the end. But she also takes the risk of losing everything by refusing simply to turn on him and allowing the possibility that he might seek to kill her. Catniss has a potential to love that is both the potential not to love and the potential to actually love. As will be seen in the next chapter on Agamben, the potentiality for something to not be is just as fundamental to the proper thinking of potentiality as the potentiality for something to be. In the story of Catniss we see just this imponderable situation, a situation in which it is strictly speaking undecidable whether Catniss loves or does not love. She has the potential to love and the potential not to love. By reading her actions *as if* they are love, we could be wrong, but we open up the possibility of making more sense of the story by allowing that reading.

Hermeneutically, what I have hoped to show is that the strategy of acting *as if* there is love is not a safe, secure, or easy one. Love exposes one to the other. Whether we love or whether we pretend to love, we cannot be assured of any certain response. But when it comes to interpreting the Scriptures the story of Catniss and Peeta surely offers us a way of understanding why an Augustinian reading is worth trying, even if it means simulating love.

The Good Samaritan

In case this argument from popular fiction seems remote from the stories of the Scriptures it is helpful to examine one particular biblical story. As David Lyle Jeffrey observes, the story of the Good Samaritan is one of the most famous and archetypically Christian stories of the New Testament.[9] Found in the center of Luke's Gospel the story appears to be at the literal and figurative heart of the Gospel. The Good Samaritan is the one who stops to help the man who has been attacked and left for dead. And while the holy and respectable pass by on the other side, it is a Samaritan, an outsider to both Jewish law and society, who stops to assist the man in need. This apparently simple story forms the key to many attempts to understand, teach, and replicate the Christian life.

What does not always take center stage in renditions of this story is its context. The story of the Good Samaritan emerges out of a dialogue between Jesus and a lawyer. According to the gospel telling it seems more like an interrogation of Jesus by the lawyer. A couple of features of this interaction are significant for our purposes. First, Jesus does not answer the lawyer's question directly. He answers a question with a question. To the question, "What must I do to inherit eternal life?" he responds Socratically, asking the lawyer what is written in the law. After the lawyer quotes the law, and receives Jesus's approbation, "You have given the right answer" the lawyer poses the follow-up question, "And who is my neighbor?" It is in reply to the lawyer's second question that Jesus tells what

9. Jeffrey, *Luke*, 149.

we think of as the story of the Good Samaritan. However, what is often glossed over is that this story is of course simply a story. It is a story that is devoted to making a point. Jesus does not claim that it is historically true, and there is no evidence to suggest that it is anything other than fiction. Just as importantly, when Jesus has finished telling the story he does not explain the moral of the story. Instead he asks another question of his own, "Which of these three, do you think, was a neighbor to the man who fell into the hands of the robbers?"

Jeffrey quotes Paul Ricoeur's observation that the point the story of the Good Samaritan seems to be making goes against the predilection in the modern world for abstract and anonymous relationships.[10] By contrast, the purpose of the parable is to help us discover the neighbor for ourselves. Jesus does not identify who the neighbor is for the lawyer. Instead he tells a fictional story whose sole purpose is to prod the lawyer into working out for himself who the neighbor might be. This practice of Jesus is one that encourages uncertainty, a strategic choice that encourages doubt and puzzlement within the listener over certainty or complacency. As Jeffrey puts it, there is a "polyvalent aspect to the good Samaritan."[11] Time and time again in the Gospels Jesus tells stories to illustrate his points. He also refuses to explain what his point might be, preferring instead to tell stories that require the hearers to make connections for themselves. What is remarkable about the story of the Good Samaritan is that while the Good Samaritan only exists within the fiction of the story, the story is no less true for it. The truth of the story of the Good Samaritan emerges in the wrestling of the hearer with the story. And whether we are separated by millennia or mere decades from the original telling, we are in no worse a position to be able to learn the truth of the story. The truth, pace *The X-Files*, is not out there. The truth emerges out of the interaction between the text and the hearer or reader.

Fiction Sets You Free

Russell Berman has made a comprehensive and powerful case for fiction leading to a flourishing of human freedom.[12] Assuming this case to be sound, the Scriptures themselves deserve to be seen within this wider

10. Ibid., 150.

11. Ibid.

12. Berman, *Fiction Sets You Free*.

framework of the efficacy of fiction. As literature, if nothing else, the Scriptures have required an interpretative engagement that deepens the ability of the interpreter to understand the range of possibilities open to them. If it can be successfully argued that the novels of Victorian England have contributed to setting humans free, it would seem churlish to suggest anything less of the Scriptures.

No one can objectively know whether the Scriptures are the story of God's love for humanity. At least, no more than we can know whether Robin Hood was the villain of Thorpe or the hero of folk legends. It is entirely sensible to doubt the Scriptures are divine, just as it makes sense to question the character of the historical Hood. We have no clear way of deciding either question. Historians might want to suggest that it is probably highly unlikely that Hood was either the villain of revisionist storytelling or the saintly hero of ancient yarns. However, the historical truth behind a figure woven out of so many fictions as Hood is but one thread in a very complex weave. In the same way, to judge the truths of the Scriptures solely against the historical record is to profoundly delimit their capacity for generating and revealing truth. To recognize that Scriptures are not solely circumscribed by history is not to recognize that they are not true. Rather, it is to recognize that their capacity for fiction is part of what allows them to be revelation. If truth is less a question of propositions, and more as the Greeks believed an *alethia*, an unconcealing or unforgetting, then the stories of the Scriptures generate truth well and apart from the question of whether they correspond with an historical record.

Scriptural truth is not a form of correlation against historical, scientific, or empirical evidence. Instead, it is a truth that is found in the friction that comes about when stories bring us up short and force us to doubt and challenge the anodyne and oversimplifying accounts of reality that masquerade as human understanding. On the other hand, if the Scriptures have something to say as a story of God's love then the story they tell can only be heard by one who is willing to take the leap of reading them *as if* they were the beloved. Reading *as if* does not provide a transparent or certain understanding of the story. Neither does it offer a way of avoiding the ambiguity or difficulty inherent in trying to discern the meaning of the story. As we saw with the Good Samaritan, simply knowing that the text is holy as the lawyer does is not to suspend or remove all questions. The lawyer can recite the law, but that does not answer his questions of interpretation. It simply constitutes a starting point for further questions. And as we saw, Jesus was realistic about knowing that sometimes the best answer to a reasonable question is a good story. Choosing to read the Scriptures *as if* they were a love story from God does not answer all the questions that they generate. Rather, it provides a trajectory along which the story may produce its own existential meaning in the life of the beloved. This is not to preclude other readings of the Scriptures. However, when an individual follows Catniss and acts as if they are loved (whether or not it feels that way) it is possible to see how Augustine's theory of interpretation might make sense of Scripture. The rule of faith is not an abstract rule. Rather, it is the standard against which those who believe (or simulate they believe) that they are loved are able to make sense of how love is manifest in the story. While this does not eliminate all, or indeed any, of the specific problems involved in making sense of the Scriptures, what it does do is provide the intrepid with a point of departure.

One of the ironies of our present cultural situation is that this truth is more likely to be recognized outside of the academy and church, and certainly not within structures like fundamentalism or scientism that seek certainty or clarity above all else. The lyrics to "Storytime" by the Finnish symphonic metal band *Nightwish* remind us of an important dimension to the power of story and fiction not simply to inspire and guide, but also to "read" us "real" (the precise quotation is, "I am the story that will read you real"). This is a welcome insight that deserves to be balanced against a scrupulous historicity or scientism that recollects the fabrications involved in the stories of the Scriptures. While it is clearly true that narratives are made up, the more significant truth is how the Scriptures, along with other powerful stories, have fabricated us or read us real. Even in the most secular parts of the West it is culturally and socially impossible to imagine a human being without recourse to how humans have been constructed by the Scriptures. Theologians teach that humans are made in the image of God, and this is clearly contentious to those of a non-religious disposition. By contrast, the truth that narrative (and Scripture is a form of story if it is nothing else) generates and constructs humanity is surely clear to all, whether of a religious or non-religious disposition. The real fiction is not the banal fiction that the Scriptures were "made up," so much as the insidious fiction that this somehow obviates their importance. In the final chapter, we will return to the importance of fiction within the psychoanalytic framework of Lacan. For now it is helpful to anticipate Lacan's positive appreciation of fiction: "The fictitious is not, in effect, in its essence that which deceives, but is precisely what I call the symbolic."[13] Without fiction it is impossible to get to truth. For it is the fictional that enables us to speak about that which is most real. As Žižek explains:

> [H]owever, as soon as we renounced fiction and illusion, we lose reality itself; *the moment we subtract fictions from reality, reality loses its discursive-logical consistency.*[14]

Fiction is essential to who we understand ourselves to be, and how we attempt to make sense of the world. We, ourselves, are collections of the stories we have been told and, in turn, tell to others. Stories have the potential to transform, liberate, and deepen human understanding. Yet this is only possible when we treat them as narratives that require a willing suspension of disbelief. Learning that fiction might be more profoundly true for our existential flourishing than non-fiction is part of what it means to be a human being. It remains possible to doubt the scientific and historical accuracy of a text without also doubting the capacity for the text to generate truth. If truth is that which sets you free, fiction is a critical arena for the work of emancipation.

13. Lacan, *The Ethics of Psychoananalysis*, book 7, 12, quoted in Žižek, *Tarrying with the Negative*, 87n6.

14. Žižek, *Tarrying with the Negative*, 88.

7

REDEEMING ATHEISM

[L]et the atheists themselves choose a god. They will find only one divinity
who ever uttered their isolation; only one religion in which God seemed for
an instant to be an atheist.[1]

—G. K. CHESTERTON

When I, a human being, experience myself as cut off from God, at that very
moment of the utmost abjection, I am absolutely close to God, since I find
myself in the position of the abandoned Christ.[2]

—SLAVOJ ŽIŽEK

WHILE MUCH PUBLIC SPACE and heat has been taken up by explorations of
the new atheism little attention has been given to the old atheism. Given
some of the absolutely remarkable utterances to have come out of quarters
traditionally hostile to religious belief this is regrettable. In recent years
there has been a veritable profusion of positive treatments of Christianity
from scholars whose natural inclinations tend more to Marxist materialism or Lacanian psychoanalysis than to Christian thought. A decade after
his death Derrida's fascination with religious tropes now looks less unusual, and more like a herald of wider philosophical trends. Thinkers as

1. Chesterton, *Orthodoxy*, 145.
2. Žižek, *On Belief*, 146; emphasis in the original.

diverse as Giorgio Agamben, Alain Badiou, Simon Critchley, and Slavoj Žižek have each found Christianity to be intellectually fertile for their respective projects while remaining resolutely atheist. While none of their philosophical projects are particularly religious in nature, they have each advanced important arguments that re-engage with specific areas of theology. Perhaps it is simply the manifestation of the intellectual desire to go against the grain. Yet, at a time when populist atheism has gone on the offensive, these academic atheists have focused on elucidating and examining previously neglected aspects of Christianity.

That Agamben, Badiou, Critchley, and Žižek have approached the Christian tradition as a subject worthy of analysis rather than dismissal or caricature is noteworthy in itself. However, they have also been responsible for forms of intellectual archaeology, revealing the radical nature of Christian thought and the often hidden and misunderstood traces that it has left in the secular world. A concrete example of this is seen in the flurry of scholarly examinations of the apostle Paul, and how his theological vision provides a foundation for wider philosophical needs. Each has recognized something philosophically extraordinary and enduringly important in Paul.[3] The analysis of human foolishness in relation to divine wisdom, the establishment of the universal implications of faith, and Paul's messianism have all been highlighted as gifts to philosophy that do not have to remain within a purely Christian sphere of understanding. In increasingly parochial postmodern times, part of the appeal of Paul is his breadth of vision, providing the intellectual basis for the transformation of a minor local sect into a philosophically coherent religion with universal relevance.

At the same time, it is not that Agamben, Badiou, Critchley, or Žižek have suddenly become religious. Far from it. Each is at pains to state how they remain firmly within another tradition, be it primarily materialistic, psychoanalytic, or philosophical. However, in different ways each has alighted on Paul's version of Christianity as revealing an intellectually sophisticated framework that overlaps at significant points their own philosophical commitments. Remaining personally wary of religion, they have found a fellow revolutionary in both Paul and the wider theological tradition he founds. With such academic atheists unearthing wisdom in Christian thought it seems particularly timely to explore how theology might discover some wisdom of its own within atheist thought.

3. Badiou, *Saint Paul*; Agamben, *The Time That Remains*; Žižek, Milbank, and Davis, *Paul's New Moment*; Critchley, *The Faith of the Faithless*.

As Paul Griffiths notes, just as the pagan classical archive was of essential importance to early Christianity, so now the Christian archive is now equally "indispensable, attractive, and dangerous" for these European atheist intellectuals.[4]

When contextualized against the trench warfare between partisans of atheism and religion, there is something exceptional about a situation in which those who would normally be hostile to religion advocate for greater attention to be spent on key parts of the theological tradition. It might be objected that these positive religious encounters are tangential or minor themes within the wider trajectories of each thinker's though. Nevertheless, the situation is more complex than that. Christianity, and specifically Paul, offers resources for each thinker to strengthen their own resistance to what they see as the inherent problems of uncritical liberal capitalism. Žižek, for example, is notoriously playful and difficult to pin down. Yet, his interest in the liberating potential of Christianity is a recurring theme throughout his writings. Žižek's interest in Paul is illustrative of his wider concern with the counter-capitalist (theo-)logic of Christianity. He also has no difficulty identifying similarities between Paul and his chief concern, Lacan's psychoanalysis:

> As a good Pauline, I claim that Law and "sin" form a vicious cycle, reinforcing each other, so that there is no way to "line up" Law and Agape: we attain Agape only when we break out of the entire cycle of Law and "sin."[5]

Such a positive use of Paul would be unimaginable for most atheists, but this fluent understanding of religion, and specifically Christianity, is far from rare in Žižek's writings. Part of the excitement of reading Žižek for those interested in questions of faith is surely the dawning realization that here is someone *outside* the fold who understands and grasps the truly radical nature of Christianity. He is certainly able to disagree with theologians, as when he (somewhat tongue in cheek) accuses John Milbank of being at heart pagan: "[I]n my atheism, I am more Christian than Milbank."[6] However, this should not blind us to the simple truth that there are few non-theologians capable of engaging in serious dialogue with the theological tradition, let alone the complexity of a theologian like Milbank. The intellectual distance between a Žižek and a Dawkins or

4. Griffiths, "Cross as the Fulcrum of Politics," 180.

5. Žižek, *The Monstrosity of Christ*, 246.

6. Ibid., 248.

Hitchens is less quantitative than qualitative. For all his rhetorical jocularity Žižek is deeply serious about exposing the failings of much recent Western thought. He does not dispense praise lightly. And yet where Christianity could simply be a symptom or example of that failure, he repeatedly points to it as a possible way out, maybe even offering salvation of a sort. As Žižek even puts it at one point, to be a proper materialist one should first go through Christianity.[7]

Ironically enough, one of Žižek's strengths is that he understands that the failure of exponents of Christianity to live authentically Christian lives is not in itself a justifiable argument for ignoring Christianity. As G. K. Chesterton put it (a thinker Žižek translated into Slovenian and is fond of quoting), "The Christian ideal has not been tried and found wanting. It has been found difficult; and left untried."[8] One rather suspects that it is actually the difficulty of authentic Christian thought that is one of the major attractants for Žižek in the first place. Just as Derrida underlines impossibility or aporia as inherent in language and thought, so it is the paradoxicality of Christianity that makes it fertile territory for Žižek's investigations. Ever the good Lacanian, Žižek knows that one's deepest desires are often for things that are unattainable (a topic that will be examined further in the next chapter). Instead of rejecting Christianity on the basis that it is a simplistic and contradictory framework for understanding the world, it is precisely its complexity, contradiction, and paradoxicality that make it worthy of attention.

What is remarkable about Agamben, Badiou, Critchley and Žižek, is how they present Christianity not as worthy of belief so much as crucial to understanding who human beings are and what the structure of life is ultimately about. As thinkers who inhabit intellectual traditions that are often perceived as inimical to religious belief their ability to excavate theology is hardly less sincere for the fact that it originates in a practice of thinking that has no reason to praise theology. Lacking any individual commitment to the practices of theology or faith makes their appropriation and engagement with theological ideas even more remarkable.

It could almost be argued in the case of Žižek how his own professed denials of Christian teaching are hard to take seriously given the repeated interest he takes in the central theological mystery of the relation between God and the Son of God. Žižek interprets, reads, and riffs upon the

7. Žižek, *Puppet and the Dwarf*, 6.
8. Chesterton, *What's Wrong with the World*, 35.

drama of theology so fluently that it is impossible not to wonder about the precise nature of his atheism. Unlike most atheists, Žižek believes that Christianity is revelatory. However, what Christianity reveals is not what orthodox theology traditionally thinks it reveals. For Žižek the central revelation of Christianity is that there is no big Other who will come to save the day. Instead, it reveals that God is, ultimately, like us, one of us, and just as incapable of saving himself as we are of saving ourselves. Like orthodox Christianity, this revelation only occurs because of the figure of Christ. Whether Žižek's rejection of the idea that God is a big Other (as revealed by Christ on the cross) is really qualitatively different from John Robinson's own rejection of a transcendent God who is "out there" remains something of an open question. One suspects Žižek would think it is different, but this is by no means obvious, and we will return to the question of what Christ reveals about God later. For now, let it suffice to note just how radically christocentric this particular atheist is.

Against the placing of theology exclusively in churches, seminaries, theological colleges, and departments of religion, Agamben, Badiou, Critchley, and Žižek reveal how theology continues to have a more decisive and ubiquitous significance. If this is true, and it shall be assumed to be true in what follows, it will have implications not just for theology but also for social, political and economic life. It may take an atheist to realize it, but the fact may very well be that theology is far too important to be left to theologians.

The Divinity of Atheism

Before going any further it is important to underline the venerable connections between theology and atheism. Twenty-first-century atheism's fascination with theology is not an altogether unexpected development. The work of mystics throughout the centuries has often bordered on atheism, and as a result confused and often caused concern for the church. In the Middle Ages, Meister Eckhart declared that one must let go of God for the sake of God. For Eckhart, as so many other mystics, the faithful should never allow themselves to be taken in by their conceptions of God. The real God is not the God of human metaphors. Nor is the real God a "thing" that can be described. God is not one type of being among others. Rather, God is beyond being, strictly speaking unknowable. For Eckhart and for the vast majority of Christian theologians to even talk of

God's existence is to talk nonsense. To exist implies a time when one did not exist, and a time when one shall cease to exist. All such talk of God is clearly meaningless if God is truly beyond our ordinary conception of beings within time.

Theologians who have been charged with atheism in the past were by and large Eckhartian in their commitment to the unknowability and unrepresentability of God. So when they denied God's existence, or when they denied a specific attribute of God, they were really denying anthropomorphic human conceptions of God. Without these kind of denials of idols or false divinity theology risks turning human imagination into a false deity. This concern with idolatry is such a part of the theological tradition that when in the nineteenth century Schopenhauer argued that God is a projection of the human spirit an entirely correct theological response could be to commend him for realizing something theologians had been discussing for centuries.

Part of the task of theology has always been to determine the difference between the "real" God and the God that is a human construct. One might define heretics less as those who flee theology than as those whose theology is skewed, prioritizing one theme or one insight to the exclusion of all others. By contrast, atheism is normally thought of as being the belief system of those who contend that there is no real God at all, only a sea of human constructs.

In a sense, atheism is therefore theologically necessary to enable theologians to free themselves from taking their theological views too seriously. Without a denial of a certain God or gods, theology is not possible. Note this is in stark contrast to the defenders of modern liberal relativism who would assert that only an affirmation of all Gods and gods makes belief in any God or gods possible. Much more radical than the banality of such easy-come-easy-go inclusivity is the realization that theology might actually call forth atheism: the denial of God.

Without atheism as part of the theological dialectic, theology threatens to turn into idolatry. By contrast, with a necessary atheism as part of the process of developing theology, theology can stay true to the God who is beyond being: the God beyond the human capacity to imagine. So there are internal methodological reasons for theology to countenance atheism. Without atheism theology risks turning into idolatry.

One important formulation of atheism has been the rejection of a rationally argued theistic being who can be both described and rationally argued as being necessary. As we saw with J. L. Mackie's argument against

God coexisting with evil, the God defined by philosophical theism cannot stand up to the burden of rationality. This theistic God, as much as the anthropomorphic God, demands our disbelief, and makes atheism the logical choice. Atheism of this sort is also absolutely fundamental to theology. It could even be said that it is nothing less than a gift to theology: the gift of realizing that the God of philosophical argument can never be the real God. Theology can never proffer a rationally argued theistic being who can be described as being necessary. Philosophers may spend their time conjuring up such linguistic tricks, but theologians and atheists alike know that they are mere human constructs.

Here it is important to note that most of the so-called "arguments for the existence of God" that are taught in the academy as an important part of philosophy all began life as explorations of God in the hearts and minds of believers. Perhaps the most famous of these is the "ontological argument" of Anselm of Canterbury. Anselm called this his *Proslogion*, and imagined it as a way of exploring his faith.[9] It even begins in prayer to God. Transferred to the academic setting Anselm's prayerful discussion is now presented as an attempt to prove the existence of God: specifically through the notion in human understanding that if we have an idea of God that idea must also be real (for if God were not real then our idea of God would not be perfect. And if anything is perfect it is God). For our present purposes we simply need to reflect how Anselm's argument began life as a monk's *meditatio*, a meditation or reflection on the nature of God. It was never conceived as a winning argument with which to defeat atheism. Instead, it arose out of one thinker's prayerful examination of what it means to have faith in God.

In this respect, there is more in common between Anselm and atheists than the rationalist theologians who would use an Anselmian methodology to attempt to prove the existence of God. Anselm would have none of it. Only by first beginning in faith can he then develop the argument toward demonstrating what it means for there to be a God. There are, however, even more powerful reasons to give atheism a respected place within Christian theology. Atheism provides a critique of the arrogance of rationality and the overreaching of human intellectualizing of the divine. However, even more importantly, atheism can also be found at the heart of the Christian story.

9. Anselm, *Prayers and Meditations*, 238–67.

When Jesus is recorded as having cried out from the cross, "My God, My God, why have you forsaken me?" what is this cry other than the cry of an atheist? For too long this plaintive call has been glossed over by theologians. Nonetheless, what is clearly happening here is the separation and alienation of Jesus from God. Far from presenting a problem for theology, this cry actually takes us to the heart of Christianity. Theology has always assumed that the Passion is at the heart of faith. Unfortunately, theology has not always paid attention to the drama and precise choreography of that Passion. Too often theologians have been anxious to theorize about what the Passion and death on the cross achieves. However, what is even more remarkable are the details of how the story of the Passion and death on the cross are related in Scripture. As Chesterton realized long ago:

> But in that terrific tale of the passion there is a distinct emotion-
> al suggestion that the author of all things (in some unthinkable
> way) went not only through agony, but through doubt.[10]

If Jesus did not cry out in forsakenness the death of God in Christ on the cross would appear to be nothing more than some costly charade. However, because of this cry, and because of the brutal finality of the death of Jesus, it is possible to see that God is alienated from God's very self on the cross. Alienated, in agony and doubt, God dies on the cross. For MacKinnon, the cry of forsakenness is nothing less than, "the supremely revealing and the supremely authoritative moment in human history."[11] It reveals the utterly real humanity of Jesus, making it impossible to doubt his position as "one of us." However, if this episode is supremely revealing and authoritative it is just as much a supremely atheistic moment in the heart of the Godhead.

Žižek also grasps the importance of Jesus's cry of forsakenness. In his reading Christ's cry is a clue that the significance of his death lies in exposing the absence of God. For Žižek, Christianity is therefore at its core a religion of "atheism." Christ's death in this reading is not just an atheistic moment, rather it is an affirmation that God is no longer "other." It takes the cross to discover that God has died, end of story.[12] This gets to the heart of Žižek's predilection for Christianity. The reason he finds favor with Christianity is that, unlike all other religions, Christianity is able

10. Chesterton, *Orthodoxy*, 145
11. MacKinnon, *Borderlands of Theology*, 81.
12. Žižek, *The Puppet and the Dwarf*, 171.

to proclaim the elimination of God as the Other. For Žižek it is, therefore, not just Jesus who dies on the cross, it is also the transcendence and the otherness of God that die. Frederiek Depoortere captures the heart of Žižek's position when he summarizes: "Christianity makes the transition from God as 'Wholly Other Thing' to God as 'Barely Nothing.'"[13]

Decades before Žižek, and writing from a position of faith, the theologian Jürgen Moltmann described the cross as the place where a certain view of God definitively dies. For Moltmann it is not simply Jesus who dies on the cross, it is also theism itself, the very idea of a philosophical way of conceiving God. Moltmann's interpretation of the cross also reveals the atheism at the heart of the Christian faith. No longer can we believe in a transcendent or all-powerful God. Instead we are left believing in the presence of God where there is suffering. In illustration of this Moltmann quotes Elie Wiesel's story of the SS hanging two Jews on a tree. Faced with the inaction of God in the face of such terrible loss, the question is asked where was God in all the horror? The reply comes that God is there, hanging from the tree.[14] The God who dies on the cross cannot be the philosopher's God, distant and untroubled by human pain, so much as a God fundamentally found in the experience of isolation, suffering, and trauma. As Moltmann explains, "To speak here of a God who could not suffer would make God a demon."

And yet, for theologians the story has not always ended there. Rather, the death of God has always been construed as the central redemptive act for the Christian church—which is not to say that theologians have ever had unanimity about what it really means. For centuries theologians have disagreed about what the atoning work of Christ on the cross really consists of. In the eleventh century, disagreements between Anselm's theory of substitutionary atonement and Abelard's concentration on a theory of Christ as exemplar emerged. Ever since this split has remained essential to the history of Christian thought. Conservatives have generally appropriated Anselm's ideas, taken out of context and hideously distorted. Liberals have done the same with Abelard, believing Christ provides nothing more than a good example. While both theories have thrived throughout the succeeding centuries, it is only in the last hundred years or so that conservatives and liberals have both forgotten that the theories they espouse owe more to two medieval monks than either

13. Depoortere, *Christ in Postmodern Philosophy*, 145.
14. Moltmann, *The Crucified God*, 273–74.

Scripture or reason. Moreover, as Gustav Aulén showed generations ago these are not the only two competing theories, but they have become the best known.[15]

Within both these drastically opposed interpretations of atonement the death of Christ remains essential. For Anselm it is the means by which the debt owed by humans to God is repaid by a God who is also a human. For Abelard it reveals the length to which Christ goes to be a good example, not even turning away from his course of loving humanity, even when death looked inevitable. However, neither Anselm nor Abelard can make much sense of the cry of forsakenness.

To understand the forsakenness of Christ on the cross, it is necessary to acknowledge how the story of the death of Jesus also bears witness to the destruction of God. It is not play acting. God truly dies. And before God dies God experiences absolute abandonment, isolation, and separation. For at least some kind of time, Jesus apparently believes that he has been let down. Whatever the human chronology involved here, this sundering between Father and Son must also, at least for orthodox interpretations, take place at an eternal level. Which means that if the death of God really happens, God actually disbelieves, and one who was God (whatever that actually means) questions the existence of God.

Theologically this is earth-shattering news. It could be avoided by not believing in the divinity of Christ. It can also be avoided by not believing in the death of Christ. But for the theologically orthodox who are asked to believe in both Christ's death and Christ's divinity the truth is unavoidable: in order to redeem humanity God became an atheist.

If the purpose of the cross is the emancipation of humanity, the redemption of humans from enslavement and oppression, it is only natural to ask about others who are driven by their own hopes of emancipation. Karl Marx is perhaps the most famous atheist thinker to have transposed the religious desire for justice onto a secular canvass. Consciously or unconsciously reshaping Judaism's trust in God making good on God's promises to bring liberation from oppression, Marx argued for the eventual universal emancipation of all. This trust in emancipation has been characterized by many thinkers as a secularized version of Jewish messianism. Marx was not a traditional believer in Judaism, but he was rooted in Judaism and his thought is marked with the hope of an emancipation

15. Aulén, *Christus Victor*.

"to come" that could not be proven simply by his reading of class struggle or economic theory alone.

The Marxist trust in the future emancipation of the working class is a theological commitment of the highest order. Needless to say, in the wake of subsequent philosophical and cultural developments such a commitment now seems decidedly anachronistic. Beliefs in progress have taken a beating. However, as we saw earlier with Derrida, and as will shortly be seen with Agamben, Marx is far from alone in incorporating the theological theme of something redemptive that is "to come" into his secular theory.

One of the points that simply cannot be emphasized enough is just how receptive theologians have been to such heathen Marxian borrowings. The complicated and constructive relationship of left-wing atheist philosophers to traditional Christian teaching is a subject beyond the abilities of this volume. However, it is relevant to remember the significant connections between Christian thought and socialism. The legacy of Marx remains immensely significant around the world. In Britain the Christian Socialism of F. D. Maurice and the pronouncements of Archbishop William Temple played an important role in demonstrating that there is no particular contradiction between left of center political thought and the highest aspirations of Christian devotion. In South America liberation theology would be unimaginable without the foundation provided by the Marxist critique of economic injustice. Since the collapse of communism, however, it has been increasingly assumed that there is no real alternative to some form of liberal capitalism. Instead, the issue for many is simply whether capitalism is relatively well heeled and regulated with a social conscience, as it is in the Nordic countries, left pretty much to its own devices as it is in the United States, or a form of autocratic capitalism as is emerging in China and other parts of the world.

In the light of this necessarily brief view of the relationship of theology to those who seek emancipation from injustice and oppression it is easier to see why thinkers like Agamben, Badiou, Critchley, and Žižek might make common cause with Christian theology. Of course, there is theology and there is theology. There are those like Eckhart, Kierkegaard, and Maurice who want to hold theology to high account, questioning whether it really is doing the work of freeing people from the bonds of unjust social structures. Then there are modern-day indulgence sellers: televangelists who have turned theology into a particularly successful form of commodity capitalism. Within theology there is a definitive split between theologians who have done everything possible to accommodate their thinking to the market and those who have not.

It is easy to dismiss those who have handed over the theological store to the excesses of capitalism. On the other hand, according to many theorists a certain form of Christianity was necessary to the evolution of capitalism itself. Over a hundred years ago Max Weber examined the emergence of capitalism from the belief system of Calvinism.[16] In the deterministic world of Calvinism, the only way a believer could demonstrate salvation came to be identified with the achievement of material success. Calvinist theology severely limited free will as salvation was thought to be entirely a matter predestined by God. Having no real control over their eternal fate, believers were instead led to view achievements in the world of commerce and industry as a substitute field where the effects of human choice could be seen for real. Success in acquiring wealth was not a guarantee of salvation, but it surely indicated a benevolent and charmed life that must also bode well for the ultimate destination of one's eternal soul. As Brad Gregory has explored in more detail, there were also other good ecclesiastical reasons for the growth of the system of capitalism.[17] Transcending divisions between Catholics and Protestants, the pursuit of wealth offered a field of equilibrium within which religious beliefs were no longer primary. In the aftermath of the thirty years war, with Europe having torn itself apart, the goal of wealth creation offered an understandably appealing escape from the life-and-death conflict of religious dispute.

Returning to the present, Mark C. Taylor has examined other more theoretical connections between free-market capitalism and theological models of God. For Taylor the transition from the gold standard is equivalent to the transition in postmodernism from the "God" standard. God like gold used to guarantee the stability of the economic (either theological or fiscal). That is no longer the case for Taylor, and the current chaos within capitalism is simply illustrative of a wider cultural and theological chaos. The old idea that there is a central theological or economic authority has disappeared for Taylor, and along with it the sense that markets can be regulated.[18] However, the fact that unfettered capitalism increases

16. Weber, *The Protestant Work Ethic and the Spirit of Capitalism*. Weber's work was originally published in 1904.

17. Gregory, *The Unintended Reformation*.

18. Taylor, *Confidence Games*.

the gap between rich and poor presents a huge challenge to theologians who are not content to rest with the triumph of market forces. Understanding the complexity and adaptability of capitalism is surely essential if theologians are to be able to have anything to say to the wider world. However, unless there is also an understanding of how and where capitalism is failing society, theologians will not be able to fundamentally address the work of emancipation.[19]

At the heart of the Christian faith there has always been a drive to search for God in the vulnerable and the oppressed. Part of the mystery of the Christian story of the incarnation is the idea that God chose to be born into a human family near the bottom of the social pyramid. God did not choose a religious, military, or professional elite within which to be revealed. Nor did God choose to be born to the propertied or wealthy. As a result, an important part of the work of those who identify as members of the body of Christ has been to draw attention to the needs of the powerless, the dispossessed, and those who live on the margins.

It is for these concrete social and political reasons that there is a symmetry of belief between atheist theorists like Agamben, Badiou, Critchley, and Žižek and the Christian church. Both share a profound commitment to overcoming the inequalities of the world. They recognize that the ideology that sustains capitalism is just that, ideology. They also know that the only significant possibility of escaping from that ideology requires a commitment to an alternative way of being in the world. For the four atheists that alternative is brought into being through a sustained critique of capitalism. For theologians the alternative is brought into being through a faith in God that requires forging a community of resistance to all that is oppressive, namely, the church. Redemption in theology has always been a question of freeing humans from all that oppresses and dominates. The argument of this chapter is that it also makes sense to talk of redemption whenever others, even atheists, attempt the work of freeing humans from that which is oppressive, destructive, and dehumanizing.

Within theology life is a gift, and the freedom to choose that which is infinitely good is God-given. By contrast, freedom within the market is simply the finite, limited, ability to choose goods—to consume. Theologically it is necessary to recover how the gift of freedom has at its heart the flourishing of human beings. The freedom of Christianity has more

19. For an excellent analysis and critique of the mechanisms of capitalism, see Harvey, *The Enigma of Capital.*

in common with the freedom of emancipatory atheism that it has with the freedom of liberal capitalism. Freedom to flourish is not synonymous with the ability to have whatever we might desire as consumers.

Christian theology is, of course, not simply a critique of current socioeconomic ideological arrangements. Christianity draws on a venerable tradition that human desiring is not always optimal. We do not always choose the good. As Augustine realized as a young man, we often choose the wrong thing just for the sheer desire to fit in and go with the flow. This visceral realization that we mess things up is really at the heart of what becomes the Augustinian doctrine of original sin. Unfortunately, though, original sin is often equated with Augustine's theory of its transmission through sexuality, a theory that has left horrific psychic scars on human culture and experience. Setting aside the unhelpful history of Augustine's view on procreation, the deeper idea that humanity is wired to make mistakes continues to flourish. As we will see in the next chapter, Žižek's Lacanian thought also reminds us that human beings have an unerring ability to desire the things that are not necessarily conducive to human flourishing. From a less theoretical perspective Frances Spufford has minted the acronym HPtFtU the "human propensity to fuck things up," precisely to get away from the sexual baggage associated with the phrase original sin. Spufford knows that the mere invocation of the word sin reeks of negativity toward pleasure or sex.[20] Nomenclature aside, whether we name this sin, HPtFtU, or whether we call it something else, it is impossible not to be aware just how flawed human beings are. We will now turn to Giorgio Agamben for one unusual diagnosis of why this might be and what might be done about it. For atheists and theologians alike there is no room for misty-eyed optimism about the nature of humanity. Yet, there is still room to imagine that the HPtFtU may not be the last word on the subject.

The Potentiality of Atheism

For Giorgio Agamben the original sin facing humankind is the knowledge that we are formed by language and yet unable to account for this by returning to a pre-linguistic state. The human animal is the one that knows it is fundamentally an animal, yet also knows that it is capable of thought. This provides the central paradox of thought for Agamben,

20. Spufford, *Unapologetic*, 27.

and much of his work is aimed at recovering this truth in the face of all our sophisticated attempts to repress this knowledge. In the same way that Derrida sought to free us from the illusions generated by the way language signifies, so Agamben's project is also fundamentally a linguistic one, aimed at recognizing the centrality of language and the possibilities that language presents. If for Derrida the age of the sign is essentially theological, this is no less true for Agamben.

In an important essay on "The Idea of Language" Agamben analyzes what it means to talk of revelation.[21] Taking his cue from theology, he realizes that revelation is not simply a revealing of some new content. It is also the revealing of the condition of possibility for knowing in general. For Agamben the realization that there is language is precisely the core revelation of human thought: one that theology attempted to frame as God, but a revelation that is equally accessible to those who have left behind theology. And yet, the very act of naming the revelation of human dependence on language automatically takes us back to wondering whether we can ever leave behind some form of theology:

> The proper sense of all revelation is therefore that all human speech and knowledge has its roots and foundation in an openness that infinitely transcends it.[22]

The language of naming "an openness that infinitely transcends it" does not immediately suggest that Agamben is able to entirely refute the possibility of the divine, even if the divine is simply an act of language. However, as Agamben himself will argue, there is no such thing as a mere act of language. Understanding the revelation that there is language is absolutely fundamental to understanding everything. Theological categories therefore play the role of both poison and cure in Agamben. Agamben's atheism is not an atheism that utterly rejects religion so much as an atheism that both recuperates and draws strength from themes within theology—even while distancing his project from that of religion.

For Agamben the most pressing political and philosophical questions require an examination of linguistic and philological roots. And as we have seen, at the root of language there is a revelation that is nothing less than theological. While standing outside of the theological tradition, Agamben senses that it is the Christian tradition that gets closest to understanding something of the mystery of what it means to be human,

21. Agamben, *Potentialities*, 39–47.
22. Ibid., 41.

and, most importantly, what it means to be embedded in language. It is in this light, as a sophisticated recognition of just how complex the nature of our relationship to language is, that Agamben repeatedly returns to the doctrine of the Trinity.[23]

While theologians have primarily seen the Trinity as a way of understanding the interrelationship of the threefold God to the world, Agamben sees the Trinity as illuminating the central paradox of the linguisticality of humanity. For Agamben what is remarkable is that the Trinity, "says nothing about *how* the world is, but rather reveals *that* the world is, that language exists."[24] As Colby Dickinson explains, "the Trinity is the summit of the expression of the existence of language."[25] The Trinity is a natural topic of study for Agamben because it presents the inherently unpresentability, or unknowability, of ultimate reality. The fact that most of us fail to understand the Trinity is precisely the point. The doctrine of the Trinity establishes that the most "truly real" is not inherently graspable. Nonetheless, despite resisting understanding, the development of the doctrine of the Trinity is an attempt to explore through language the central mystery of what it means to talk of God.

If language is the defining feature of human existence and the constrictions of language the "original sin" of humanity, this is, nevertheless, not to be interpreted entirely negatively. Here it is helpful to remember the way the Fall, the site of original sin, has been described by theologians not as an entirely negative event, but also as a *felix culpa*, a happy curse. Agamben also talks about language as if it were a kind of sacrament.[26] Language is not something to be feared. Instead, like the role of the sacraments in theology, language is that which connects us to that which is most essential to the human condition.

Agamben also recognizes how language use rests on elementary divisions between ideas of the sacred and that which is not. Much of Agamben's work is spent elucidating how the creation of the designations "sacred" and "secular" arise through the human experience of language. Negotiating a way beyond distinctions between the sacred and secular of language is part of Agamben's project. For Agamben this first division lies at the root of all subsequent cultural, political, and theological

23. For the most extensive treatment of the Trinity see Agamben, *The Kingdom and the Glory*.

24. *Potentialities*, 40–41.

25. Dickinson, *Agamben and Theology*, 35.

26. Agamben, *The Sacrament of Language*.

developments. The task as he sees it is to "profane," to escape to, or rather regress to, an infancy that lies before this disjunction between the sacred and the secular. Strictly speaking Agamben therefore critiques *both* the secular and the sacred. Rather than identifying with either realm, the task of philosophy is to assist humanity in regressing back to a place before this split. Until we effect a regression to the point *before* the sacred/secular division, we will always find ourselves encumbered by representation of the sacred and the secular whichever side of the split one gravitates toward. Just as Derrida cautions against polar opposites determining the way reality is viewed, so Agamben reminds us that being truly secular is simply inhabiting a world that has repressed the sacred, not a world that has moved away from it.

So against siding with either the sacred or the secular, Agamben's project is about moving to a time prior to the split through the work of profaning. Agamben makes it clear that profanation, against the more common interpretation of this word, is not simply a denial of the sacred:

> Philologists never cease to be surprised by the double, contra-dictory meaning that the verb *profanare* seems to have in Latin: it means, on the one hand, to render profane and, on the other (in only a few cases) to sacrifice.[27]

The task of moving away from the split between the sacred and the secular to a time *before* the split allows for a form of unity between the two. Moreover, as Dickinson astutely observes, this is not the first time such a suggestion has been made. The work of profaning also correlates with the actions of Jesus.[28] What was Jesus doing when he taught the kingdom was around every corner, dined with prostitutes, and healed the unclean, if not *profaning*? In overturning the divisions of his day between the sacred and the secular, and making common those things that were not com-mon Jesus was already doing the work of profanation.

As Agamben notes, the work of profaning is not about destroying the sacred, so much as renewing a sense of what is truly common to all people. What makes this particularly interesting is that, while Agamben sees a proximity between the actions of Jesus and the work of profana-tion, he argues that the work of profaning is something intrinsically be-yond the capacities of capitalism:

27. Agamben, *Profanations*, 77.
28. Dickinson, *Agamben and Theology*, 45.

> If to profane means to return to common use that which has
> been removed to the sphere of the sacred, the capitalist religion
> in its extreme phase aims at creating something absolutely
> unprofanable.[29]

The classic distinction that Agamben is working with, then, is between approaches that divide humanity up against themselves (from capitalism to politics) and those (we might call them the profaners) who are able to point back to things that humans have in common, before the divisions of the anthropological machinery take place.

We see further examples of Agamben's relevance to theology when in order to explore the nature of government Agamben returns to the early church and the history of the development of the Trinity. Analyzing the doctrine of the Trinity Agamben notes that a fundamental split has always characterized the theological understanding of God. The Trinity is revealed through the threefold action of God in the world as Father, Son, and Holy Spirit. Theologically, these actions of God in the world are known as the economy of God. At the same time, this economy of God does not affect or change the nature of who God "really is" in God's inner self. This ultimate inner nature is also threefold, Trinitarian. This is known as the immanent Godhead, in contrast with the economic Godhead of God in relation to the world. The issue at stake here is how this division between the immanent and the economic is fundamental to God. It is a necessary division, and yet there is no real or ontic division between the immanent and the economic Trinity. There is just one Trinity, but two different ways of understanding. In other words, it is a division of representation, an artificial division, not a division in reality. But without such a division we cannot grasp hold of the reality of God.

While kingdom or glory constitutes the immanent Trinity, the economic Trinity raises questions of externals, such as government and ministry. God's immanence is self-sufficient. However, God's economy enfolds and administers creation, requiring engagement and participation with that creation. Agamben believes in turn, that in politics this split between the glory of sovereignty and the exercise of sovereignty (in administration and government) is a theological reality specifically born out of the doctrine of the Trinity. What makes this remarkable is that even after secularization occurs this fundamental dichotomy persists in

---

29. Agamben, *Profanations*, 82.

the field of sovereignty and government. Agamben anticipates and explains why this might be:

> Secularization is a form of repression. It leaves intact the forces it deals with by simply moving them from one place to another. Thus the political secularization of theological concepts (the transcendence of God as a paradigm of sovereign power) does nothing but displace the heavenly monarchy onto an earthly monarchy, leaving its power intact.[30]

In other words, far from disappearing with secularization, theology fundamentally shapes the secular articulation of the separation of powers between sovereignty and government, or glory and power. Each pair is fundamentally connected, but the reasons for the separation make no sense unless one understands their theological, and more specifically Trinitarian, origins.

Taking things further, Agamben analyzes the after effects of the way the glory of God is constituted liturgically through acclamation. When it comes to contemporary politics, liturgical acclamation is no longer pertinent. Instead, acclamation is offered in other places, most especially through the media. In the same way that the rule of God could not be understood or conceived of without liturgical acclamation, so the contemporary formulation of sovereignty is impossible without its own forms of acclamation. It is well known how within pre-democratic societies the trappings of ceremony were essential to a monarchy's ability to project power to the throne. The intriguing reality of contemporary democracy is not that it has shed these trappings, but that they are to be found in unexpected places, such as the approval of the media and the acclamation of the public. Just as God cannot be conceived without legions of angels and worshippers, so sovereignty today is premised upon those who can dispense non-liturgical forms of acclaim. Sovereignty is not self-founding. Instead, it is dependent on the approval of those who cede their power to it.

It is important to realize that Agamben is not offering an ingenious argument for a return to monarchical government. Nor is he merely affirming that power requires the demonstration of power. Instead he is pointing out how contemporary secular politics is already predicated upon a theological view of sovereignty and administration that is taken

30. Ibid., 77.

right from the Trinitarian distinction between God's immanence and God's economy. As he puts it:

> Modernity, removing God from the world, has not only failed to leave theology behind, but in some ways has done nothing other than to lead the project of the providential *oikonomia* [economy] to completion.[31]

The really fascinating thing here is not what it says about theology, so much as what it says about highest secular values. If the way in which government is construed at its base is irrevocably theological, where does that leave understandings of secular politics? Can theology ever be left behind when so many apparently "secular" thought-patterns remain ineluctably bound up with theological ideas and relations that are absolutely foreign to the secular mind?

Although the connection between theology and contemporary politics is made particularly clear in *The Kingdom and the Glory*, this is far from the only place where Agamben connects the two. A key area of his thought charts the emergence of the political through what Agamben calls the state of the exception. The question of sovereignty and how it shapes political realities is a theme that runs through much of Agamben's work. Once again, the way sovereignty is developed and maintained also calls to mind questions of both the sacred and sacrifice. In doing this, categories of the sacred and the secular emerge as fundamentally interconnected. Agamben's purpose here is to point out how the exclusions and divisions that create the sacred/secular division seep down throughout all later political and cultural developments. In other words, there is something ineluctably sacrificial about the way politics rests on a state of exception.

Agamben repeatedly reminds us that the sacred itself is, "necessarily an ambiguous and circular notion," resting as it does on a Latin word for the sacred (*sacer*) that simultaneously means both "abject, ignominious" as well as "august, reserved to the gods."[32] At its heart the sacred is Janus-faced, pointing both to that which is holy as well as to that which is excluded. This central interface between the sacred, sacrifice, politics, and sovereignty is explored in detail through the *Homo Sacer* sequence of books.[33] Agamben reveals how sovereignty always presumes a funda-

---

31. Agamben, *The Kingdom and the Glory*, 287.
32. Agamben, *Potentialities*, 136. See also Agamben, *Profanations*, 77.
33. Agamben, *Homo Sacer*; *State of Exception*; and *Remnants of Auschwitz*.

mental state of exception, a moment in which sovereignty is shown to rest on fundamental exceptions to lawful sovereignty. This is the paradox of sovereignty, and it is similar to the paradox of the law, namely, that law arises out of something unlawful. Both American and French revolutions stand as witness to this fundamental paradox. Neither was lawful at the time, but each provided the beginning for a new way of construing law and justice. The founding of a new law and a new sovereignty entails a repudiation that is itself illegal by the standards of the previous law and the previous sovereignty. However, this is not simply an historical moment within the origins of sovereignty. The one who is sovereign, in the classic formulation of the German political philosopher Carl Schmitt, is always the one who decides on the exception: on where the rule of law is suspended.

For Agamben we see a similar suspension of law in the way that the *homo sacer* is treated. *Homo sacer* is literally the one whose bare life exists outside of the system of life lived within the law. But this foundation to sovereignty is not simply a matter of excluding others from the political system. *Homo sacer* also reveals how the sacred emerges as part of the constitution of sovereignty. As Agamben explains:

> Life is sacred only insofar as it is taken into the sovereign exception, and to have exchanged a juridico-political phenomenon (*homo sacer*'s capacity to be killed but not sacrificed) for a genuinely religious phenomenon is the root of the equivocations that have marked studies both of the sacred and of sovereignty of our time.[34]

In case this all sounds somewhat abstract it is critical to understand the implications. Agamben sees the truth of this bare life removed from the protections of politics epitomized in the death camps: "Today it is not the city but rather the camp that is the fundamental biopolitical paradigm of the West."[35] The reality behind the thesis about sovereignty and bare life forms a continuum connecting all those states of exception in which law is suspended by sovereign fiat from Auschwitz and Guantanamo Bay to the overwhelming situation of the third-world poor. These are lives that do not benefit from the political protections of the law, and yet this is not an anomaly of the law or sovereignty, but revelatory of how politics *always* rests on some fundamental exclusion.

34. Agamben, *Homo Sacer*, 85.
35. Ibid., 181.

In articulating the connection between the sacred, sacrifice, and sovereignty, Agamben shows once again how an "anthropological machinery" determines the difference between insiders and outsiders. In thinking through this fundamental difference Agamben is indebted to the work of Schmitt who sees the division between the friend and enemy as central to politics and theology. With this in mind, the exclusion of "bare life" from full membership in political structures as seen in the death camps is not something that theology can simply evade responsibility for. Theology by its very nature, Agamben suggests, rests upon a similar division to that of Schmitt between friend and enemy, only for theology it is the division between believer and unbeliever. However, there are other parts of the theological tradition, as we saw in chapter 4, that dispute attempts to set up firm demarcations between those who believe and those who do not. The most pressing reason that theology has to resist efforts at eschatological separation between heaven and hell is that such efforts almost always contribute to the creation and maintenance of states of exception in the present.

In revealing how impossible it is to distance secular politics from religious ideas Agamben demonstrates two possibilities for theology. Theology can simply be the necessary other side of the secular coin, part of the exclusionary anthropological machinery that generates the *homo sacer* and the state of exception. Alternatively, theology offers the possibility of being different, altogether more liberating, and as we saw earlier, radically profane. Theological universalism is, in effect, profane in just this kind of way. Universalism affirms that all are treated in common, denying that some pay an eternal sacrifice while others do not. To risk stretching the metaphor somewhat, universalists take issue with the idea that hell might be some kind of state of exception to heaven (or vice versa). Rather, for universalists, the sacrificial logic that divides humans into the clean and the unclean, goats and sheep, or believers and unbelievers is itself overturned (profaned) by the arrival of the kingdom of heaven.

Even in a postsecular world, the central division between those who should be sacrificed and those who should not be sacrificed is inherent in the way that political communities are constructed. We may think politics has come a long way from that of the Roman senate, but fundamentally, as Agamben shows, politics and sovereignty continues to depend upon the sacrifice and exclusion of others.

In contrast to this, Agamben desires the overcoming of social divisions premised on these fundamental divisions between the sacred and secular, the friend and the enemy, or between insiders and outsiders. Here it is important to recognize that like the universalist theologians, Agamben has utopian commitments of his own. Agamben seeks what he calls a "coming community," a construction of community that would *not* rest on the state of exception. In his work on the coming community it is clear that for all Agamben is critical of the religious roots and associations of current politics, there are also other more positive religious resources that can offer hope for release from our current predicament. And so, as with Derrida, the idea of the messianic also has an important role here. The messianic offers Agamben a way of trying to think an alternative to the current state of exclusionary politics without being able to precisely determine or explain what that alternative might be.

Religious messianism is always construed as a form of hope in that which is as yet unknown. The coming community is Agamben's analogue to religious messianism, sharing the promise of an unknowable and undefinable hope of release and freedom from unjust and repressive structures. At one point in his writing on this coming community Agamben draws attention to the figure of a halo. The halo is, "a zone in which possibility and reality, potentiality and actuality, become indistinguishable."[36] Time and again Agamben's most powerful metaphors draw on religious tropes. Like those who wait for a messiah, Agamben cannot tell us when or how the coming community will arrive. Instead, the coming community represents, like the halos of the saints, a trust in the possibility and the potentiality of emancipation from political, cultural, and linguistic chains.

One reason that Agamben is keen to engage with the apostle Paul is that Paul reveals the truly radical nature of messianism (before the church comes in to tidy up, bureaucratize, and fossilize). Unlike later interpreters, Paul understands that faith in Christ is about transforming current affiliations and structures into a new relationship with that which is fundamentally new (and also fundamentally unknowable). As Richard Kearney explains, what matters for both the messianic and Agamben's coming community is potentiality:

> The coming community of the kingdom, announced by Paul in specifically eschatological and messianic terms, reveals itself accordingly as pure potentiality.[37]

36. Agamben, *The Coming Community*, 56
37. Caputo and Alcoff, *St. Paul among the Philosophers*, 152.

Potentiality is a key concept for Agamben, and messianism reveals both the power and the possibility of potentiality. Potentiality is inherently indescribable and beyond codification or explanation, in the same way that messianism is at its core a trust in something that cannot be accounted for. Against the dominant historical and philosophical conceptualizations of humanity within the West, Agamben believes that it is potentiality rather than actuality that defines humans. Strictly speaking, it is language that creates the field of potentiality within which we find ourselves situated. More precisely, potentiality is not simply the potentiality for something to be. It is also the potentiality not to be. As Agamben repeatedly stresses in his readings of Aristotle, potentiality is only truly potentiality when it does *not* turn immediately into actuality.[38] Which means that for potentiality to be possibility it must also be the possibility of something *not* actually occurring. This bifurcation between what might and what might not be possible is, of course, also at the heart of messianism. The fact is that most of the time the Messiah doesn't arrive. However, it is only the non-arrival of the Messiah that allows for thinking about the messianic in the first place.

Messianism gives Agamben a framework for talking about a concrete form of potentiality that is to come (the coming community). The messianic, like potentiality, reveals the power in possibility, the potentiality of what is to come. It hardly needs to be said that all three of these important concepts (the messianic, the coming community, potentiality) have doubt and uncertainty inscribed into them: in the same way thinking about the messianic is always thinking about the potential of the Messiah *not* to come. However, it is important to note that the messianism of Agamben is not a messianism of endless deferral or waiting. Similarly, the potentiality he writes of is not the potentiality for some future experience, it is the potentiality that grounds the present.

Agamben makes this explicit in his criticism of how the church shifts the meaning of God's kingdom from being a present possibility to some state way off in the future. For Agamben, when the church opts for a strategy of deferral, rather than realizing the potentiality *within* the present, it misunderstands the radical nature of what it means to speak of *kairos*, God's time, as simply time in the future:

---

38. Agamben, *Potentialities*, 250–51.

> [T]he time of the messiah cannot be, for Paul, a future time. The
> expression he uses to refer to this time is always *ho nyn kairos*,
> 'now time.' [39]

As Durantaye reiterates, messianic time is not one of "apocalypse" so much as "immediacy," grasping the full potential of the possibilities in the present.[40] The question of time is not, however, the only area in which messianism articulates the task of uncovering potentiality and the coming community. Just as Paul's messianism reveals how strength and power is found in weakness, so Agamben's notion of potentiality is the possibility of this type of messianic power-in-weakness.

If the Cartesian cogito represented a concern for certainty and clarity in the founding of the thinking subject, Agamben's project seems to be diametrically opposite. Agamben's thought of potentiality represents a way of doubting the straightjacket of traditional Western thought. Like the messianism of Paul, the potentiality of Agamben reminds us that the task of becoming fully human is not the task of settling for certainties, but the task of being open to the fullness of unexpected possibilities and inversions. Here it is instructive to note the resemblance between Agamben's profanation and Pauline messianism. Dickinson goes as far to suggest that "the task of profanation is nearly identical to Paul's understanding of messianic vocation."[41] Both Agamben and Paul are looking for ways of opening up a new future premised not on exclusionary power, but on transformative weakness.

When Dickinson states that the task Agamben sets is "nothing if not seemingly impossible" it is hard not to be reminded of Derrida's own affirmation of the impossible that we encountered in chapter 3.[42] For escape to be possible from the state of the current linguistic situation Agamben proposes a regression to what he has repeatedly called infancy. Viewing infancy as somehow more determinative of humanity than adulthood, Agamben sees infancy as the uniquely human situation. The fact that children are much better at acquiring language only serves to heighten the force of this argument that equates the essential identity of humanity with an essential linguisticality. It is not a coincidence that this call for a return to infancy also sounds remarkably like Christian language of

39. Agamben, *The Church and the Kingdom*, 26.

40. Ibid., 59.

41. Dickinson, *Agamben and Theology*, 137.

42. Ibid., 107.

being "born again." Clearly, regressing to infancy is not something that can be simply achieved. However, for Agamben it is in such things that cannot simply be achieved, or that have never been achieved, that we discover the identity of humanity:

> But this—what has *never happened*—is the historical and wholly actual homeland of humanity.[43]

The heart of Agamben's project lies in positing the possibility of such impossibilities. Again the similarities to Derrida are revealing. For both thinkers, the "impossible" does not signify something that cannot be attempted, so much as a zone that reveals the most profound truth to our situation as creatures determined to a greater extent than we might care to believe by language.

Agamben reveals how the designations of language provide the illusion of control, when in fact it is language that is doing the controlling. The theory of the state of exception is nothing other than the reminder that the linguistic desires for certainty and clarity are the very same phenomena behind the exclusions of the *homo sacer*. The figure of the *homo sacer* shows how the comfortable representations of political systems are themselves dependent on a fundamental exclusion of some others as "bare life," unworthy of the protections of the law. Politics and law offer a type of certainty, but against those certainties Agamben wishes to cast doubt on the way in which language divides and rules. Theology and faith can be found on both sides of this debate. Theology can be a conservative force, enabling and sustaining the accommodations of politics with exclusion. Nonetheless, theology can also be revolutionary, aligned with Agamben's recuperation of Paul's suggestion of a new way of thinking that is "to come." It is both the strength and weakness of Agamben's work that his analysis of messianism cannot be separated from a biblical messianism that uncertainly awaits the presence of God not in strength but in weakness.

Locating this search for that which is to come that is in weakness rather than strength has led to this being called Agamben's Franciscan ontology.[44] Against the pretensions of both western metaphysics and contemporary society, Agamben's cure is not inherently opposed to the parts of the Christian tradition that see God revealed in vulnerability rather

43. Agamben, *Potentialities*, 159.

44. The terminology is used by both Lorenzo Chiesa and Alain Badiou. See Dickinson, *Agamben and Theology*, 104n19.

than power. The ultimate gift of Agamben's work to theology, like the gift of Derrida, is to cast doubt on the certainties of traditional Western metaphysical assumptions, as well as the political divisions that result from them. Each doubts the controlling, dividing, and dominating logic that privileges power, and each open a space for allowing weakness (messianic or not) to emerge as a site for hope rather than despair.

These emancipatory uses of doubt indicate both a way in which atheism might be redeeming as well as new potentialities for the renewal of faith. Like the ones and zeros of binary code, the apparent opposites of atheism and faith require the other to fully express anything of significance. Faith that has not been forged in the fire of atheism is at best stillborn. If, however fleeting, some form of atheism was experienced by Christ forsaken on the cross, there can be no good theological reason why some forms of atheism cannot continue to be redeeming.

8

BREACH

Our faith is not assured, because faith can never be, it must never be a
certainty.

—JACQUES DERRIDA[1]

The bracing oscillation between doubt and faith, withdrawal and consent is
the aperture that precedes and follows each wager ... The choice to believe
or not believe is indispensable to the anatheist wager. And it is a choice made
over and over, never once and for all.

—RICHARD KEARNEY[2]

Faithful Fragments

THE THREAD CONNECTING THE thinkers examined up to this point has
concerned the variety of ways in which doubt has been intellectually
productive. It is now time to examine someone who in many ways represents the antithesis of the doubting intellectual, the Danish thinker Søren
Kierkegaard. While Kierkegaard cast doubt on many prevailing ortho-
doxies, both religious and philosophical, he is more properly a thinker of
the limits of doubt. Although he is one of the most important doubters of

1. Derrida, *Gift of Death*, 80.
2. Kearney, *Anatheism*, 56.

nineteenth-century philosophical certainty, Kierkegaard's doubt was always in the service of faith. Kierkegaard points to the inseparability of the attitudes of faith and doubt. Hailed as the grandfather of existentialism, Kierkegaard is often mentioned in the same breath as Nietzsche. Both lived in the nineteenth century, and both had sharp things to say about the practice of Christianity. In their own way each took on the dominant philosophical systems of European philosophy, arguing for an uprooting and discarding of metaphysical assumptions. Both iconoclasts and intellectual loners, neither had much time for moral or metaphysical certainties as purveyed by the philosophical system builders Kant and Hegel. There are numerous other points of similarity between the two thinkers. Yet they are also incredibly different. While both believed that organized religion, and Christianity in particular, had led to a shackling of the human spirit, where Nietzsche repudiated faith, Kierkegaard dedicated his literary life to intensifying it.[3]

Born in 1813 Kierkegaard is one of a select number of theologians to have made almost as much an impact on philosophy as on theology, and on the faithless as much as the faithful. Raised within the established Lutheran church in Denmark Kierkegaard devoted his life to criticizing the establishment, both philosophical and ecclesiastical. From an early age his stooped back marked him out as different, and his childhood was a time of merciless teasing. But by the time he attended university he had a reputation for having an incisive wit. His first work *Fear and Trembling* was published in 1843 and targeted both contemporary philosophy and the comfortable religious pieties of his day. Unafraid of stirring up controversy, Kierkegaard continued writing until his untimely death in 1855 aged just forty-two.

Despite relative ignominy during his lifetime, Kierkegaard has been a remarkably enduring hero to succeeding generations. Taken up by the likes of Jean-Paul Sartre and Albert Camus, Kierkegaard has had a powerful influence on those who are not remotely religious, through the philosophy of existentialism. For Kierkegaard knowledge is personal, and authenticity is one of the highest values humans can aspire to. But unlike the secular existentialists who appropriated his thought a hundred years later, Kierkegaard had no inclination to atheism.

The main philosophical targets of Kierkegaard's attacks were Kant and Hegel and their privileging of reason as capable of explaining pretty

---

3. For important perspectives on what theology can nonetheless learn from Nietzsche, see Westphal, *Suspicion and Faith*; and Fraser, *Redeeming Nietzsche*.

much everything. Against those attempts to make rationality the ultimate arbiter, Kierkegaard wanted to recover the strangeness and radical nature of faith. For him faith was not a type of knowledge that could be laboriously proved and argued into being. Far from being rational, faith is better described as a passion: something that cannot be explained by rational argument. The passion of faith can only be acted upon, or analyzed indirectly. In Stump's terminology he was devoted to faith as a form of Franciscan knowledge, rather than Dominican knowledge. The passion that is faith requires the recognition of an inherent conflict between theology and reason. Kierkegaard therefore despaired at the conventional morality and bourgeois practices of the nineteenth-century Danish church. He wanted his readers to free themselves from the rational constraints of Enlightenment thought, and instead discover for themselves the radical nature of trust in God.

Today Kierkegaard remains an attractive figure for a culture that prides itself in the importance of individuality, choice, and authenticity. In the West, while the power of science to explain reality is foundational to society, we also believe in the right of each person to decide what is real for them. Part of the irony of Western experience is that these two incommensurable beliefs are held up as self-evident. The objectivity of science is relied on for providing a framework for making sense of the external world. Yet at the same time, it is assumed that each individual should rely upon themselves to make sense of the interior world of values, choices, and beliefs.

Kierkegaard anticipated the need for individuals to have just this kind of personal relationship to truth. For him truth is not something "out there," independent of the subject and waiting to be discovered. Rather, truth is something that requires an individual to enter into, it is something that has to be claimed personally. Nevertheless, Kierkegaard would have been horrified to discover the now commonplace notion that all personal choices and beliefs are equally valid. For Kierkegaard ultimate truth is not located solely in individual choice. Ultimate truth is divine, and participation in that truth only occurs when the individual is in relation with the divine. Part of the paradox here is that while things only become true when there is a genuine relationship to the truth, that truth is not generated by the individual. Until an individual realizes their need for a passionate relationship to the truth that is beyond them they remain in untruth and an accompanying sense of anxiety. So while the existentialists were correct to note that authenticity requires an active laying hold of what is true, they were less close to Kierkegaard when they implied that the individual could lay hold of simply anything and proclaim it true. As individuals it is not possible to ever attain a complete hold of truth. Truth resists the efforts of the individual to lay hold of it, and in that essential problem Kierkegaard reveals both the reality of human subjectivity and what he believed was the reality of the divine.

One of Kierkegaard's most enduring intellectual legacies is his powerful exploration of the nature of faith. Through the pseudonym Johannes de Silentio (John the Silent) he attempted to make sense of God's command to Abraham to sacrifice his son Isaac.[4] It remains one of the most disturbing passages in the Scriptures. What kind of God orders a father to kill a son? Just as importantly, what kind of father obeys such a command, giving every indication of preparing all he needs to sacrifice his son? Kierkegaard's purpose here is to frame the inherently inexplicable and unreasonable nature of faith. John the Silent explicitly does not have faith. With him as our guide we discover that by the standards of ethics and philosophy Abraham makes no sense: rather, he is mad, bad, or dangerous. Nor can Abraham be understood as a hero. Heroism would have refused the command to kill one's son, rather than conforming right down to the moment he raises the axe with which to make the sacrifice. It is no coincidence that in this famous story Abraham displays no doubts and does not second guess God. He does not seek to bargain or delay, he simply responds to what God commands.

Faced with trying to make sense of this terrible story, John the Silent is left with a final explanation. Where ethics, philosophy, and heroism cannot offer any kind of explanation of Abraham's motives in the narrative, faith can. It is a hard conclusion to a hard story. But it takes us right to the heart of Kierkegaard's theology. For Kierkegaard, God is not to be explained by rationality. For where reason can never provide access to God, faith alone can.

Over the next sixteen years Kierkegaard elaborated this fundamental insight about the priority of faith. Writing prolifically he challenged the church to repudiate the role it had assumed as arbiter of conventional morality. For Kierkegaard this idea of the church as social glue holding everything together was nothing short of a failure of nerve and a loss of faithfulness.

---

4. Kierkegaard, *Fear and Trembling*.

A year later, in 1844 Kierkegaard developed an elegant description of the contrasting fields of reason and faith.[5] Through another pseudonym, Johannes Climacus (John the Climber), Kierkegaard posed the conundrum: How does knowledge of the infinite come to be known in the finite? Reason, or what he calls Truth A, is finite. Given its finitude rationality cannot possibly point to the infinite. But if there is to be knowledge of the infinite, that knowledge will need to be known within the finite world. If humans cannot use their reason to escape Truth A, the movement will have to come from a different direction. Kierkegaard's solution is to pose a Truth B in which the infinite is able to teach knowledge of the infinite within Truth A.

To do this the infinite needs to place itself within the finite. This is the experience of Truth B, where knowledge is particular, within time, and yet also utterly connected to the infinite. Or to use more traditional language, Truth B reveals the possibility of the paradox of the incarnation, where God is spoken of as being completely human.

In this thought experiment incarnation is stripped down to the bare philosophical essentials. Kierkegaard is concerned to answer the question of how God might communicate with humanity. If God is infinite and humanity finite, the only way the infinite can be comprehended by finite beings is if the infinite coincides at one particular point and time with the finite. For Kierkegaard, that is why Christ is both human and divine. The presence of the infinite within time itself in a particular person is the only way for there to be a real interconnection between God and humanity. In this reading, incarnation is not a mere prelude to providing a blood sacrifice, but the central purpose of the person of Christ. Incarnation makes it possible for communication to flow from the infinite reality of the divine to the finite world of humanity.

Kierkegaard points to Socrates as the model teacher within Truth A. Socrates is the consummate midwife, helping others to see the rational truth that is always true in all times and in all places. There is no necessity for Socrates to be the one to show the way, the way is clear whenever reason is used properly. By contrast, within Truth B the only way the infinite can be grasped is when there is a relationship with the truth-giver, in this case Christ. Human reason needs no particular teacher. Divine truth reveals a coincidence between the content of the truth and the carrier of that truth. Hence the wonder of the incarnation.

5. Kierkegaard, *Philosophical Fragments*.

Philosophical Fragments is a fascinating argument for the incarnation. But it is not really an argument about the objective necessity of incarnation. If it were, Kierkegaard would have a lot more in common with the philosophers whom he critiques. What makes his argument unique is that it is an affirmation of the irreducibility of subjectivity. Kierkegaard is not suggesting that the incarnation is objectively proved. Rather, he is demonstrating that the only real kind of knowledge of the divine is knowledge that is relational and personal.

For Kierkegaard approaching the divine is not a matter of understanding philosophical theories. To approach the divine is to trust the passion that is faith. There can, strictly speaking, be no objective knowledge of God. All there can really be are individual lives oriented in relation to God through the faculty of faith. Reason will not help, other than to reveal its limits. Faith alone can allow the individual a subjective relationship with God. And for Kierkegaard, it does not matter how much information one has (or thinks one has) about God. All that matters is whether one is prepared to take the leap of faith and acknowledge that reason will always come up short when trying to explain faith.

On Somewhat Disagreeing with Kierkegaard

One of the problems with Kierkegaard's thought is that while he doubts the certainties of philosophers there is not enough room for faithful doubting, or what has been called *docta ignorantia*, learned ignorance. Few today would disagree with Kierkegaard placing the individual's faith at the center of the relationship with God. However, in Kierkegaard's rush to disagree with the totalizing philosophical attempts of Kant and Hegel to explain everything, he takes the opposite extreme. Humans cannot explain everything, they are wrong to do so, and, instead, they should recognize the limits of reason. Reason can only take one so far, after which faith must take over.

On the one hand this makes perfect sense. If God is God, then how can God be understood by the created world of which God is the creator? It is a little like expecting an iPad to understand the emotions of a software engineer. While the iPad is a wonderfully capable "magical" piece of equipment, it is a product of another's intelligence, and it cannot comprehend that intelligence. Humans have somewhat more self-consciousness than iPads, but even we are hard pressed to make the mental leap from our position as creatures to having a God's eye view of the world. So, Kierkegaard is absolutely right. Reason cannot entirely explain God. It never has, and if the history of philosophy and theology is anything to go by, it never will.

At the same time, various forms of reason have always played an important part in the history of Christianity. Reason has enabled theologians to recognize that Christian belief is not static. While reason cannot lay bare the inner working of God, it is not true that reason has no role in reappraising, challenging, and interrogating beliefs and traditions. Saying that reason cannot explain all is not the same as saying that reason can reveal nothing.

Kierkegaard shows how faith should be the preeminent faculty of Christian belief. However, this does not provide a license to ignore the challenges to Christianity generated by reason. In other words, it cannot be a simple matter of opposing faith to reason. Both faith and reason are required, but both are required different ways and at different times. Or to put it in Derridean terms, it is necessary to understand the differential nature of faith and reason: faith and reason each have their limits, and each always ends up needing the other.

Borrowing the language of *différance* it is possible to imagine how faith and reason are not opposing poles so much as overlapping fields. Simply put, there is no one "faith" and there is no single "rationality." Both faith and reason are constructs embedded in history. Some practices of faith are more absolute in their denial of reason, and some types of rationality leave little space for faith. But this does not hide the fact that there are other forms of faith that complement reason, and other forms of rationality that realize reason has its limits. As was seen in the first chapter the real division today is not between faith and reason. The real division is between those who believe that either faith or reason can explain everything, and those who recognize that things are more complex, and that each is irrevocably implicated in the other. To speak of a differential relationship between faith and reason is to begin to recognize that there is no pure faith and no pure reason. Faith has its reasons, and rationality can be deeply faithful. By contrast, problems arise where faith becomes over-identified with irrationality or when rationality is determined solely in opposition to faith.

This former possibility is precisely the issue facing potential followers of Kierkegaard today. The danger of a fully Kierkegaardian approach to Christianity is that reason becomes the first casualty in a paradigm shift that goes on to efface experience, tradition, and history. Pretty soon all one is left with is the dehistoricized and anchorless text of the Scriptures. Of course, for some this is perceived as desirable. *Sola scriptura*, or Scripture alone, was the rallying cry of the Reformation and remains significant to many faithful people. But to rely on Scripture *alone* is to ignore the history and experience of thousands of years of human experience. It also makes little sense theologically in that it limits the scope of how God might be revealed through creation. Moreover, historical and philosophical perspectives suggest that it is counterintuitive to think that Scripture is the only place where one can reflect on the divine. For such a thing to be true, there would have to be a qualitative and quantitative gulf between the Scriptures on the one hand and all that is non-scriptural (history, philosophy and culture to name just a few) on the other. Whether it is at all coherent to posit such a clear and decisive gulf given the tangled web of religion, history, culture, and philosophy is the question to which we now turn.

Miéville's Breach

Imagine for a moment two city states with two separate rules of law, two different cultures, two rival sets of institutions, speaking two languages. Then imagine that each of these two different city states has different political leanings. One is more free market, one is more socialist. Now imagine that both cities occupy the exact same geographical space. Two cities, one overlapping spatial presence. Two sets of customs, two different peoples, walking the same streets, but under different jurisdictions, speaking entirely different languages.

This experience of parallel cities is the extraordinary premise of China Miéville's novel *The City and the City*. From birth residents of each city lead unremarkable lives. They go to school, learn citizenship, form relationships, work, and play. In all things they are like any other citizen of any other city at any other time. Except for one exception. A resident of one city may never gaze upon the other city. At first it sounds like an absolutely extraordinary idea. It is literally fantastic to think that one might walk and drive the same territory without seeing others who lie under a different jurisdiction. But Miéville constructs an entirely believable world in which residents of each city literally "unsee" the other residents. Each city has its own distinctive fashions, architecture, and technology.

And residents are taught from birth to "unsee," to deliberately not see, both the built environment and the populace of the other city.

The City and The City constructs a powerful allegory for contemporary life. It raises questions about how people coexist while largely managing to ignore one another. And it makes us wonder about the depth to which the social construction of our own identity goes. Residents of each city have no difficulty "unseeing" the other. They learn to ignore unfamiliar patterns, colors, architecture, even sounds and noises. And instead they restrict themselves to fully participating in the city that is demarcated as their own. Objectively, or Dominicanly-speaking, both sets of residents are exposed to exactly the same stimuli and streetscapes. But Franciscanly-speaking, each set has been raised to respond properly to only one set, filtering out the others. In contrast to Coakley's account of how resurrection might be perceived more easily depending upon the level of devoutness of the individual perceiving, in Miéville's work it is the level of cultural familiarity that decides what is revealed and what is hidden.

Should a citizen inadvertently see something in the other city that resident is immediately in breach. Something of a cross between a secret police and an alien intelligence overseeing the division between the cities, breach is both a noun and verb. People breach, and then the officers of Breach come to sort things out. They are a third entity, not belonging to either of the cities, instead operating in the interstices of the two, ensuring that neither city encroaches on the other.

Working with Miéville's metaphor one could suggest that contemporary society has constructed a city of faith and a city of reason.[6] Like the two cities of the novel each seeks to see that its inhabitants are placed firmly in one or the other. And regardless of where others might be inhabitants learn to stay within the comfort zone of their chosen city. For faith this means eschewing reason, and for reason this means avoiding faith. Within this context the purpose of Kierkegaard is similar to the purpose of breach. He rigidly enforces the demarcating line between the two faculties of faith and reason, allowing no overlap.

---

6. In the United States the constitutional separation of church and state would be just one manifestation of this division but should not be confused with the entirety of what the division represents. It is a truism that while the constitutional separation precludes religion from having an official role in public, the evidence of recent politics points to how politicians remain persistently in breach in their use of religious language and categories of thought.

The problem with this is that a rigid separation of faith and reason is neither particularly desirable for the future nor historically valid. Theologians have been in breach for centuries. Jesus himself was in breach. And the people who are most invested in keeping faith and reason separate are, as chapter 1 suggested, the extremists, the fundamentalists. Similarly, in Miéville's novel it is the freedom-fighting, right-wing, ultra-nationalist separatists of both cities who have most to gain from enforcing a strict separation. They need the other city to give them their own identity, in much the same way that fundamentalists need to define others as outsiders in order to guarantee their own identity.

Like the variegated reality of cities in the real world, the relationship between faith and reason is more hybrid than we have been led to believe. Breach happens all the time for the simple reason that the approach of faith and reason is not an either/or. Faith without reason is a form of incredulous naiveté. While reason shorn of faith is terribly dreary for different reasons.

Despite setting up an incomparably difficult technical problem (how to occupy the same space without bumping into one's neighbor) Miéville succeeds because the reader knows how humans already excel at not noticing others right in front of them. Alienation from others is a vital part of the contemporary context for the novel. And it is here that Miéville and Kierkegaard are in wholehearted agreement. Alienation from the other, both the divine other and other people, is a persistent feature of human existence.

Kierkegaard understood the power and reality of alienation in human relationships and self-understanding. And he is perspicacious in realizing the part faith can play in providing existential authenticity. However, there is no particular reason for rationality to be excluded from the important role of reconciling us with the brute reality of existence. Or to put it another way, Kierkegaard was right to see that reason alone cannot argue its way to belief. Neither, however, can faith. While he rightly exposed the hubris of rationality he has no way of protecting faith from being subjected to the same fate. By contrast, serious attempts to navigate religious faith must surely be required to effect their own breach of the polarity that opposes faith to reason. Neither faith alone nor reason alone. Instead, what is needed is the thought of a hybrid relation between the two that makes it possible to live simultaneously in both the city of faith and the city of reason.

The contemporary situation of late modernity or postmodernity is of a world where everyone is always in breach. Like the cities of Miéville, contemporary cities are reminders of how important it is to doubt that any single perspective (whether of an individual or of a communal identity) can contain the whole truth. Here doubt is an important corrective to the self-assuredness and certainty of purpose that has been so destructive in the history of humanity. The classic task of religion has always been to help humans understand how they can begin to see and serve the others they have been trained for too long to ignore. That it has, in fact, also been part of the system by which people are trained to exclude and ignore others for being outsiders is incontestable. However, that it should continue to be so is as ludicrous as it is inevitable. Those who raise doubts about the usual pieties of their intellectual clan or coreligionists are needed to continue to challenge others to leave the cozy confines of the communities of rationality and religion within which they are situated.

Awareness of the delights and limitations of the city was an important part of Kierkegaard's own experience.[7] Kierkegaard railed against the comfortable parochialism of contemporary Copenhagen. Scorning Copenhagen as a small market town rather than a capital city, Kierkegaard was painfully aware of the small-minded and petty provincialism of the Danish capital. It is partly for this reason that the reception of Kierkegaard has been less than enthusiastic in his homeland. Experientially, Kierkegaard understood just how claustrophobic it was to live in a small town where everyone knew everyone and uniformity was prized above all else. So there is an understandable dimension to Kierkegaard's thought that seeks distance from sites of uniformity. Kierkegaard certainly seems to have enjoyed his visits to the much more cosmopolitan Berlin, no doubt affording him both anonymity and a much greater range of cultural and intellectual opportunities. But even there it is also worth remembering how Kierkegaard had little positive to say about the enormous philosophical project of the great thinker, Hegel, who occupied the chair of philosophy at the University of Berlin for the majority of Kierkegaard's life. For Kierkegaard, as for Miéville, cities are places of conflict and contestation, sites of ambiguity and difference.

Kierkegaard and Miéville both recognize how it is possible to inhabit the same space and never see the position of the other. That, after all, is the message of so much of Kierkegaard's pseudonymous authorship:

7. I am grateful to George Pattison for alerting me to the importance of the city in Kierkegaard's thought.

John the silent knows the story of Abraham and can point to the knight of faith, but he cannot make the jump to faith himself. Kierkegaard, then, is as fascinated in the possibility of breach as Miéville. He wants to break with the overarching sense that rationality, Hegelian or otherwise, can explain everything. The task of his writing is to help free us from the secular city (ironically enough, conjoined to the established church) and discover the city of God (purified of the curse of Christendom). Like Miéville he knows that the secular city and the city of God inhabit the same spatial dimensions. However, unlike Miéville, he does not necessarily realize that in seeking to breach from the city of rationality to the city of faith one cannot entirely leave the first behind. Miéville's two cities cannot remain entirely segregated, while Kierkegaard suggests that the city of reason and the city of faith are ultimately entirely separate. Where Miéville allows for breach to go both ways, Kierkegaard does not. Ultimately, Kierkegaard hopes that in becoming citizens of a city of faith the city of rationality may be left behind. By contrast, Miéville offers a way of conceiving how the two cities are always already in breach, interdependent of one another, never fully capable of independence or autonomy.

The Fiction That I am

Leaving the city, it is now time to address the nature of the individual, another topic central to Kierkegaard. Earlier in chapter 6 the importance of fiction as a literary genre was addressed. Fiction provides an important category of thought for approaching questions of truth outside of the dominance of scientific or historical discourse. It is now time to turn again to another sort of fiction that has helped create and sustain questions of truth and method, the Cartesian fiction that there is in fact a self that is self-possessed, rational, and in control.

In *The Sickness unto Death* Kierkegaard presents a novel way of understanding subjectivity. A self is a relation in which one relates oneself to oneself. In other words, to be a self is to be conscious, just as Descartes had argued. But Kierkegaard does not stop there. He goes on to say that a self that relates itself to itself is not yet a self. To be a self also requires the relating of oneself to oneself to discover that the self is not all that there is. For Kierkegaard, the question of subjectivity is a question of becoming. And not only is it necessary to be self-conscious, but it is also necessary to be conscious that our self depends on another relation. For Kierkegaard this other relation is God. True subjectivity only arises when we realize that our selfhood is always in relation to, and dependent upon, God.

Unlike the Cartesian cogito that grounds selfhood in thought, Kierkegaard grounds selfhood in the ability to step outside of the self. Here it is not the Cartesian affirmation, "I think therefore I am," so much as the existential realization, "I am incomplete therefore I must become." The recognition of this incompletion leads Kierkegaard to God, but it might lead others to different conclusions. What matters here is that the self is exposed as essentially dependent on that which is outside itself if it is to attain proper selfhood. Whether this is called the divine or goes by another name, Kierkegaard helps reveal the impossibility of talking about a self as something that is self-grounded, in control, or perfect. While Descartes did not need anything more than the thinking of the subject to ground his philosophical system, Kierkegaard shows us that the individual subject is always required to be in relation to something outside of itself. Secular existentialists have adopted this insight by affirming the importance of the individual self in making the decision to choose just where it can attain full subjectivity. But the original insight is clear: it is only in the absolute feeling of dependence on another that we can attain subjectivity. Only in recognizing how one particular relationship makes demands of us is it possible to properly become a subject. In both iterations of Kierkegaard, the secular and the theological, the self is seen not as a "being" so much as a "becoming." Hence the familiar existentialist motif, existence precedes essence. We are not simply given our subjectivity, we have to earn subjectivity precisely by recognizing that we are not yet subjects until we do the work of stepping outside of ourselves.

Kierkegaard's description of the subject as essentially incomplete is an interesting foreshadowing of the ideas of Jacques Lacan, the twentieth-century psychoanalyst. As an atheist Lacan does not have a role for the divine within his understanding of subjectivity. But Lacan does have a very complex understanding of what it means to speak of a self or a subject. In particular, Lacan also understands that subjects are fundamentally constructed by what they lack.

Lacan thinks that subjects are not rational, and that our identity is determined by that which is fundamentally non-rational, the unconscious. Since the subject can never know the unconscious, except in fleeting and often incomprehensible ways, the subject is never able to be stable, self-possessed, and in control of its own subjectivity. Trauma alone is the decisive way that the subject is able to connect with the unconscious. However, this in itself reminds us how difficult it is to attain subjectivity. For Lacan subjectivity is always about a lack. We lack complete understanding about who we are, and our fundamental desires are driven by the inability to fulfil them. Like Kierkegaard, what we lack is absolutely essential to who we are.

This is epitomized in the developmental stage that all humans go through, called by Lacan the mirror stage. Lacan believed that between the ages of six and eighteen months children move from being unaware of their own "being" to gaining a sense of self. What is critical about the mirror stage is that this sense of self only emerges as the child learns to see itself reflected in another person (the person who mirrors themselves back to them). There does not have to be a physical mirror in the mirror stage. However, what there does have to be is the recognition that another gives us our sense of self-identity. In other words, for Lacan we do not think ourselves into being a self. Rather, it is the process of the other recognizing us as different from them that allows an individual to become an individual rather than an extension of another. It is therefore the state of being in relation to another, and incomplete in oneself, that is primary. There is no blank slate or *tabula rasa* on which subjectivity is created. There is certainly no foundational Cartesian decision to think myself into being. Instead, my subjectivity is created in relation (remember Kierkegaard) to another, and it is only because of the attention of that other that we can learn to speak of our own subjectivity.

In Lacan's understanding, not only is a subject never alone, a subject is also never able to complete its subjectivity. The purpose of psychoanalysis is to reveal how our identity is always bound up with the question of how we relate to others and our desires. Having passed through the mirror stage the subject does not attain a perfect point of equilibrium. Instead, the subject continues to be defined by what is lacking. For Lacan the ongoing drama of subjectivity is present in the recognition that even our most intimate desires are often the desires of others, whether literally or symbolically. Lacan is therefore in complete agreement with the seventeenth-century divine and poet John Donne that no man is an island. Subjectivity is not something we produce heroically in opposition to others. Subjectivity is rather the operation by which we discover that there is nothing about our inner lives that is not connected to a wider universe of signification, either conscious or unconscious.

In explaining Lacan's view of the subject, Sean Homer notes how this contrasts with Cartesian subjectivity:

[T]he only thing one can be certain of is that *one does not exist*
. . . it is not a question of existence, of being or non-being, but
rather of the unrealized, the unknown of Cartesian doubt.[8]

We can now see just how close Lacan comes to a Kierkegaardian model of
the self in his own theory of subjectivity. Lacan agrees with Kierkegaard
in understanding that subjectivity, contra Descartes, is not self-grounded. It is not just a question of the self arriving at an understanding of
itself. Rather, selfhood is always something that begs the question of what
outside of the self makes it possible to be a self.

Žižek shares Lacan's approach to subjectivity. Unlike Kierkegaard
God is not the guarantor of selfhood. Nevertheless, unlike Descartes, the
subject is not self-grounded. Selfhood for Žižek again reminds us that
what the self lacks is what makes it possible to be a self. Similarly, it is relevant that Agamben also realizes that what we lack at our core as human
beings is central to his concept of potentiality: "To be potential means: to
be one's own lack, *to be in relation to one's own incapacity*."[9] For Agamben, the fact that humans are creatures of potentiality, creatures that lack,
is absolutely decisive to understanding who we are. Similarly, the task of
the Lacanian is in many ways like the task of the theologian: highlighting
dependence on that which we lack, while attempting to reveal that the
truth of humanity is bound up not with who we are, but with that which
is beyond us (and, more often than not, beyond our comprehension).

In different ways Agamben, Derrida, Kierkegaard, Lacan, and Žižek
understand the foolishness of attempting to have meaningful discourse
about subjectivity as a matter of pure interiority. To speak of a subject
means also to speak of what the subject lacks, another relation, that
makes subjectivity possible. This is not the same as saying that for there
to be a subject there must also be an object for the subject to relate to.
What they are saying, in radically different ways, is that it is in the nature
of a self to always be unable to completely understand itself or even have
subjectivity. The abyss at the heart of the subject for Žižek is just that—
the fact that there is no subject pure and simple.

For Lacan, thought about the self also requires a recognition that
there are always three different horizons: the Imaginary, the Symbolic,
and the Real. The impossibility of speaking of a subject pure and simple
springs from the fact that subjectivity traverses these different dimensions.

8. Homer, *Jacques Lacan*, 67.
9. Agamben, *Potentialities*, 182.

Each of us has an imaginary, a self-understanding. We also participate in a wider social order of the Symbolic (that is itself mobile and not always easy to pin down). The order of the Symbolic differs from the Imaginary in that the understanding of the symbolic has to do with shared narratives and modes of understanding. Finally, there is the relationship to that which is the Real, itself a curiously difficult concept to lay hold of. Part of the reason it is so difficult to understand is that the Real can never be spoken about, because to speak is to take part in the Symbolic. Lacan is notoriously opaque, but at one point he explains quite clearly:

> The real is the difference between what works and what doesn't work. What works is the world. The real is what doesn't work.[10]

This is not to say that the Real is neither important nor serious. It is, and for Lacan psychoanalysis is all about that which doesn't work. But as soon as we start to ponder our subjectivity we are either in the Imaginary or the Symbolic. When Derrida talks about there being nothing outside the text something similar is going on: everything is part of the Symbolic order of textuality, and to conceive of something outside (the Lacanian "Real") is to talk about that which cannot be spoken of.

From a theological perspective the Real operates a bit like God in some theologies. The Real is what it sounds like, absolutely real. Nonetheless, to talk about it, it is necessary to use language with its attendant questions of signification, metaphor, and circumlocution. Discussing Kant, Žižek notes how both the Real and God are similar in resisting reduction to empirical reality:

> Existence in the sense of empirical reality is thus the very opposite of the Lacanian Real: precisely insofar as God does not "exist" qua part of experiential, empirical reality He belongs to the Real.[11]

Just as negative theologians deny the possibility that anyone can ever say anything about God, so Lacanians deny that anyone can ever say anything about the Real. Adam Kotsko underlines the paradoxical nature of the Real, drawing an explicit parallel between it and the "contradictory" way in which God is named in one of the classic works of negative theology, Dionysius's Divine Names. Both attempts to describe God and the Real, "are so many ways to try to get at the idea of a fundamental

10. Lacan, The Triumph of Religion, 61.
11. Žižek, Tarrying with the Negative, 144n27.

self-contradiction at the heart of existence."[12] All we can talk about is the symbolic or the imaginary. Encapsulating and determining the "true" nature of subjectivity is never possible outside of these social and individual symbolic structures that create subjectivity. The Real (like God) remains elusive. Selfhood "in itself" remains caught in the gap between what we can say about the self in relation to the Symbolic, and what it really is in the Real.

The problem of the self is that just as we can never properly talk about what is Real (or divine), so we can never escape the Symbolic or the linguistic. The self straddles these different horizons of meaning, and the impossibility of determining what the self actually is lies right at the heart of psychoanalysis. Both Kierkegaard and the Lacanians realize that selfhood is an essential fiction. It is a fiction that we use in everyday life because it makes communication and thought easier. However, as soon as we evaluate the self with any kind of philosophical or theoretical rigor it dissolves right before our eyes. The only way for Lacanian psychoanalysis to think the true nature of the self is to talk about that which is not the self. The only way for Kierkegaard to understand the self is to talk about that which is outside of the self, God. Both strategies are, for the best possible reasons, equally incapable of determining or fixing stable subjectivity.

One way of framing these Lacanian and Kierkegaardian insights into subjectivity is to underline how they cast doubt on the myth of rationality found in the Cartesian cogito. Precisely by doubting the certainty of the Cartesian understanding of the self they enrich our understanding of subjectivity. Subjectivity for both is a necessary fiction, and it is only through doubting the supposed unity of the self that Kierkegaard and Lacan can enlarge our understanding. As Kotsko lucidly explains:

> This opacity of the subject, the fact that it can never find its elusive meaning in itself, drives it to seek that meaning in another subject—which is, in turn, also opaque to it (and to itself).[13]

Neither Kierkegaard nor Lacan believe the self to be fully rational. While they disagree on what it is that fundamentally determines self *qua* self (either the unconscious for Lacan or the divine for Kierkegaard), in both cases that most cherished of all modern ideas, the self, turns out to be less

12. Kotsko, *Žižek and Theology*, 33.
13. Ibid., 55.

about one's own "inner" identity and more about matters that are literally beyond our ability to conceive.

The Structure of Desire

Before we leave this exploration of subjectivity it is helpful to underline the place of desire in all this. We have already seen how for both Lacan and Žižek this difficulty of understanding the self is absolutely essential. One of the reasons for this is to do with the three horizons of meaning within which the self is located. Each self is a fable constructed in the conscious and unconscious interplay of these three dimensions. But, even without these horizons of meaning it is possible to see just how difficult it is to identify individual selfhood given the place of desire in the formation of identity. The paradox of desire functions at the core of our selfhood. On the one hand that which is most truly "ours" is our desire. However, that which we desire is often most truly the desire of another.

Žižek gives the example of the little girl who loves to eat strawberry cake. She sees the pleasure that it gives her parents to watch her eat strawberry cake. And so she desires strawberry cake. Here the structure of desire is clear. We desire something because of the fact that we are never selves alone: our selfhood is always bound up in some way with that which is other. Moreover, much of the time it is the desire of the big Other, whether that is the parent or an ideological system. For Lacan, desire is always the desire of the other. Like Kierkegaard's definition of self, desire is not just a self's reflection on its own internal consciousness. The self is dependent upon a relation to another (for Kierkegaard, God) in just the same way that desire is a response to the perceived desire or demands of another. We do not simply desire in a vacuum. We desire as a response to that which is around us.

There is another layer of difficulty to the structure of desire. Attaining the object of desire for Žižek is structurally impossible because that which we always desire (it is called the Thing) is always that which is unattainable. One of the more interesting pieces of Lacanian thought here is the question of how humans respond to this unattainability. Acknowledging the structural unattainability or impossibility of the Thing (the object of desire) is not a simple matter. Instead of choosing that path, we construct a fantasy that desire for the Thing would not be impossible if it were not for an external factor, that which is called the Law, denying it. As Depoortere carefully explains, it is this fantasy that we would be able to attain our desire for the Thing that drives desire itself:

> Moreover, *the course of desire is sustained by the illusion that full satisfaction* (the possession of the Thing) *would be possible if only the Law did prevent it.* Or, to put it differently, the Law calls into being the fantasy that the Thing is not really impossible, but only forbidden and fosters in this way the expectation that one day possession of the Thing will become possible.[14]

In other words, the impossibility of desire is that which the self hides from itself by resorting instead to fantasizing how desire would be possible if only external factors were different. However, in blaming external factors, we occlude the fact that it is precisely this impossibility of attaining what is desired that makes it the Thing worthy of desire in the first place.

The theological implications of this are absolutely staggering. One can argue that love and desire are not the same thing, and that would be correct. However, the fact is that there is an enormous correspondence between the theological teaching that God's love is the creative force that demands a response, and the structure of desire as something that reveals the interconnectedness and essential incompleteness of all human beings. Desire can, of course, be desire for things that may not be beneficent. But this does alter the fact that fundamentally, theologians and Lacanians both realize how humans are always involved in complex, difficult, relationships, and that subjectivity is always emerging (and always being failed to be fully realized) because of the structure of desire.

It is worth reiterating this central Lacanian insight that desire by its very nature can never be satisfied. It is an article of faith for Lacan that what we lack constitutes the center of our desire. If we were to sate a particular desire it would therefore by virtue of being satisfied no longer be our desire. As Homer clarifies:

> Unlike the Cartesian subject . . . the Lacanian subject does not have the certainty of self-consciousness—*I think, therefore, I am*; the Lacanian subject of the unconscious is essentially *no-thing*; it is a lacking subject who has lost his or her being.[15]

---

14. Depoortere, *Christ in Postmodern Philosophy*, 107.

15. Homer, *Jacques Lacan*, 71.

Structurally, this sets up the human subject to always be incomplete in our subjectivity. Equally, in reflecting on this inherently insatiable desire theologians cannot help but remember how Augustine also hungered and thirsted for God: "I tasted you, now I hunger and thirst for you. You touched me, and I am inflamed with love of your peace."[16] Psychoanalytic and theological accounts of desire may not be quite as distinct as their various practitioners have tended to think.

Whatever name ultimate reality goes by, for both Lacanian psychoanalysis and theology the human subject is never able to find perfect equilibrium or harmony with that ultimate reality. For Lacanians it is impossible to truly know our deepest desires, let alone have them fulfilled. For theology it is impossible to truly know the divine, let alone have a perfect relationship with the divine. But in each case, the impossible forms the horizon upon which all meaning is predicated. As we saw with both Derrida and Agamben, it is precisely the impossibilities that reveal truth. While this can at first sound like meaningless jargon, the challenge of psychoanalysis and theology is to recognize the fabricated nature of human subjectivity as a challenge not to abandon the quest for subjectivity but as the only truly authentic way of deepening our understanding of selfhood.

If subjectivity is not something that falls out of the sky fully formed then it is instead, as Kierkegaard and the existentialists suspected, something to be worked for, something to be created. Lacan shows how this process of creativity can never simply be the process of an individual manipulating the raw matter of existence. Instead, the process of becoming an individual is also the process of recognizing our dependence on the structures of desire that form our culture, language, and social reality. Part of the argument of this book is that until we give up certainty surrounding who we think we "really" are the work of becoming human cannot begin. It is not only Caputo who echoes Socrates in realizing that we do not know who we are. The fundamental realization that we do not know who we are is central to both theology and psychoanalysis. Just as a curious hospitality to theological ideas emerged from Derrida and Agamben, so Lacan and Žižek also offer ways to refine and rework existing theological ideas.

16. Augustine, *Confessions*, 232.

Beyond Faith or Doubt

Over eighteen-hundred years ago the theologian Tertullian wrote *credo quia absurdum est*, "I believe because it is absurd."[17] In an apparent repetition of this, discussing the apparent incommensurability of one of the psychoanalyst Lacan's key beliefs, Žižek notes that it is precisely the incommensurability of the position that gives it sense.[18] It is a characteristic of Žižek to argue that apparent contradiction or downright opposition is in actual fact significant of a deeper harmony or a deeper truth. In his psychoanalytic framework that which we repress or ignore is often that which is the most important. While he does not apply this insight specifically to the relationship of doubt and faith, this key insight is probably the place where psychoanalysis can most assist religious reflection.

Until now faith and doubt have always been perceived as unhappy relatives. Even in the liberal or progressive imagination, when doubt is acknowledged it is still only recognized in so far as it can open up space for a deeper faith. By contrast, the suggestion here is that serious theological thought ultimately only occurs when faith and doubt are discovered as absolutely intertwined. Where faith is prioritized over doubt or where doubt marginalizes faith there is not theology, just some other form of knowledge, whether it is a form of rationalism, fundamentalism, or scientism.

Žižek's psychoanalytic framework serves to remind us that it is the repression of doubt that reveals the true importance of doubt. The truth about doubt is that it is an intrinsic part of faith, and where doubt has been excised there is no real faith. Faith needs doubt to keep it faithful, and to prevent it from turning into certainty, religious cynicism, or simply plain denial. In this sense, doubt is not a stage on the way to faith, so much as the essential guardian of the truth of faith. Only faith that allows itself to think about the radical impossibility of faith is really faith. The experience of doubt is therefore one of the most authentically theological experiences possible. Things that are never seriously doubted or called into question are not ultimately terribly important. But paradox and impossibility (whether Derrida's aporias or Agamben's potentialities) provide a fertile ground for doubt since they are also the essential preconditions for thinking about, and experiencing, God.

17. Tertullian, *De Carne Christi* (ANF 3:525).
18. Žižek, *The Monstrosity of Christ*, 234–303.

The Faith of the Faithless

As an academic philosopher and self-professed non-believer one might expect Simon Critchley to have little enthusiasm for the general drift of the argument of this work so far. On the other hand, Critchley fundamentally grasps the importance of Kierkegaard's position. Moreover, against forms of philosophical quietism in which philosophy does little more than describe and analyze, Critchley favors the emergence of a type of philosophical activism. Here what matters is how philosophy can be used for responding and shaping social issues, not simply observing and dissecting.

Critchley gives this philosophical activism a remarkable name: "the faith of the faithless." He is unabashed in arguing that it is the faithless who are the clearest inheritors of Kierkegaard's understanding of faith. Highlighting Kierkegaard's affirmation of faith as something that does not require security or guarantees, Critchley suggests that it is those who do not have the security of a denomination or religion who are today capable of being the most faithful.

Critchley's perspective brings us around full circle to where we began on Dover beach. And yet, unlike his nineteenth-century atheist forebears, Critchley is willing and eager to embrace the fundamental theological attitude of faith. For Critchley there is nothing incoherent in speaking of the faith of the faithless. Invoking the Roman centurion whose faith Kierkegaard analyzed, Critchley is explicit that, "it is perhaps the faithless who can best sustain the rigor of faith without requiring security, guarantees, or rewards."[19] In an extraordinary culmination to an atheist's academic philosophical work, Critchley's final words are not his but the words of Jesus in Matthew's Gospel to the centurion, "Be it done for you, as you believed."[20]

Given Critchley's intricate analysis of Kierkegaard, mystics, and St. Paul we cannot dismiss his work as mere posturing. While this work has been keen to explore how certain beliefs of unbelievers can inform and help theology, Critchley's point is that the faithless are already demonstrating faithfulness in powerful ways. The question that remains to be asked is whether there can be a harmony between these two positions, or whether they reveal an unbridgeable abyss? The present work does not wish to argue that Critchley is wrong in his analysis of faith. Rather,

19. Critchley, *Faith of the Faithless*, 252.
20. Ibid. The quote is from Matt 8:13.

it seems that Critchley has grasped what is fundamental to the Christian tradition through its many iterations and developments from Paul to Kierkegaard and into the present day. Faith as an attitudinal, existential relationship is essential. And it is the passion of faith that is the bridge between the faithless and the faithful.

It seems possible to argue that there is as much in common between Critchley's faithlessness and the centurion's faithfulness as there is between religious fundamentalism and scientific fundamentalism. Critchley says as much when, avowing his own atheism, he distances himself from what he calls the "evangelical atheism" of Hitchens and Dawkins.[21] To wonder at this astonishing turn of events is to recognize from another angle the argument that underlies this present work. In avowing a faithless faith Critchley understands that faith is not a trump card that clears up all the uncertainties and answers all problems. Rather, faith is a kind of conscious decision to live as-if things were not as they are, in the sure and certain knowledge that they are really quite as terrible as they are. This seems deeply Pauline and Kierkegaardian. We recognize that things are neither happy nor perfect but we allow ourselves the leap of faith to believe that it might be other. Where this differs from the faith of the fundamentalist is that deep down we know that we might really be wrong. The faith of the faithless is not a total breach with reason, in fact it requires reason to be a continual and active partner in the shaping of understanding. By the same token, the faith of the doubtfully faithful can also never be a total breach with reason. Without reason we are unmoored and unhinged.

Critchley reveals how the task of living entails commerce and engagement between the city of reason and the city of faith. These two cities cannot be arbitrarily separated and distinguished, for they share much in common. Humans have been in breach for centuries, and our only hope is to continue to live in breach. There is no future in setting up gated communities for the like-minded premised on clear boundaries and certain rewards. Instead, we need to allow ourselves, like Critchley's centurion, to believe that something radically different and radically other might be truly transformative. As we have seen doubt and uncertainty have driven and uncovered some of the most creative and illuminating dimensions to faith. Paradoxically, only by engaging wholeheartedly with doubt and the faith of the faithless can the faithful live more authentically faithful lives.

21. Ibid., 19.

Interestingly enough, this notion that the faithless might actually have a richer sense of faith than the faithful is also hinted at by Žižek. Exploring the relationship of his own form of Marxist atheism to theism, Žižek suggests that atheism needs to find a new way between either opposition or simple indifference to belief:

> That is to say: what if, in a kind of negation of negation, true atheism were to return to belief (faith?), asserting it without reference to God—only atheists can truly believe; the only true belief is belief without any support in the authority of some presupposed figured of the "big Other."[22]

Again, what is remarkable here is not simply the hospitality toward faith that it exhibits. More importantly, it is almost as if Žižek is attempting to understand the true nature of faith. What distance, after all, truly separates this position of Žižek from that of Robinson, MacKinnon, or Eckhart? Like Žižek they too deny that faith can rest on the authority or support of some "big Other." Critical of attempts to capture God or make sense of God too easily, these theologians are exactly like Critchley and Žižek in seeking to expose the radical vulnerability and uncertainty that characterizes faith. Moreover, this is not due to any peculiarity or outlier status on behalf of these theologians. One reading of the New Testament would be as a textual escape from precisely the idea of this "big Other" providing the ultimate authority for how life should be lived. The Jesus of the New Testament does not spend an awful lot of time pointing people in the direction of fealty to a big Other. Instead, his time is spent pointing out the disturbing yet emancipatory news that humans have been set free from all the systems that conspired to confine and enslave, whether they be economic, social or religious. When Jesus heals the sick he repeatedly ascribes the healing not to the intervention of an all-powerful big Other, but instead tells the individual: "Your faith has saved you: go in peace."[23] Jesus never explains what the content of their faith is that saves and frees. Nor does he spend much time discussing the attributes of God.

It seems important to remain fairly circumspect about reading in any Dominican knowledge into the stories told by Jesus. Instead, what seems to drive his interactions with others is an experiential, Franciscan, desire to liberate all those whose lives were most on the margins: prostitutes, sinners, foreigners, tax collectors, the sick, and the unclean. When

22. Žižek, *Monstrosity of Christ*, 101.
23. Luke 7:49.

Jesus found faith in such unlikely places it was by very definition *not* the faith of the orthodox. Like emancipatory atheists of today, the faith of the marginalized and the dispossessed was not a trust in some ornate system of metaphysics so much as a trust that somehow, in spite of all evidence to the contrary, there is the possibility of hope. However, to offer any kind of certainty about the character or content of that hope would be to sever hope from faith and turn it instead into a form of wishful thinking, prophecy, or simple planning. The hope of faith is always uncertain. But, paradoxically, the uncertainty of faith is the only guarantee that it might really, just possibly, be faith that sets us free.

Divine Breach

As Kierkegaard realized, the ultimate theological breach is between the philosophical discourse of rationality and the event of incarnation. Returning to the site of this breach it is helpful to remember the struggles that have surrounded attempts to understand incarnation. It takes several centuries after the death of Jesus before the church is able to articulate something along the lines of the Kierkegaardian paradox in which the person of Christ is both fully human and fully divine. What matters here is simply the contested history of this central theological doctrine. From the deniers of Christ's full humanity to the deniers of Christ's full divinity, orthodoxy only emerges slowly. The central point is that it is the positions that come to be labeled as heresy that are the purveyors of certainty and clarity. What becomes the mystery of the incarnation was not always a mystery. For some, the person of Jesus the Son was divine, but not as divine as the Father, and not really properly human. For others, it was the humanity of Jesus that was not in doubt, and his divinity consequently much reduced. The ins and outs of these debates are notoriously complex. However, what continues to have an enduring importance is the achievement of the Chalcedonian definition of 451.

As we saw in the first chapter, Chalcedon does not explicitly state how it might be possible to be divine and human in one person. However, the Christology formed at Chalcedon of one person and two natures signifies that the person of Christ is a person who is in breach. The incarnation is a breach in two distinct ways. First, it breaches the ability of either rationality or faith to fully comprehend. Against heretical attempts to comprehend or prioritize the relationship of Christ's humanity and divinity, Chalcedon inscribes doubt into the heart of the doctrine of the incarnation. Neither reason nor faith can make sense of the Chalcedonian definition for the simple reason that it is exclusionary. It says what is *not* true of the person of Christ. It does not purport to objectively describe the way the two natures (humanity and divinity) might coexist in one person.

However, as well as being a breach with the ability of faith or reason to comprehend the mystery of the incarnation, the incarnation is also a breach of the dividing line that separates God and humanity. Chalcedon sets Christian orthodoxy decisively against Gnosticism. It rejects the Gnosticism that sought to firmly divide God and humanity, delimiting the good to the spiritual, and denying the goodness of the material world. Chalcedon affirms that there is no essential contradiction between the goodness of God and the goodness of human nature. At the same time, Chalcedon also marks a fundamental disagreement with the Gnosticism that claimed to have secret knowledge available only to an elect. The secret of Christianity is that there is no secret. The mystery of the incarnation is not a mystery that will be revealed to a faithful few. The secret of Christianity is that the mystery of the incarnation is nothing less than the public proclamation that the divide that separated God and humanity is no longer.

In summary, where the central doctrine of Christian belief is concerned, the incarnation, it is not possible to respond in any way other than disbelief and doubt. It simply does not make coherent sense by the standards of either faith or rationality to proclaim God as human. Nevertheless, the wonder of the incarnation is that the church refutes every attempt to generate sense or certainty from this central mystery. What separates the incarnation from the heresies that fail to think incarnation is very simple: where orthodoxy rejects certainty in favor of an impossible truth, heresy seeks certainty at the expense of the fullness of the truth.

The Poetry of Faith

The poet priest R. S. Thomas struggled with questions of identity throughout his life. A Welshman who was raised an English speaker, there was always a distance between the language of his poetry and the Welsh language and culture that were the subject of so much of that poetry. Many of Thomas's poems invoke S. K. (Kierkegaard), and like his hero he lived on the edge of society: both figuratively, in his occupation as a priest in a largely secular society, as well as literally, settled in a remote rural village at the edge of Wales, far from any centers of culture. There is much that is melancholy about the poetry of Thomas, something best illustrated by the Welsh title of his autobiography, *Neb*, that translates literally as "no one." Doubt played an important role in the life and poetry of R. S. Thomas. However, doubt for Thomas was never simply negative. Doubt was always connected to faith, always the spur to a greater understanding of the mysteriousness of faith and life.

Like faith, doubt is not easily reduced to simple explanation or description. However, also like faith, doubt lends itself more easily to poetic expression than either intellectual abstraction or scientific analysis. The type of doubt that we have been exploring is no more the sibling of skepticism than faith is the twin of fideism. Instead, this sketch of doubt has attempted to uncover the deeper family resemblance between faith and faithlessness, between the study of God and the study of the impossibilities at the heart of human existence.

The poetry of Thomas shows us that the languages of love and science, nationality and religion, hearth and home are not all the same. And yet, it is possible to express wonder about chromosomes and calculus at the same time as marveling at redemption and forgiveness. Incorporating the worlds of science and religion through poetry, Thomas revealed the possibility of faithfulness to both the deepest human instincts to understand and the realization that we can never grasp everything. Doubt for Thomas was not a question of negating, so much as a way of unearthing new possibilities. If doubt is to claim a kinship with faith it will also be necessary to recognize the power of the poetic in theology. Uncertainty, ambiguity and polyvalence are as intrinsic to poetry as they are to faith. As Spufford writes, "You never stop doubting—how could you?—but you learn to live with doubt and faith unresolved, because unresolvable."[24]

A doubt that also entertains the hope of poetry is one way to guarantee a faith that is less certain and more faithful to the dimension of possibility that is God. At the end of a breathtaking tour through the central drama of faith Thomas concludes that just such doubtful faith might also be all that is ultimately required:

> I think that maybe
> I will be a little surer

24. Spufford, *Unapologetic*, 208.

of being a little nearer.
That's all. Eternity
is in the understanding
that that little is more than enough.[25]

There is an honest ambiguity here. But what more could one possibly hope for? Faith is, after all, not an escape from doubt so much as a recognition that without doubt there is no belief worthy of the name. Faith can never be removed or separated from doubt, precisely because faith is itself a form of doubt. Faith consists in doubting that one can grasp the totality of all that has been, is, and is yet to come. Against false certainties that ultimately fail to satisfy, faith is an attitude of radical uncertainty that self-authenticates in the midst of things we can never fully understand. We do not know, we imagine. Faithful doubt suggests that somehow this imaginative capacity is what counts. Doubt does not have to lead to denial. It can also breathe life into the mystery of faith.

25. Thomas, "AD."

BIBLIOGRAPHY

Agamben, Giorgio. *The Church and the Kingdom*. Photographs by Alice Attie. Translated by Leland De La Durantaye. London: Seagull, 2012.

———. *The Coming Community*. Translated by Michael Hardt. Minneapolis: University of Minnesota Press, 1993.

———. *Homo Sacer: Sovereign Power and Bare Life*. Translated by Daniel Heller-Roazen. Stanford: Stanford University Press, 1998.

———. *Infancy and History: On the Destruction of Experience*. Translated by Liz Heron. London: Verso, 1993.

———. *The Kingdom and the Glory: For a Theological Genealogy of Economy and Government*. Translated by Lorenzo Chiesa with Matteo Mandarini. Stanford: Stanford University Press, 2011.

———. *Language and Death: The Place of Negativity*. Translated by Karen E. Pinkus with Michael Hardt. Minneapolis: University of Minnesota Press, 1991.

———. *Potentialities: Collected Essays in Philosophy*. Translated and edited by Daniel Heller-Roazen. Stanford: Stanford University Press, 1999.

———. *Profanations*. Translated by Jeff Fort. New York: Zone, 2007.

———. *Remnants of Auschwitz: The Witness and the Archive*. Translated by Daniel Heller-Roazen. New York: Zone, 1999.

———. *The Sacrament of Language: An Archaeology of the Oath*. Translated by Adam Kotsko. Stanford: Stanford University Press, 2011.

———. *State of Exception*. Translated by Kevin Attell. Chicago: University of Chicago Press, 2005.

———. *The Time that Remains: A Commentary on the Letter to the Romans*. Translated by Patricia Dailey. Stanford: Stanford University Press, 2005.

Anselm. *Prayers and Meditations*. Translated by Benedicta Ward. London: Penguin, 1979.

Arendt, Hannah. *Eichmann in Jerusalem: A Report on the Banality of Evil*. London: Penguin, 2006.

Aulén, Gustav. *Christus Victor*. London: SPCK, 1931.

Augustine, *Confessions*. Translated by R. S. Pine-Coffin. London: Penguin, 1961.

———. *De Doctrina Christiana*. Translated and edited by R. P. H. Green. Oxford: Clarendon, 1995.

Bacon, Francis. *The New Organon: Or True Directions Concerning the Interpretation of Nature*. Edited by Lisa Jardine and Michael Silverthorne. Cambridge: Cambridge University Press, 2000.

Badiou, Alain. *Saint Paul: The Foundation of Universalism*. Stanford: Stanford University Press, 2003.

Bauman, Zygmunt. *Postmodernity and its Discontents*. Cambridge: Polity, 1997.

Bell, Rob. *Love Wins*. New York: HarperOne, 2011.

Berman, Russell A. *Fiction Sets You Free: Literature, Liberty, and Western Culture*. Iowa City: University of Iowa Press, 2007.

Burrell, David. *Deconstructing Theodicy: Why Job Has Nothing to Say to the Puzzle of Suffering*. Grand Rapids: Brazos, 2008.

Caputo, John D. *On Religion*. London: Routledge, 2001.

———. "The Poetics of the Impossible and the Kingdom of God." In *The Blackwell Guide to Postmodern Theology*, edited by Graham Ward, 469–81. Oxford: Blackwell, 2001.

———. *The Prayers and Tears of Jacques Derrida*. Bloomington: Indiana University Press, 1997.

Caputo, John D., and Linda Martin Alcoff. *St Paul among the Philosophers*. Bloomington: Indiana University Press, 2009.

Chesterton, G. K. *The Man Who Was Thursday*. San Francisco: Ignatius, 2004.

———. *Orthodoxy*. San Francisco: Ignatius, 1995.

———. *What's Wrong with the World*. Charleston, SC: BiblioBazaar, 2007.

Coakley, Sarah. *Powers and Submissions: Spirituality, Philosophy and Gender*. Oxford: Blackwell, 2002.

Collins, Suzanne. *The Hunger Games*. New York: Scholastic, 2008.

Critchley, Simon. *The Faith of the Faithless: Experiments in Political Theology*. London: Verso, 2012.

Crossan, John Dominic. *Cliffs of Fall: Paradox and Polyvalence in the Parables of Jesus*. Eugene, OR: Wipf and Stock, 2008.

Cupitt, Don. *The Sea of Faith*. 2nd ed. London: SCM, 1994.

Depoortere, Frederiek. *Christ in Postmodern Philosophy: Gianni Vattimo, René Girard and Slavoj Žižek*. London: T. & T. Clark, 2008.

Derrida, Jacques. *Aporias*. Translated by Thomas Dutoit. Stanford: Stanford University Press, 1993.

———. "Circumfession." In *Jacques Derrida*, edited by Geoffrey Bennington, 3–315. Chicago: University of Chicago Press, 1993.

———. "Des Tours de Babel." In *Difference in Translation*, edited and translated by Joseph F. Graham, 165–207. Ithaca, NY: Cornell University Press, 1985.

———. *Dissemination*. Translated by Barbara Johnson. London: Athlone, 1981.

———. "Force of Law: The 'Mystical Foundation of Authority.'" In *Deconstruction and the Possibility of Justice*, edited by Drucilla Cornell, Michel Rosenfeld, and David Gray Carlson, 3–67. London: Routledge, 1992.

———. *The Gift of Death*. Translated by David Wills. Chicago: University of Chicago Press, 1995.

———. "How to Avoid Speaking: Denials." In *Languages of the Unsayable: The Play of Negativity in Literature and Literary Theory*, edited by Sanford Budick and Wolfgang Ider, translated by Ken Frieden, 3–70. New York: Columbia University Press, 1989.

———. *Limited Inc*. Translated by Samuel Weber. Evanston, IL: Northwestern University Press, 1988.

———. *Margins of Philosophy*. Translated by Alan Bass. New York: Harvester Wheatsheaf, 1982.

————. "Not Apocalypse, Not Now (full speed ahead, seven missiles, seven missives)." Translated by Catherine Porter and Philip Lewis. *Diacritics* 14, no. 2 (1984) 20–31.

————. "Of an Apocalyptic Tone Recently Adopted in Philosophy." *Semeia* 23 (1982) 63–96.

————. *Of Grammatology*. Translated by Gayatri Chakravorty Spivak. Baltimore: Johns Hopkins University Press, 1976.

————. *On Cosmopolitanism and Forgiveness*. London: Routledge, 2001.

————. *On the Name*. Translated by David Wood, John P. Leavey, and Ian McLeod. Stanford: Stanford University Press, 1995.

————. "Psyche: Inventions of the Other." In *Reading De Man Reading*, edited by Lindsay Waters and Wlad Godzich, translated by Catherine Porter, 25–65. Minneapolis: University of Minnesota Press, 1989.

————. *Resistances of Psychoanalysis*. Translated by Peggy Kamuf, Pascale-Anne Brault and Michael Naas. Stanford: Stanford University Press, 1998.

————. *Specters of Marx*. Translated by Peggy Kamuf. London: Routledge, 1994.

————. "Two Words for Joyce." In *Post-structuralist Joyce*, edited by Derek Attridge and Daniel Ferrer, translated by Geoffrey Bennington, 145–59. London: Cambridge University Press, 1984.

————. *Writing and Difference*. Translated by Alan Bass. London: Routledge, 1978.

Derrida, Jacques, and Gianni Vattimo. *On Religion*. Oxford: Polity, 1998.

Descartes, René. *Meditations on First Philosophy*. 3rd ed. Indianapolis, IN: Hackett, 1993.

Dickinson, Colby. *Agamben and Theology*. London: T. & T. Clark, 2011.

Donne, John. "Satyre III." *Poetical Works*, edited by Herbert J. C. Grierson, 136–40. Oxford: Oxford University Press, 1971.

Eagleton, Terry. *On Evil*. New Haven: Yale University Press, 2010.

Erasmus, Desiderius. *Praise of Folly*. Translated by Leonard Dean. Chicago: Packard, 1946.

Fergusson, David. *Faith and its Critics*. Oxford: Oxford University Press, 2009.

Fraser, Giles. *Redeeming Nietzsche: On the Piety of Unbelief*. London: Routledge, 2002.

Gasché, Rodolphe. *The Tain of the Mirror: Derrida and the Philosophy of Reflection*. Cambridge, MA: Harvard University Press, 1986.

Gray, John. *Straw Dogs: Thoughts on Humans and Other Animals*. New York: Farrar, Straus and Giroux, 2002.

Gregory, Brad. *The Unintended Reformation*. Cambridge, MA: Harvard University Press, 2012.

Griffiths, Paul J. "The Cross as the Fulcrum of Politics: Expropriating Agamben on Paul." In *Paul, Philosophy and the Theopolitical Vision*, edited by Douglas Harink, 179–97. Eugene, OR: Wipf and Stock, 2010.

Gschwandtner, Christina. *Postmodern Apologetics? Arguments for God in Contemporary Philosophy*. New York: Fordham University Press, 2013.

Hart, Kevin. *The Trespass of the Sign*. Cambridge: Cambridge University Press, 1989.

Harvey, David. *The Enigma of Capital: and the Crises of Capitalism*. Oxford: Oxford University Press, 2010.

Hick, John. *Evil and the God of Love*. 2nd ed. London: Macmillan, 1977.

Hitchens, Christopher. *God Is Not Great*. New York: Hachette, 2007.

Homer, Sean. *Jacques Lacan*. London: Routledge, 2005.

Hyman, Gavin. *A Short History of Atheism*. London: Taurus, 2010.

The International Necronautical Society. "INS Founding Manifesto." *The Times*, December 14, 1999, http://necronauts.net/manifestos/1999_times_manifesto.html.

Jeffrey, David Lyle. *Luke*. Grand Rapids: Brazos, 2012.

Kant, Immanuel. "An Answer to the Question: 'What is Enlightenment?'" [From the Preface to *Critique of Pure Reason* (1784).] In *From Modernism to Postmodernism*, edited by Lawrence Cahoone, 45–49. Oxford: Blackwell, 2003.

Kearney, Richard. *Anatheism: Returning to God after God*. New York: Columbia University Press, 2010.

Kierkegaard, Søren. *Attack Upon "Christendom."* Translated by Walter Lowrie. Princeton: Princeton University Press, 1968.

———. *Fear and Trembling*. Translated by Alastair Hannay. London: Penguin, 1985.

———. *Philosophical Fragments*. Edited and Translated by Howard V. Hong and Edna H. Hong. Princeton: Princeton University Press, 1995.

———. *The Sickness Unto Death: A Christian Psychological Exposition for Upbuilding and Awakening*. Edited and Translated by Howard V. Hong and Edna H. Hong. Princeton: Princeton University Press, 1980.

Kort, Wesley A. *"Take, Read": Scripture, Textuality, and Cultural Practice*. University Park: Pennsylvania State University Press, 1996.

Kotsko, Adam. *Žižek and Theology*. London: T. & T. Clark, 2008.

Lacan, Jacques. *Écrits*. Translated by Bruce Fink. New York: Norton, 2002.

———. *The Triumph of Religion*. Translated by Bruce Fink. Cambridge: Polity, 2013.

Le Guin, Ursula K. *The Telling*. New York: Harcourt, 2000.

Loughlin, Gerard. *Telling God's Story*. Cambridge: Cambridge University Press, 1996.

Luther, Martin. *On the Bondage of the Will*. London: Clarke, 1957.

Lyotard, Jean-François. *The Postmodern Condition: A Report on Knowledge*. Translated by Geoff Bennington and Brian Massumi. Foreword by Fredric Jameson. Manchester: Manchester University Press, 1986.

Mackie, J.K. "Evil and Omnipotence." *Mind* 64, no. 254 (1955) 200-212.

MacKinnon, Donald. *Borderlands of Theology and other essays*. Eugene, OR: Wipf and Stock, 2011.

McLuhan, Marshall. *Understanding Media: The Extensions of Man*. Cambridge, MA: MIT Press, 1994.

Miéville, China. *The City and The City*. New York: Random House, 2010.

Milbank, John. "Darkness and Silence: Evil and the Western Legacy." In *The Religious*, edited by John D. Caputo, 277–300. Oxford: Blackwell, 2002.

Miller, Walter. *A Canticle for Leibovitz*. Boston: Gregg, 1975.

Moltmann, Jürgen. *The Crucified God*. Translated by R. A. Wilson and John Bowden. London: SCM, 1974.

Murray, Alex. *Giorgio Agamben*. London: Routledge, 2010.

Nightwish, "Storytime." In *Imaginaerum*. Donzdorf: Nuclear Blast Records, 2011.

Pascal, Blaise. *Pensées and Other Writings*. Translated by Honor Levi. Oxford: Oxford University Press, 1995.

Popkin, Richard. *The History of Scepticism: From Savonarola to Bayle*. Rev. and exp. ed. Oxford: Oxford University Press, 2003.

Pullman, Philip. *His Dark Materials*. London: Scholastic, 2002.

Robinson, John. *Honest to God*, London: SCM, 1963.

Schleiermacher, Friedrich. *On Religion: Speeches to its Cultured Despisers.* Edited by Richard Crouter. Cambridge: Cambridge University Press, 1988.

Shakespeare, Steven. *Derrida and Theology.* London: T. & T. Clark, 2009.

Simpson, James. *Burning to Read: English Fundamentalism and Its Reformation Opponents.* Cambridge, MA: Harvard University Press, 2010.

Spufford, Francis. *Unapologetic: Why, Despite Everything, Christianity Can Still Make Surprising Emotional Sense.* London: Faber, 2012.

Stephenson, Neal. *Anathem.* New York: Morrow, 2008.

Stump, Eleanore. *Wandering and Darkness: Narrative and the Problem of Suffering.* Oxford: Oxford University Press, 2010.

Taylor, Mark C. *Altarity.* Chicago: University of Chicago Press, 1987.

———. *Confidence Games: Money and Markets in a World Without Redemption.* Chicago: University of Chicago Press, 2004.

———. *The Moment of Complexity: Emergent Network Culture.* Chicago: University of Chicago Press, 2001.

Tertullian. *De Carne Christi.* In *The Ante-Nicene Fathers*, edited by Alexander Roberts and James Donaldson, 3:521–42. Edinburgh: T. & T. Clark, 1997.

Thomas, R. S. "AD." In *Collected Later Poems, 1988–2000*, 109–31. Newcastle: Bloodaxe, 2011.

Thorpe, Adam. *Hodd.* London: Cape, 2009.

Tracy, David. *Plurality and Ambiguity: Hermeneutics, Religion and Hope.* Chicago: University of Chicago, 1994.

Wittgenstein, Ludwig. *Philosophical Investigations.* Translated by G. E. M. Anscombe. 3rd ed. New York: Macmillan, 1973.

Ward, Graham. *Barth, Derrida and the Language of Theology.* Cambridge: Cambridge University Press, 1995.

———. *The Politics of Discipleship: Becoming Postmaterial Citizens.* Grand Rapids: Baker Academic, 2009.

———. "Why is Derrida Important for Theology?" *Theology* 95 (1992) 263–70.

Weber, Max. *The Protestant Work Ethic and the Spirit of Capitalism.* Translated by Talcott Parsons. 2nd ed. London: Routledge, 2001.

Westphal, Merold. *Suspicion and Faith: The Religious Uses of Modern Atheism.* New York: Fordham University Press, 1998.

Wyschogrod, Edith. *Spirit in Ashes: Hegel, Heidegger, and Man-Made Death.* New Haven: Yale University Press, 1990.

Žižek, Slavoj. *Demanding the Impossible.* Edited by Yong-june Park. Cambridge: Polity, 2013.

———. *On Belief.* London: Routledge, 2001.

———. *The Puppet and the Dwarf: The Perverse Core of Christianity.* Cambridge: MIT Press, 2003.

———. *Tarrying with the Negative: Kant, Hegel, and the Critique of Ideology.* Durham, NC: Duke University Press, 1993.

Žižek, Slavoj, and Boris Gunjević. *God in Pain: Inversions of Apocalypse.* New York: Seven Stories, 2012.

Žižek, Slavoj, and John Milbank. *The Monstrosity of Christ: Paradox or Dialectic?* Edited by Creston Davis. Cambridge: MIT Press, 2009.

Žižek, Slavoj, John Milbank, and Creston Davis. *Paul's New Moment: Continental Philosophy and the Future of Christian Theology.* Grand Rapids: Brazos, 2010.

Index

8174896R00133

Printed in Great Britain
by Amazon.co.uk, Ltd.,
Marston Gate.